I0824825

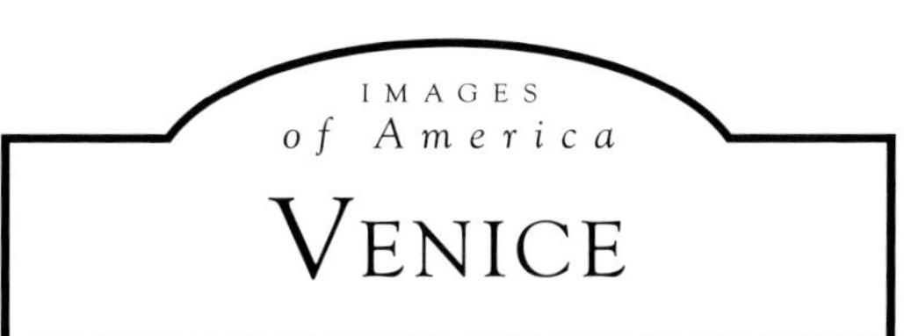
IMAGES
of America
VENICE

On the Cover: Beachgoers look for millions-of-years-old shark teeth and other fossils washed ashore each day from the offshore Hawthorn Group onto Venice beaches. This image was taken in the 1960s on Caspersen Beach. (Venice Museum & Archives, Venice Historical Resources, 2008.21.100, CD 36 of 48.)

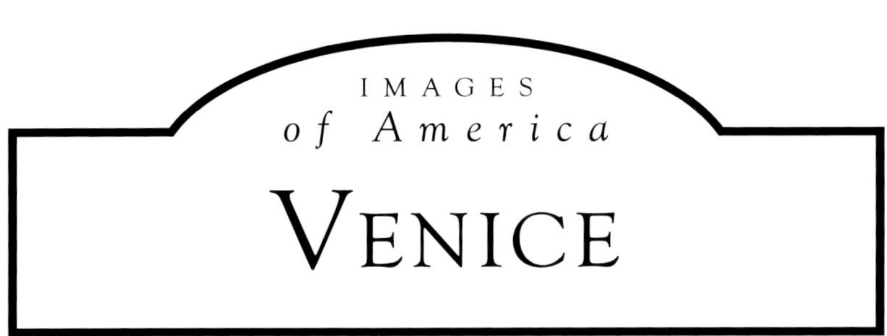

Margaret Mackle Kapustiak

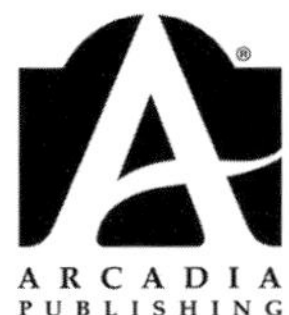

ISBN 9781-4671-6295-1

Published by Arcadia Publishing
Charleston, South Carolina

Printed in the United States of America

Library of Congress Control Number: 2025937174

For all general information, please contact Arcadia Publishing:
Telephone 843-853-2070
Fax 843-853-0044
E-mail sales@arcadiapublishing.com

Visit us on the Internet at www.arcadiapublishing.com

Dedicated to Mary Charles, 50-year volunteer; Dorothy Korwek, historian and author extraordinaire; and Wendell, my rock and strongest supporter

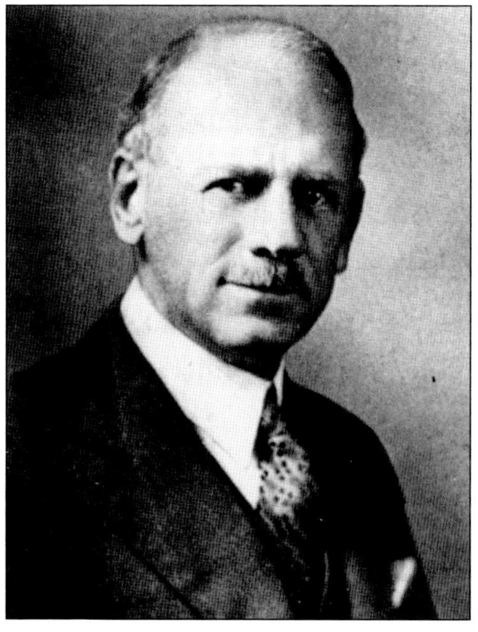

John Nolen's 1926 Venice plan included streets, parks, business areas, housing, and landscaping still visible today. Venice is a planned community with numerous national, county, and local historic districts. There are around 90 Mediterranean Revival buildings, initially erected by the Brotherhood of Locomotive Engineers from 1925 to 1928. Parks and streets still remain as planned over 100 years ago. (Venice Museum & Archives, Venice Historical Resources, MS179 Box 1 Folder 3.)

Contents

Acknowledgments

The City of Venice celebrated 100 years of incorporation on November 30, 2025. Venice has unique features and people, so not everyone can be mentioned in one book. For that, I apologize. It soon became apparent that a second book would be needed to cover the circus's winter home for 30 years, the shell mounds, early settlers, and members of the Venice and Nokomis communities.

Many images are online and/or in the collections of the Division of Historical Resources, Venice Museum & Archives, where one can visit and ask research questions. Thank you to Harry Klinkhamer, historical resources manager; Rhonda Rogers, administrative coordinator; and Jon Watson, curator. Also, thanks to the many people and organizations who donated or scanned their photographs, maps, brochures, and memorabilia. It takes a village to write a history book, so the bibliography is intended to help the reader investigate more details and dates.

Thank you to the technical experts and reviewers: Dorothy Korwek, Rhonda Rogers, Jim Nemec, Larry Humes, and Abigail and Wendell Kapustiak.

Thank you to the Lord-Higel volunteers, who often as winter residents never gave up, worked on the house, and made donations: Jack and Judie Bauer, Ron Higel, Lynda Adamczyk, Robert Brooke, Bob Copeland, Judie Foote, Louise Giovenco, Jim Hazelton, Dorothy Korwek, Bernard Matthey, Jim Middleton, Joyce Higel Norton, Jerry Valente, and Ron Wentworth.

Also, thanks to history volunteers: Mary Charles, 50-year archivist; Clarke Presley, researcher; and particularly Dorothy Korwek, volunteer extraordinaire, without whom much of Venice's and Sarasota County's history would be forgotten or never investigated and updated with new findings.

Thank you to the many photographers whose work has been donated: the Hauser family, Dorothy Korwek, Rhonda Rogers, Woody Thayer, Sunshine Press, Vaughan Pitman, the chamber of commerce, Koons Studios, Jay Brown, Burnell Brothers, Pete Conover, and others that have donated images.

Thank you also to Erin Vosgien, acquisitions editor, Michael Litchfield, production editor, and particularly Amy Jarvis, content editor, and the copy editors of Arcadia Publishing for their much-appreciated guidance and support.

Images and research help were provided by Krystin Miner and Jonathan Torkos at Manatee County Historical Records Library (MCHRL), Leah Lapszynski of the Sarasota County History Center (SCHC), Ronda Rogers (RR), Sarasota Alliance for Historic Preservation (SAHP), myself as author (MMK), Robert L. Fuqua, Buzz and Wendy Fink, Rev. James Mitchell of the Union Missionary Baptist Church, the *Venice Gondolier* newspaper, and Eric Duda, grandson of Vaughan Pitman. Unless otherwise noted, all images appear courtesy of the Venice Museum & Archives, Venice Historical Resources (VHR), where I have been a volunteer since 2011.

INTRODUCTION

People are drawn to the Venice, Florida, area for many different reasons. Some like the climate, some gather ancient shark teeth and other fossils, some come for the history and the livability, and others come to support the tourist trade or because their employer moves to the area. Many people have families that have lived in the area for generations. The history of Venice is a series of highlights. This book will talk about the geological rationale for millions-of-years-old shark teeth and other fossils found on the beach and why there are no keys or offshore islands. It will cover a few of the early settlers (with more to come in another book) and some of the early promoters of the area.

Joseph H. Lord was one of the first promoters. Starting in the 1890s, he established a citrus grove and purchased or leased, with a number of investors, over 100,000 acres in the county. Lord brought the second promoter, Bertha Honoré Palmer, from Chicago. Her Sarasota-Venice Company in the 1910s established Eagle Point, the area's first resort. She moved the post office and railroad to Venice and even took Nokomis's original name of Venice and moved it a mile south as the name of her new town. Dr. Fred Albee and his wife, Louella, from New York, came to the Nokomis area in 1917 and stayed to establish a second resort with plans for housing. Dr. Albee also developed the first airfield and the first hospital.

The Brotherhood of Locomotive Engineers (BLE), a union based in Ohio looking for investment opportunities and willing to spend money for its members, hired noted city planner John Nolen in 1926. Many of his concept drawings and plans survive to this day and are architectural works of art in themselves. Along with Nolen, the BLE hired young landscape architect Prentiss French. His impact can be seen in the many oak trees shading Venice streets as well as the number and varieties of palm trees planted around the city. French went on to a distinguished career, and his designs have been carried forward in many locations in Venice and elsewhere. The BLE built numerous hotels, homes, and businesses, with plans for small farms, a shipping port, and a waterway around the city. Unfortunately, those plans came tumbling down as the Great Depression began and sales bottomed out in Florida. The BLE abandoned Venice in 1928, leaving the immediate area with fewer than 300 residents.

However, the BLE had built hotels that were perfect for the Kentucky Military Institute (KMI), a school that had begun searching for new winter quarters for its cadets in 1930. It modified the BLE hotels to its use, and the first class of cadets arrived in 1932. The cadets and their visiting families took full advantage of the railroad pushed by the Palmer family, which arrived at the depot built by the BLE. KMI stayed for 40 years until 1972.

In 1941, Finn Caspersen contacted the US Army, promoting the idea of building an Air Corps base in Venice. By July 1942, the base was partially operational. It eventually trained 22,000 men for World War II. In 1945, when the war ended, the Army left an intact airfield that became the Venice Municipal Airport.

After Dr. Albee died, a second hospital, the Venice Hospital, was established in the early 1950s. Also, in the 1950s and 1960s, architects from the Sarasota School of Architecture designed a number of Mid-Century Modern homes and buildings that were situated among the Mediterranean Revival buildings created by the BLE and others. Housing developments proliferated over the years as the owners of citrus groves and cattle ranches sold their lands to property developers. Venice gradually expanded its city boundaries to accommodate those new developments.

The 1960s also brought to Venice the Ringling Bros. and Barnum & Bailey Circus (RB&BBC), which established its winter headquarters in Venice. The circus maintained this connection for 30 years. Eventually, it even established a clown school here.

In 1967, the Intracoastal Waterway (ICW), circling the original city and airport, was finally completed after 70 years of controversy and planning. This led to the building of the three bridges that we see today and gave rise to the term "island of Venice" to refer to that part of the city west of the Intracoastal.

All of the individuals and companies described above brought new residents and visitors to the area, from the early settlers to Lord, Palmer, and Albee to the BLE, KMI, RB&BBC, and the ICW. They did this directly through their companies and projects but also through the many businesses and individuals needed to support their efforts.

A major reason people visited Venice or decided to stay probably stems from the John Nolen Plan and the livability it imparts. Streets are walker-friendly, parks are close at hand, and historic districts of housing and businesses are a few examples of the many facets of his design. Another is the great boulevard, West Venice Avenue, with Heritage Park down its center, and a winding tree-shaded path that still draws people to the beach.

We need to take one further moment to talk about volunteers. Some are mentioned in the text of this book, but this understates the influence that broad groups of volunteers, both permanent residents and those who only come in the winter, have had. These unpaid individuals have had a direct and far-reaching impact on the community. They include those who have saved and treasured historical documents and photographs and those who educate the interested public by acting as docents and explainers. Many participate in service projects, in gardening, or in the arts and theater. Scuba divers organize to clean up trash found in many of the waterways. Local businesses are a generous source of funding with a wellspring of volunteers among their staff. Beyond all this, volunteer groups have taken concrete action in the areas of local beautification, championing the preservation of Venice's history, and have worked directly with city government and agencies on the common goal of making certain that Venice retains the qualities that have made it the city that it is.

One

Shark Teeth, Beaches, and Storms

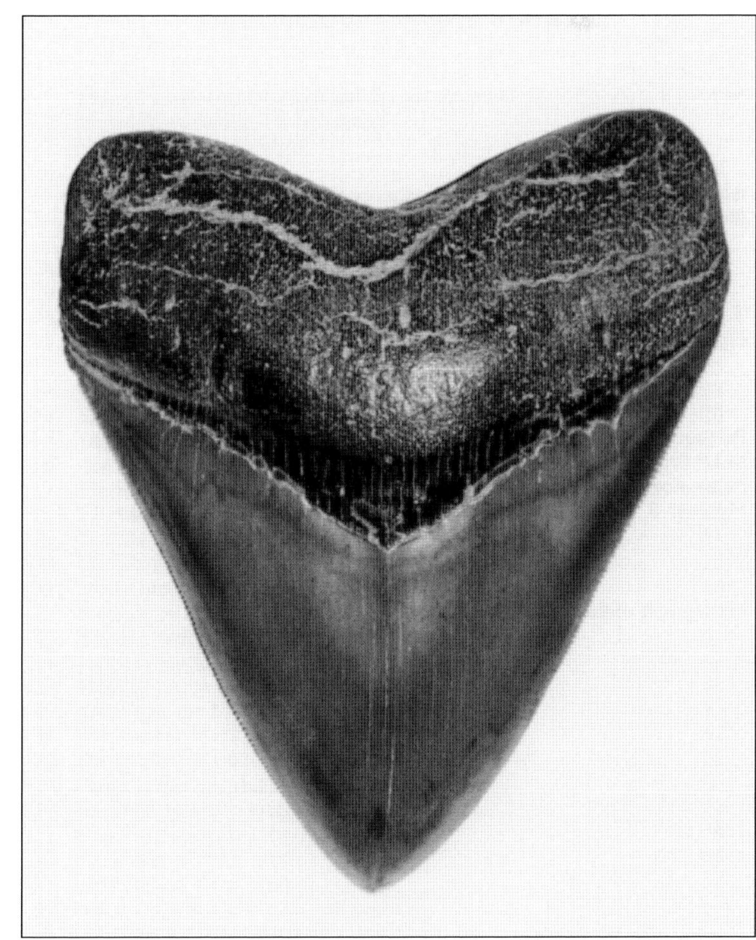

Welcome to "Venice—the Shark Tooth Capital of the World." It is not often that one will find shark teeth this size (four to five inches in width) on the beach. Sea levels have varied over the years, so these 2- to 35-million-year-old beauties are more often found inland, miles from the beach. (Robert L. Fuqua.)

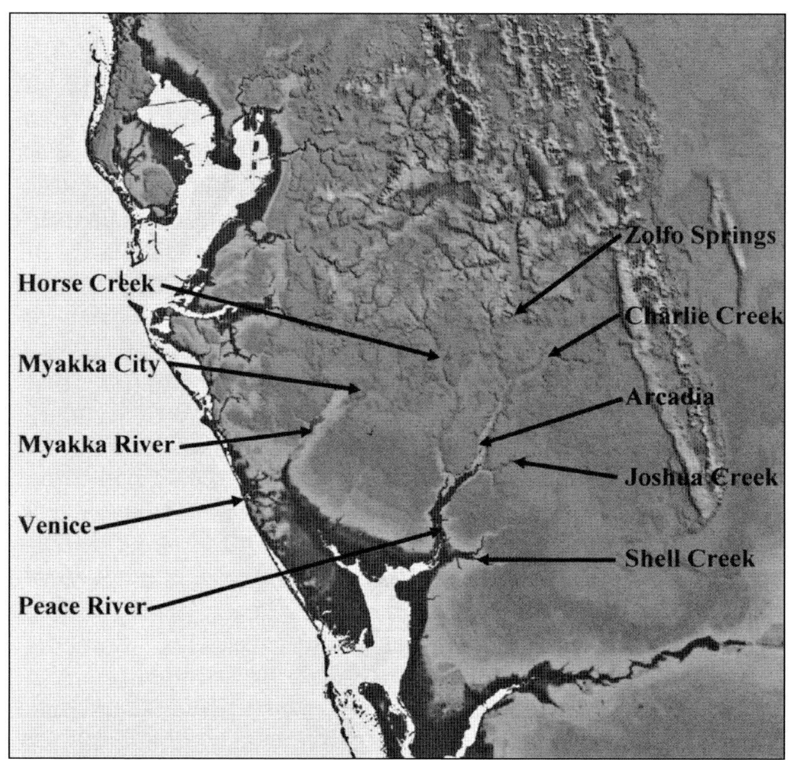

Often, these exquisite treasures have broken shoulders or points resulting from millions of years of being buried and then tumbled about in rivers or seawater on their ride to the beach. Fossils are found in many locations in southwest Florida but particularly in Venice. (Robert L. Fuqua.)

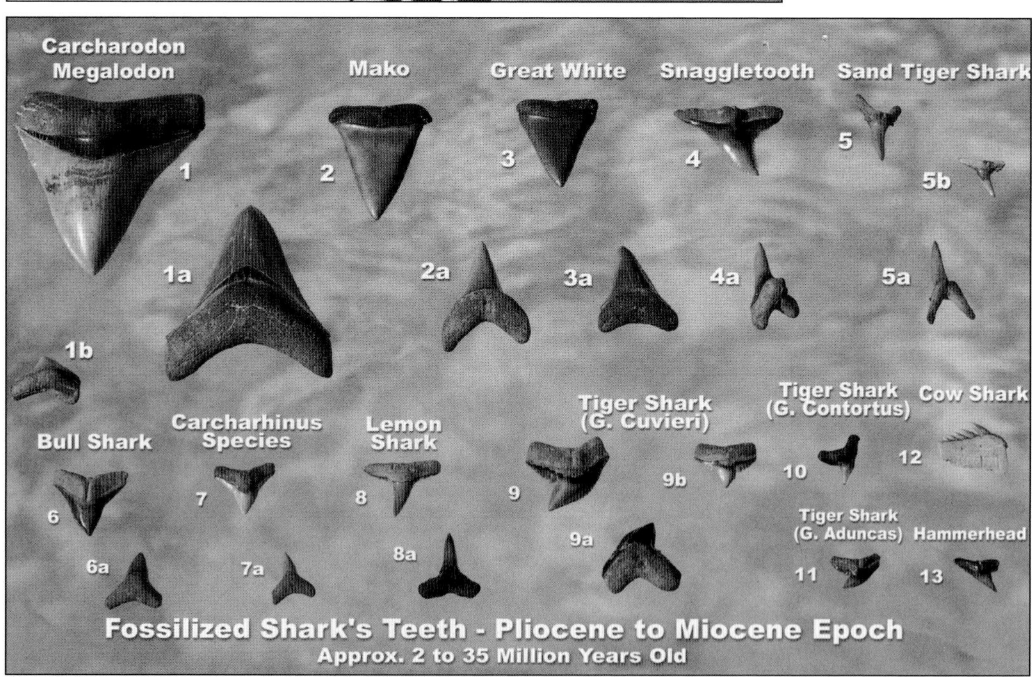

Charts, books, and online sources can help identify the fossil remains of shark teeth, turtles, mammals, stingrays, and other ocean creatures found on the beach and in the water. This chart by a local shark tooth diver showing many extinct species is particularly helpful. (Buzz and Wendy Fink.)

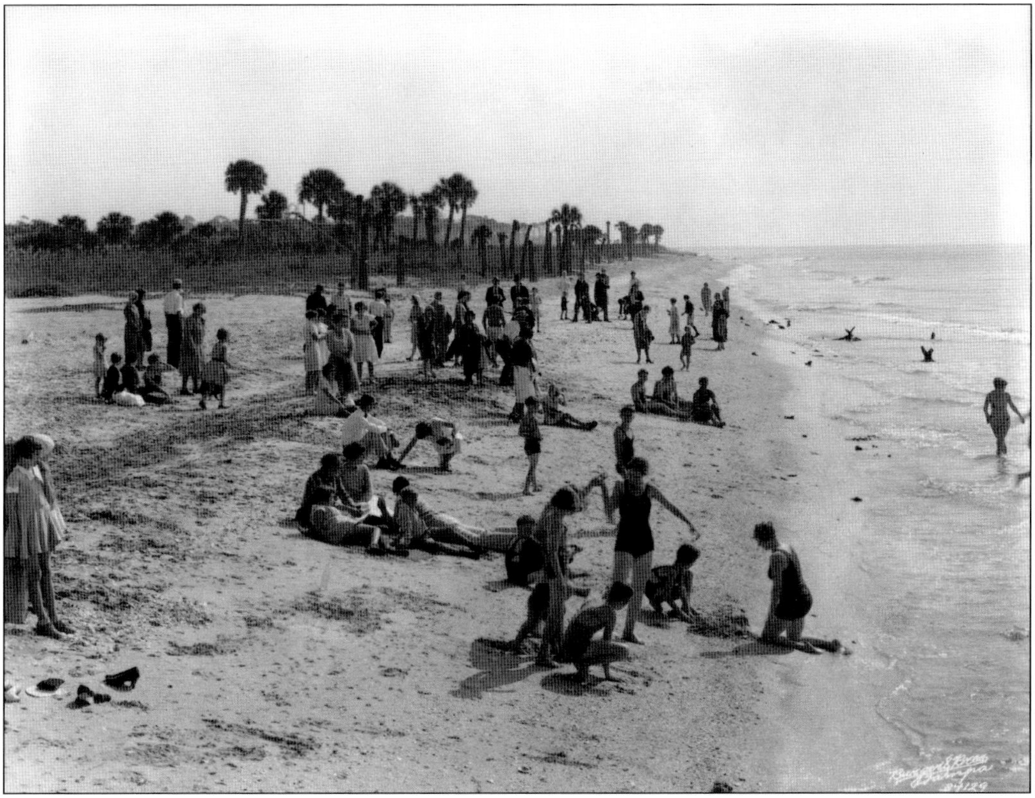

This 1960s image of Caspersen Beach has the salt-and-pepper speckles of the original Venice beaches prior to beach replacement. The black bits are minerals, plus a variety of fossils, such as shark teeth, whale and dugong bones, and stingrays, that have been fossilized over millions of years. (2008.21.100, CD 36 of 48.)

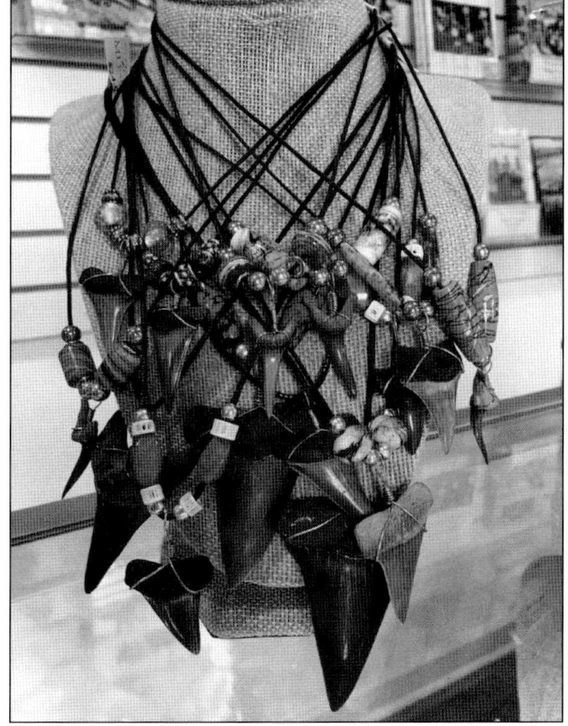

Many locally found shark teeth, plus numerous other fossils, are displayed and sold at the Venice Museum & Archives at the Triangle Inn. This city museum, with themed exhibits changing every few months, is operated by the Historical Resources Department and is located on Nassau Street in East Blalock Park. (RR.)

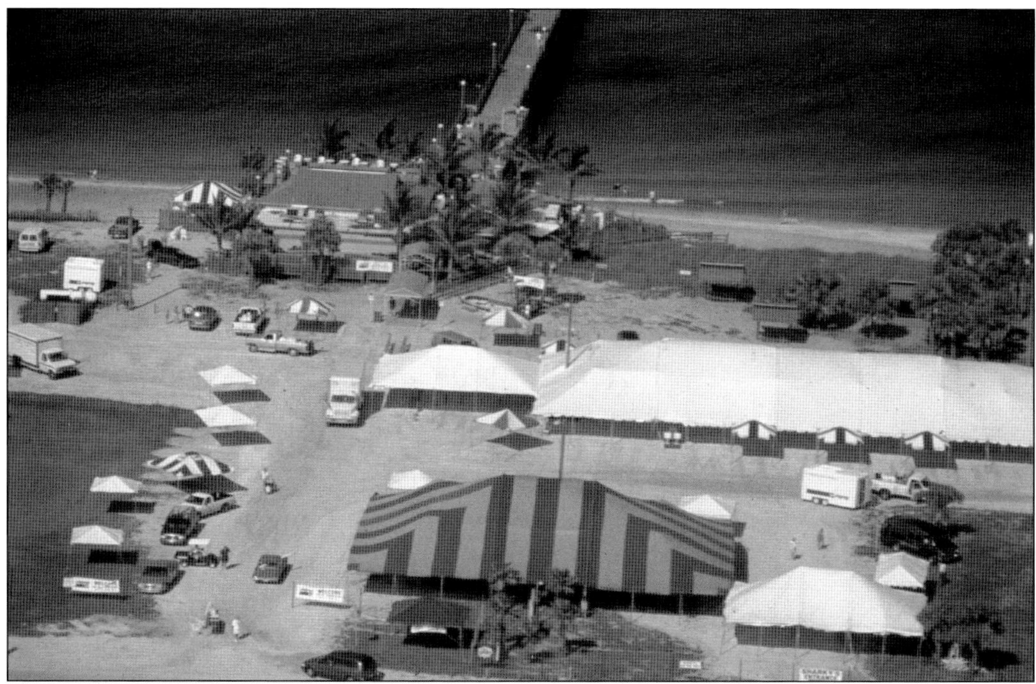

At the annual Sharks Tooth Festival, shoppers can buy shells and shark teeth or jewelry made with fossils. This 1960s aerial of the festival shows tents in the parking lot of the original Sharky's Restaurant, with the Venice Fishing Pier also seen. (PH26.0158, image 5 of 5.)

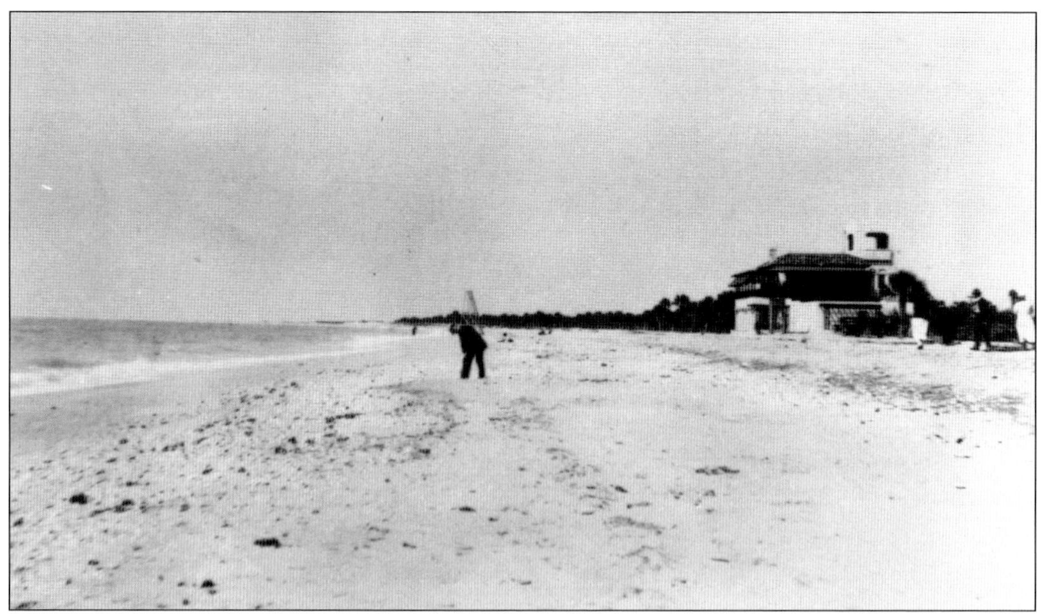

Try concentrating on the many fossils and broken bits of minerals found on the beach, as this 1920s gentleman is. Generally, black or brown shark teeth are the oldest. Occasionally, one may find white teeth shed by a recent shark, maybe still out in the water, hunting for dolphins, fish, turtles, or smaller sharks. (SCHC.)

Why are there so many fossils in the Venice area? This book by Tonya Clayton makes over 30 references to Venice, Caspersen Beach, Casey Key, and Manasota Key. It explains why Venice has no barrier islands, and it explains why Venice's beach structure is so unique. (MMK.)

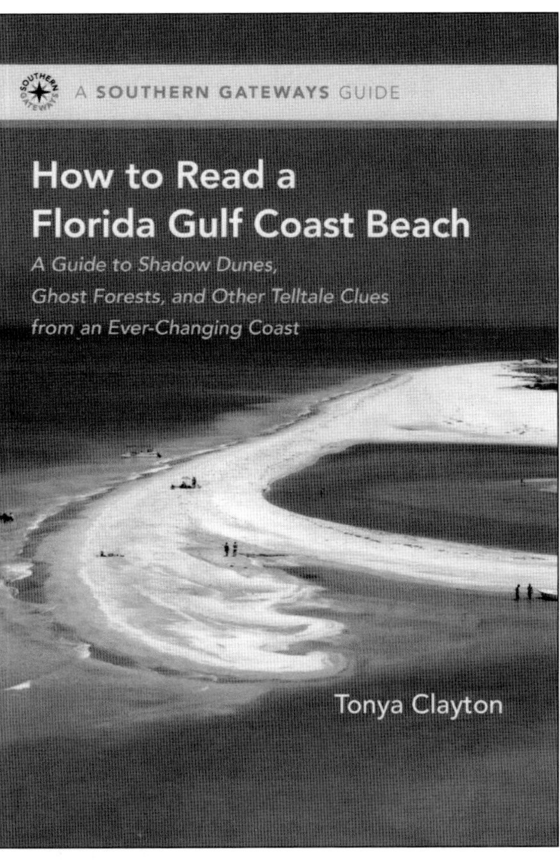

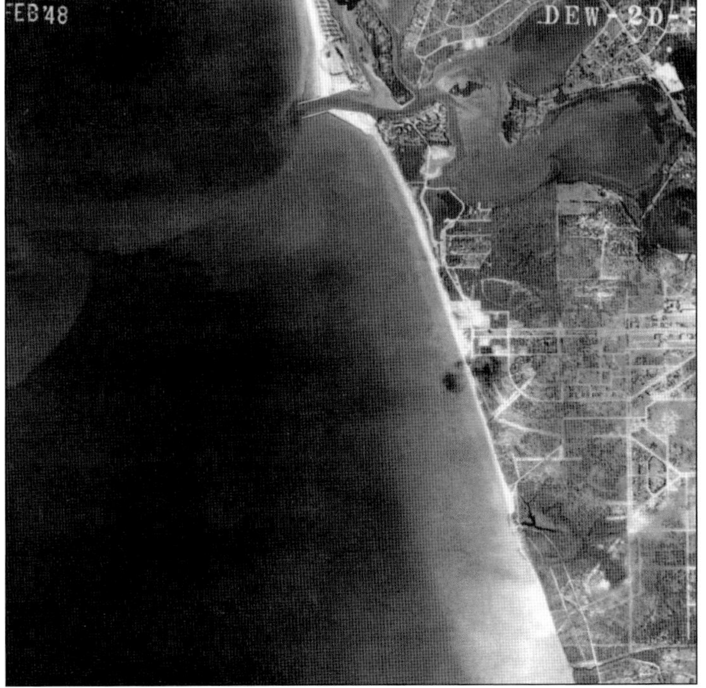

A section of the Peace River Formation of the Hawthorn Group is just offshore. It prevents a barrier island, or a key, from forming off Venice Beach. It sheds the many black and brown fossils and minerals that once created the uniquely colored salt-and-pepper sand. Thus Venice is a natural peninsula, as seen in this 1948 aerial from the map collection of the University of Florida. (PH26.0464, image 1 of 15.)

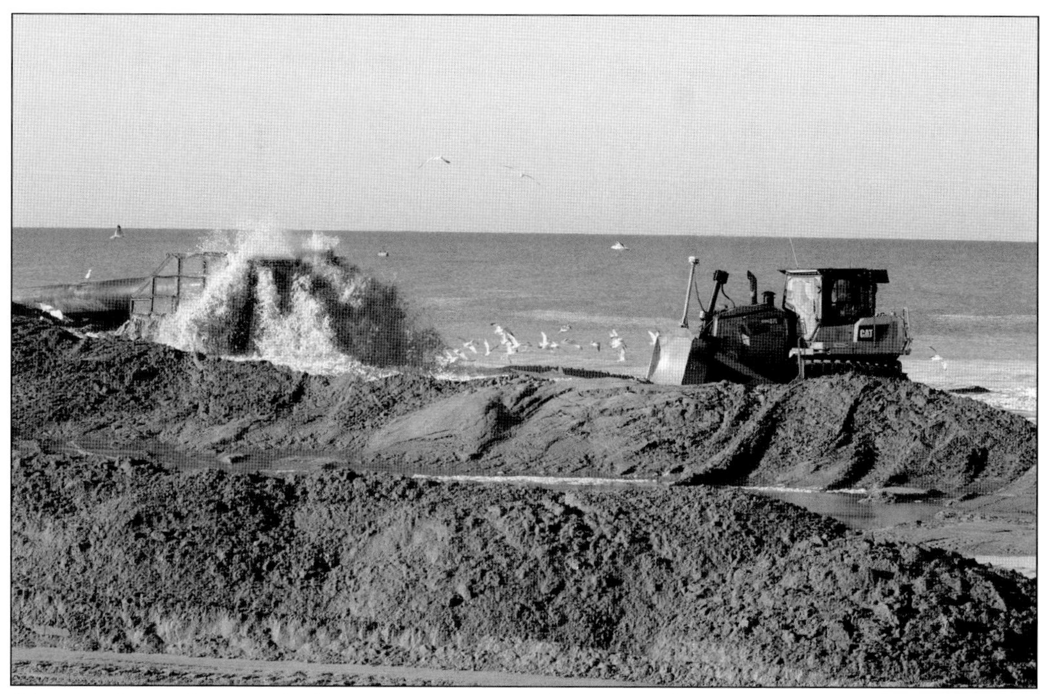

Climate change has resulted in rising waters and increasingly intense storms that wash away beaches. Property owners and visitors expect attractive beaches, which may require expensive sand replacement to replenish beach erosion. These 2015 photographs show sand being pumped onshore from far beyond the Peace River Formation. Sand can also be dredged onto flat barges and then pumped onshore. (PH26.0543, CD011, image 11 of 263.)

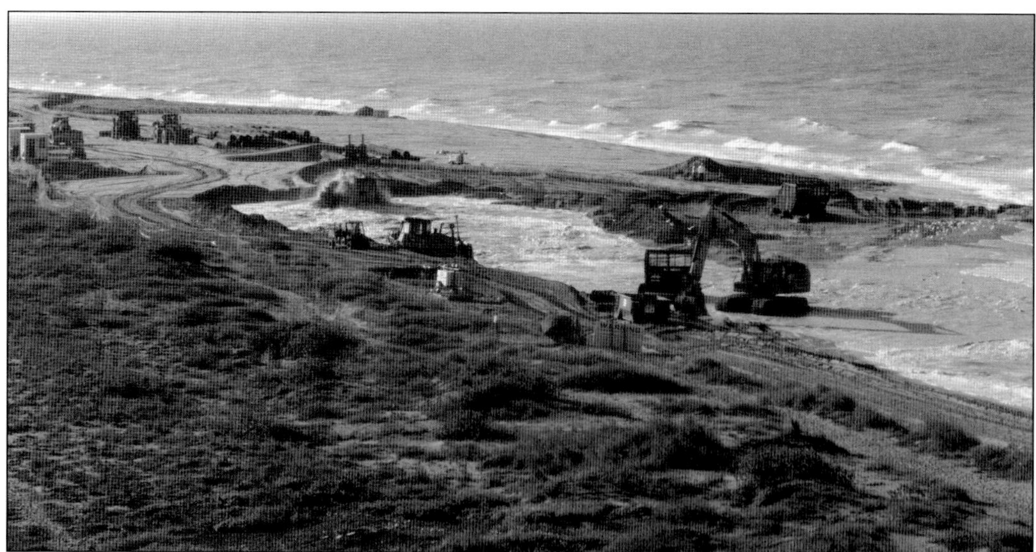

It is hard to call these 2015 photographs beach "renourishment." It is much better described as beach "replacement." Consider this when sitting on a sandy beach and question why, after sand replacement, even in the early morning, there are few fossils on the beach. (PH26.0543, CD036, image 35 of 263.)

Jetties, including the two at the Venice Inlet, commonly disrupt the natural flow of sand, as seen in this 1970s aerial view. Sand flows from the north to the south in the Gulf near Venice, so it gathers on the north side of the jetty but recedes on the south side. (NP0934.)

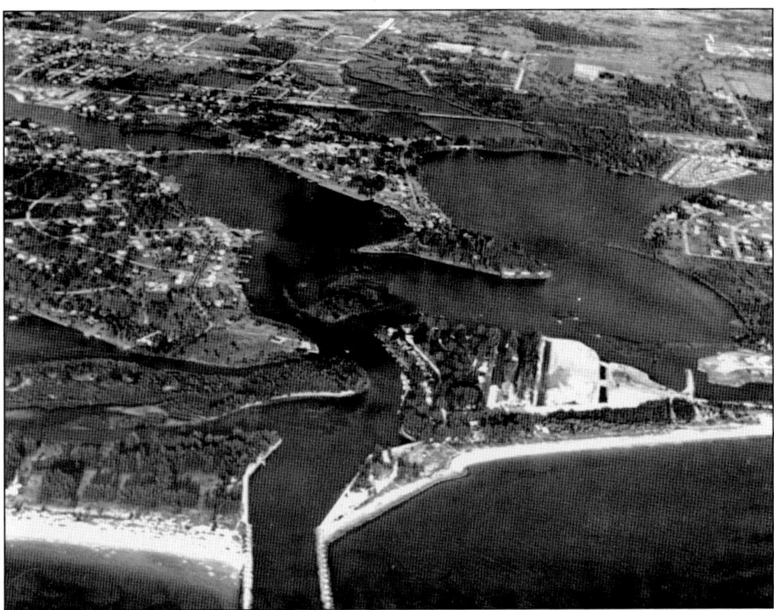

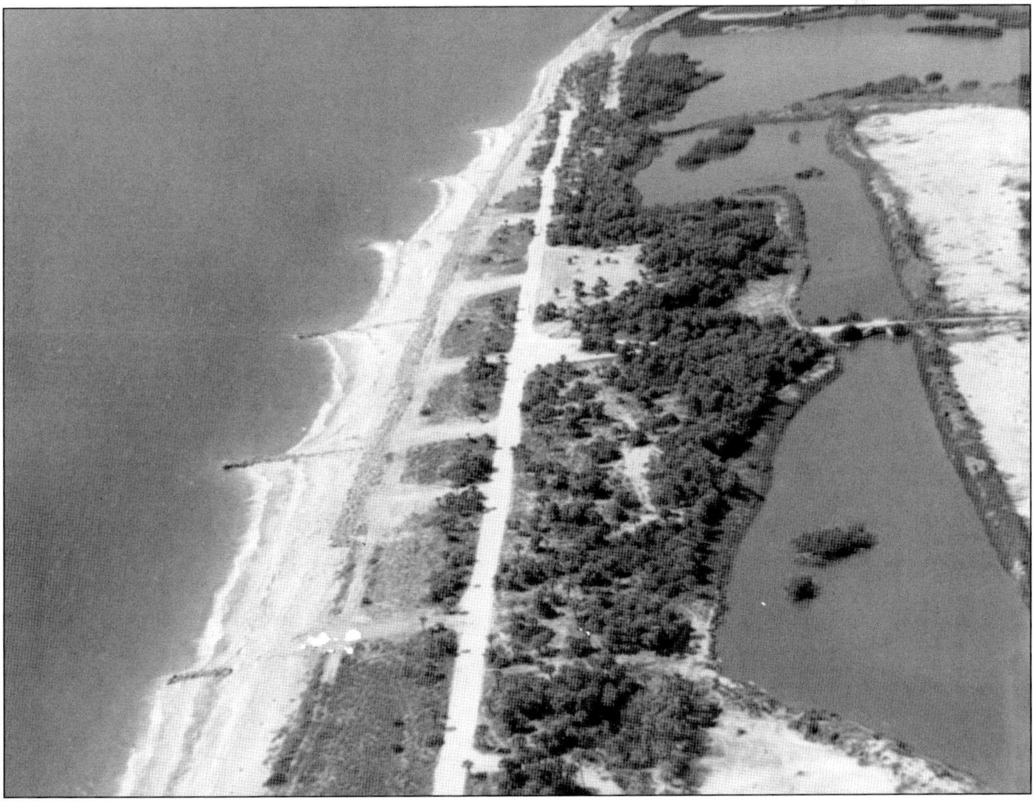

The afore-mentioned Clayton book quotes an estimate that 6,300 dump truck–sized loads of sand move along the Venice-area beaches each year. In the 1970s at Caspersen Beach, man-made structures extended into the water. They were envisioned to catch sand but actually made erosion worse. After removing them, only piles of rocks now remain. (PH26.0168.)

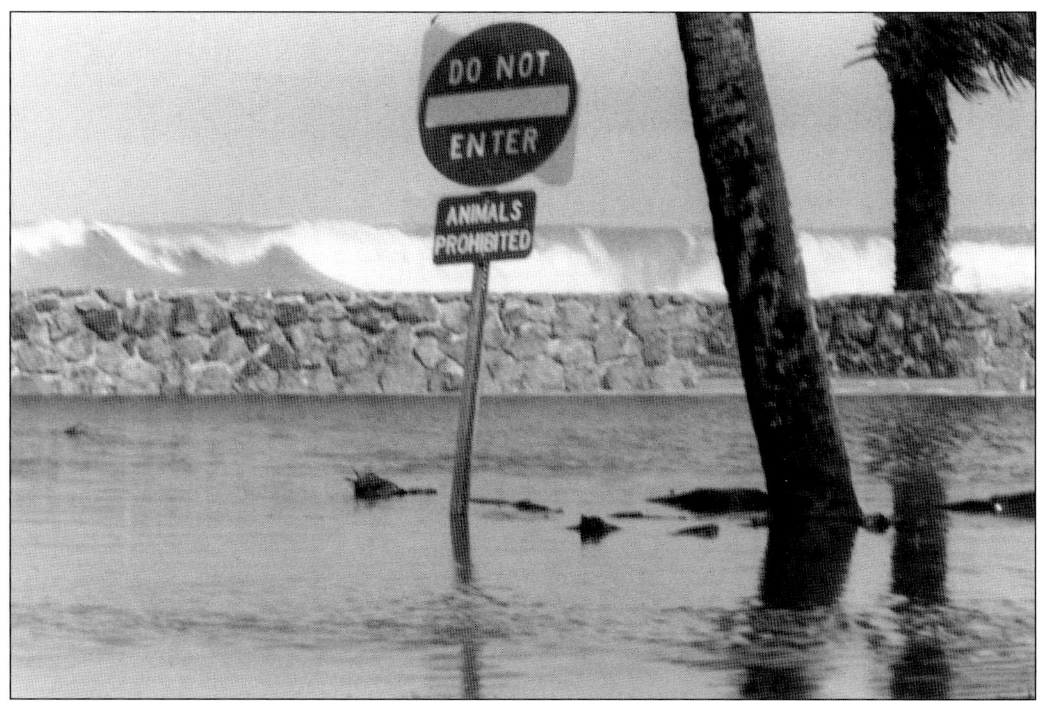

A hurricane or storm does not have to strike Venice to do damage. The worst winds and waves are often in the northeast quadrant of a storm. So, as it is chugging northward, miles out in the Gulf, a storm can, depending upon how wide it is, send multiple high waves and surges toward Venice, as seen from this 1982 storm. (PH26.0233.)

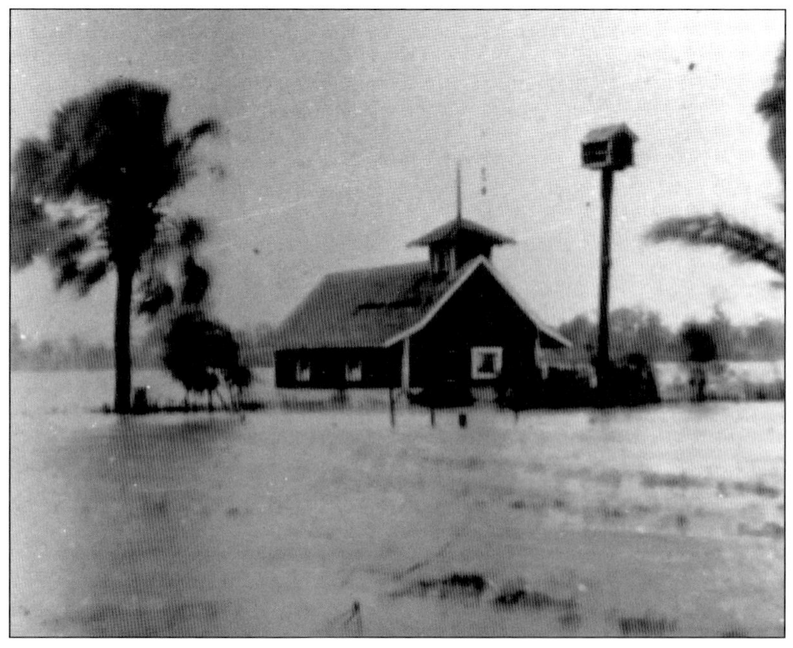

Venice's shallow bays, low-lying land, and inland creeks can overflow in heavy rain storms. Salty storm-surge water undermines buildings, pushing high tides inland, as this 100-year-old fuzzy image taken in the pouring rain a mile from the beach demonstrates. High winds create higher waves, tear off roofs, and bring down trees. (PH26.0420.)

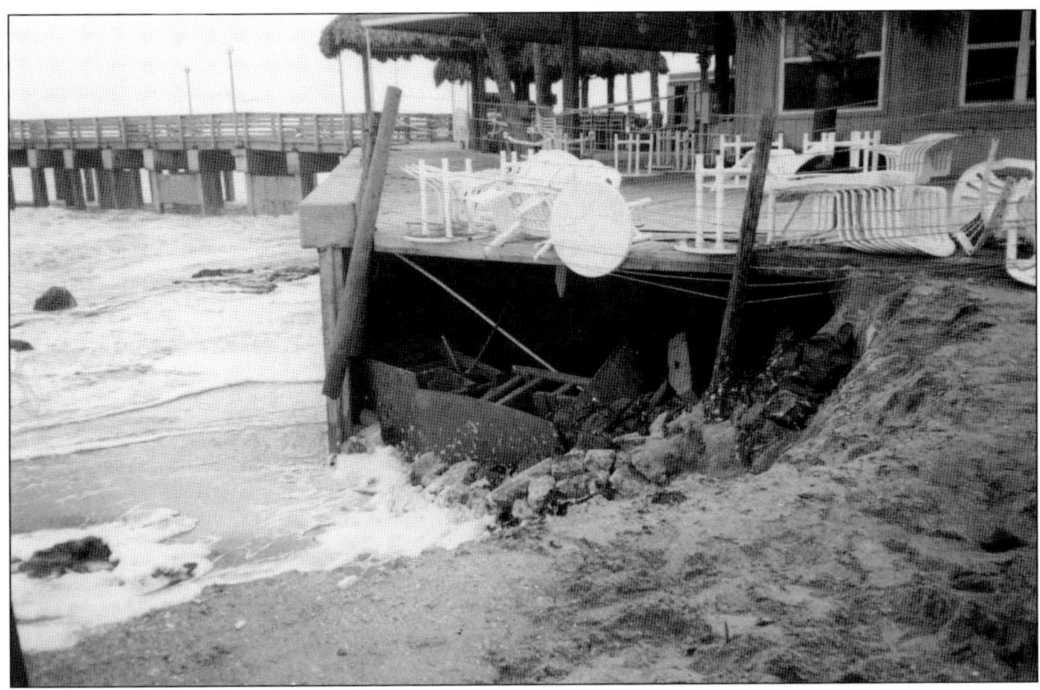

On March 13, 1999, a tropical storm referred to as "No Name" undermined the shore and decking of the first rendition of Sharky's Restaurant. Many storms before and since have resulted in both the restaurant's and the pier's damage, requiring extensive repair or even rebuilding. (PH26.0619.)

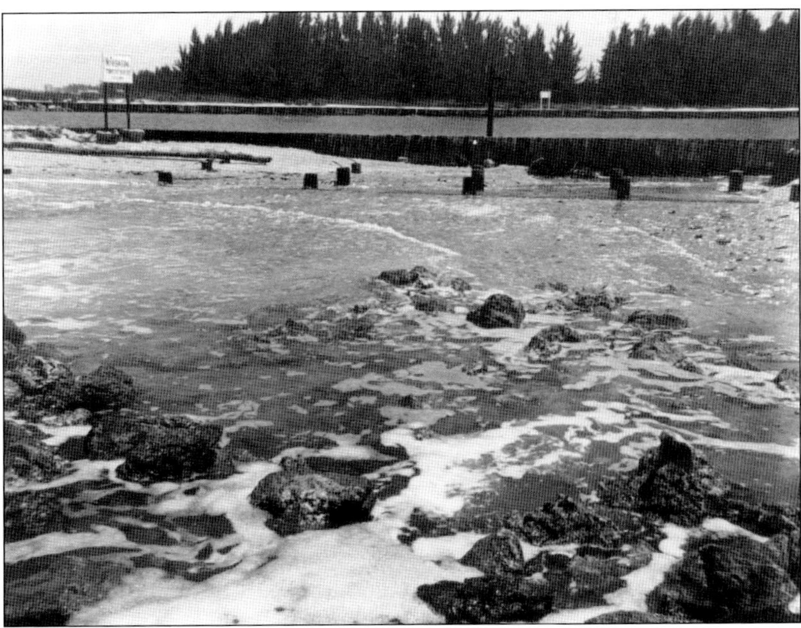

Look at the waves rushing over the remains of the jetty on the Venice side of the Venice Inlet in the 1960s. Even the large boulders protecting the jetties can be washed over and carried away. This is an aftermath photograph, so one can imagine what the waves were like during the actual storm. (NP0157.)

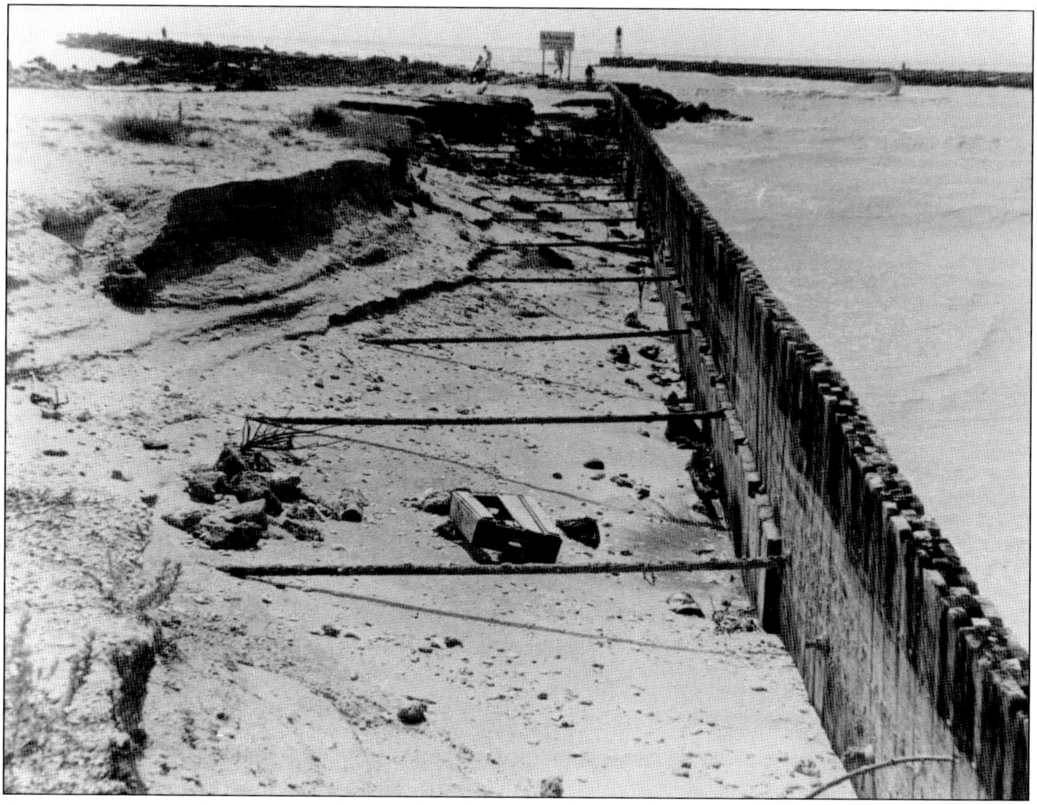

Repairs are expensive, such as this sand washout on the South Jetty in the 1960s, and are passed along to taxpayers and renters. The legend that Native American mounds provide protection for Venice seems inconsistent with the fact that mounds were used years ago to build roads. (NP0158.)

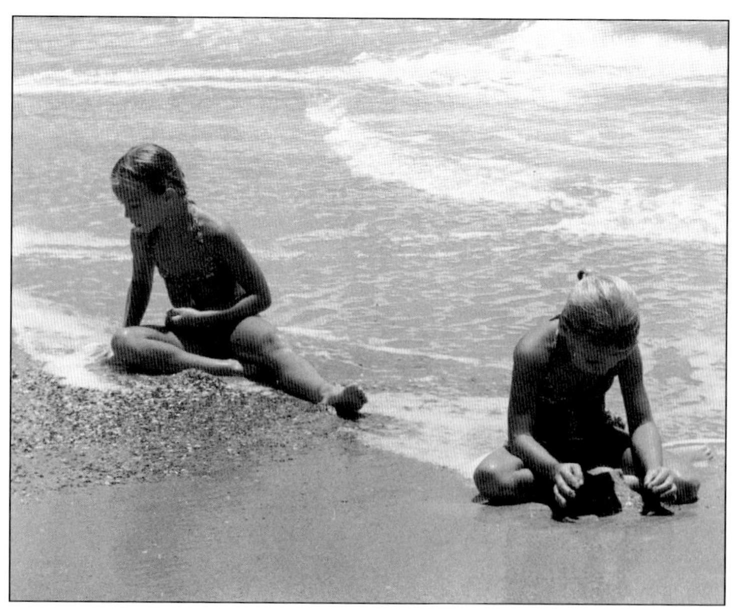

The older beachgoer is a seeker, working tirelessly in her search for shark teeth and fossils, while the younger one is actively engaged in building with sand. Along with surf casting, bird watching, kite surfing, strolling, or just whiling away the hours with a good book, these are familiar activities to beachgoers. (PH01.032.1, Box 1.)

In the 1960s, with a flowered swim cap or with wet hair, these three admire a recent find on Caspersen Beach. Note how the beach is salt-and-pepper in color. This was prior to the 1990s, when beach sand replacement took priority. (PH01.032.2, Box 1.)

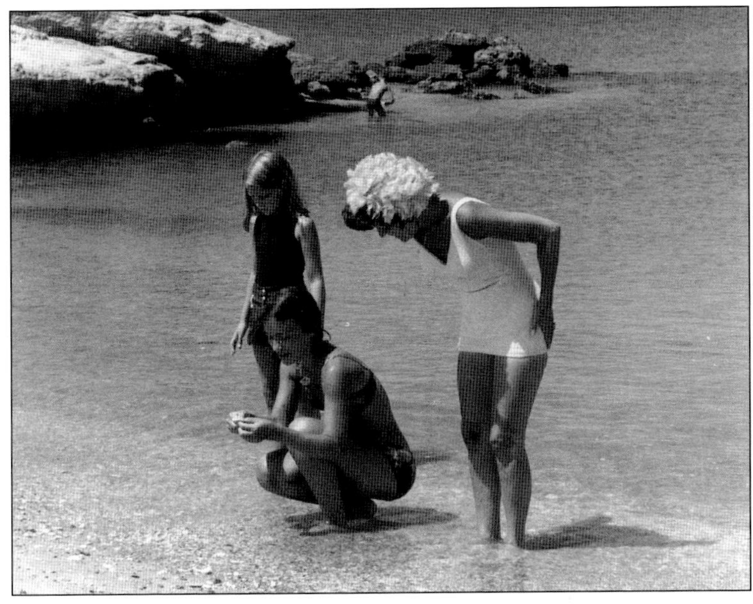

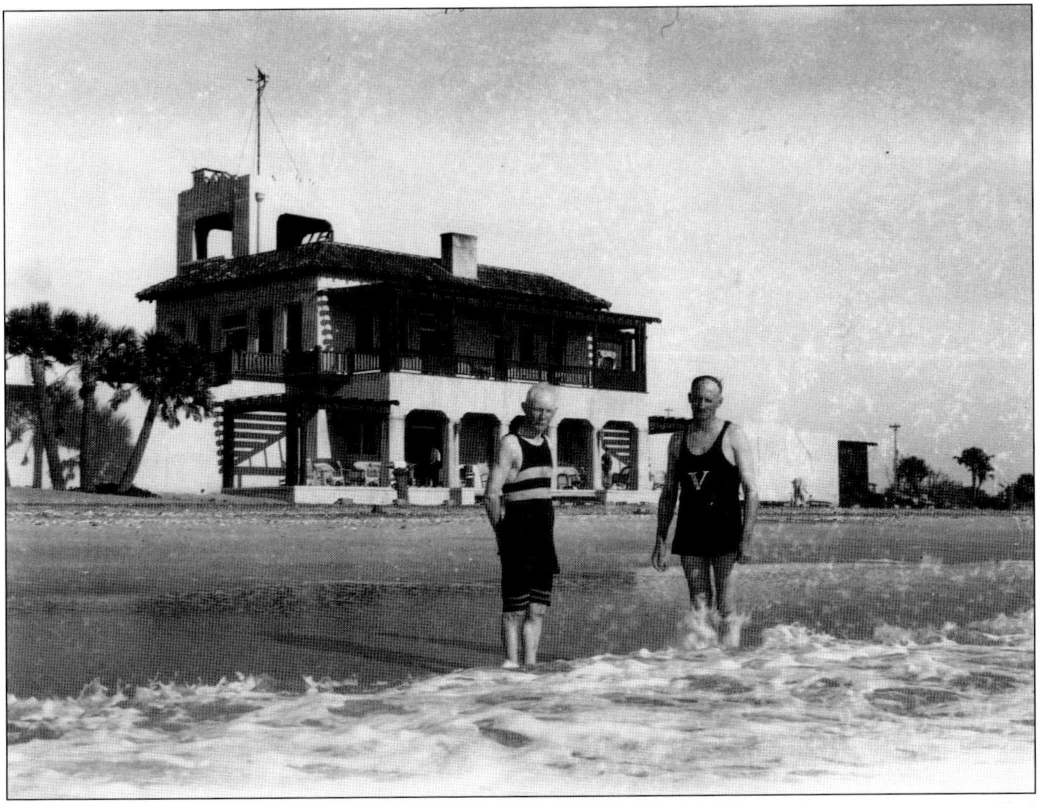

In 1925, Dr. Fred Albee started his planned resort with the first Beach Pavilion, sometimes called "the Beach House and Casino." It was at 811 The Esplanade, near Ormond Street. Then, realizing how expensive building a resort would be, he soon sold nearly 1,500 acres to the BLE. In 1927, Henry Hauser (left) and Gus Reike are at the Albee Beach House. (NP0879.)

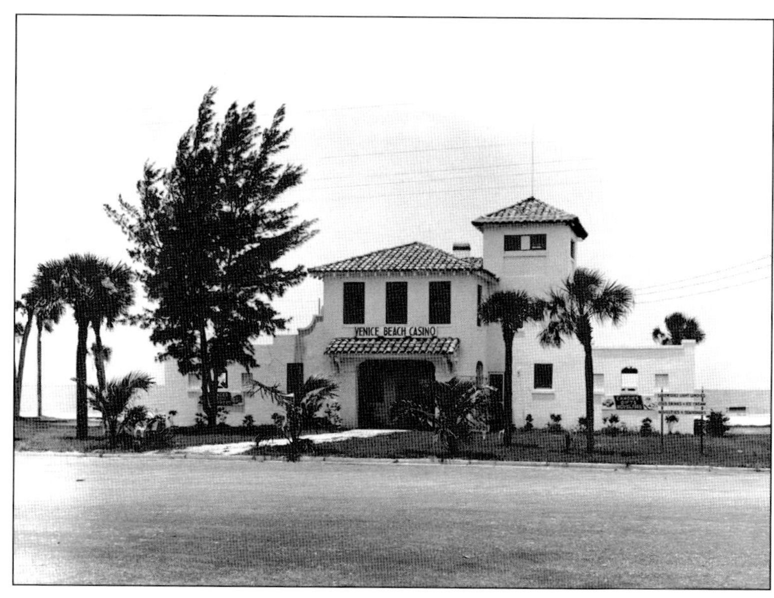

Albee's Beach Pavilion was destroyed in the 1932 hurricane, which bypassed Venice but struck Tampa. A second Mediterranean Revival–style Beach House and Casino was built in 1932–1933 by contractor Mitt Cousins using parts of Albee's building. Erected south of the original Beach House, its placement adhered to John Nolen's 1925 plan. (NP0218.)

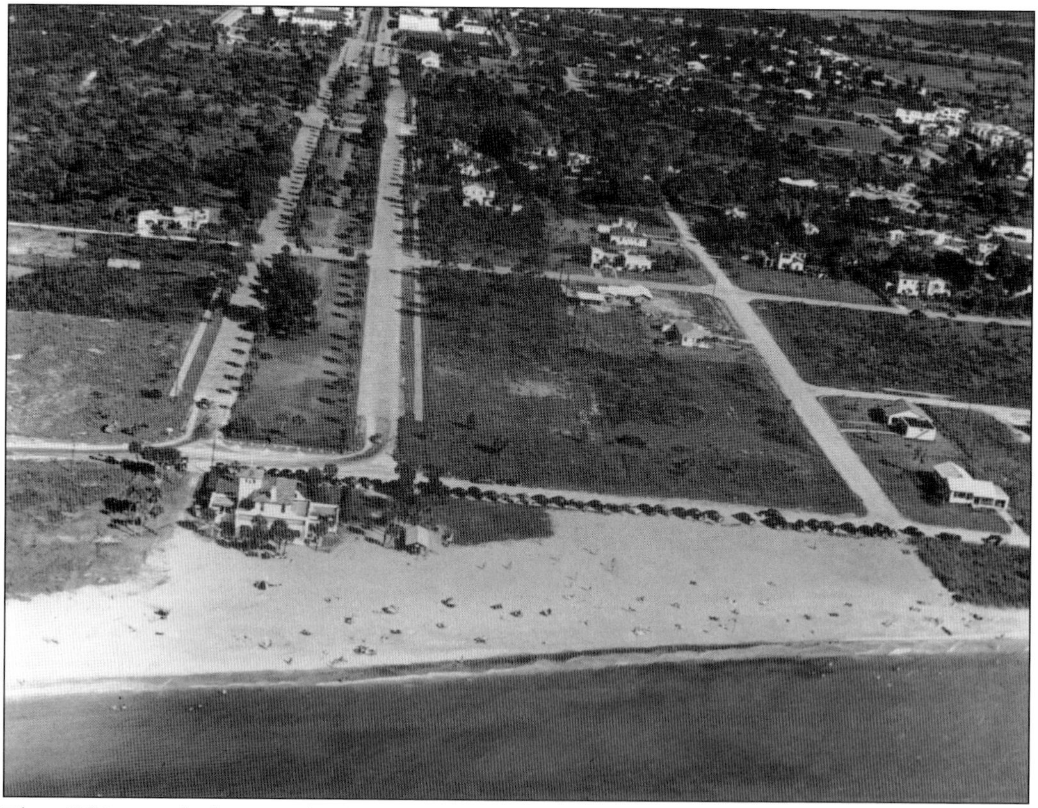

This 1950s aerial photograph shows the second Beach House and Casino at the end of West Venice Avenue. The word "casino" at that time did not mean gambling; instead, it meant a social gathering place. The second floor initially housed the mayor and city council, because a city hall had never been built by the BLE. (PH26.0465, 4 of 9.)

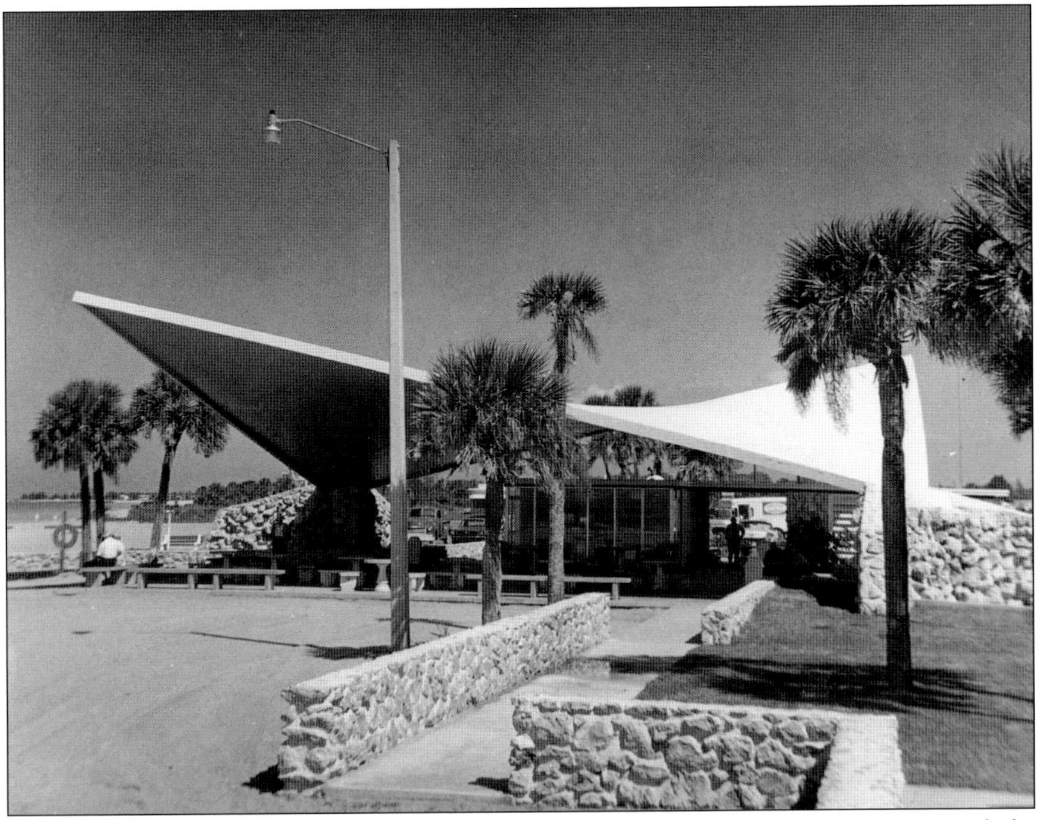

In 1963, the second Beach House was replaced with this unique and historic Hyperbolic Paraboloid Beach House on Venice Beach. Dedicated on February 8, 1964, William H. Lindh was the engineer, and Cyril T. Tucker was the architect. It was listed in the Local Register of Historical Resources in 2025. (MS26 Box 3 File 11.)

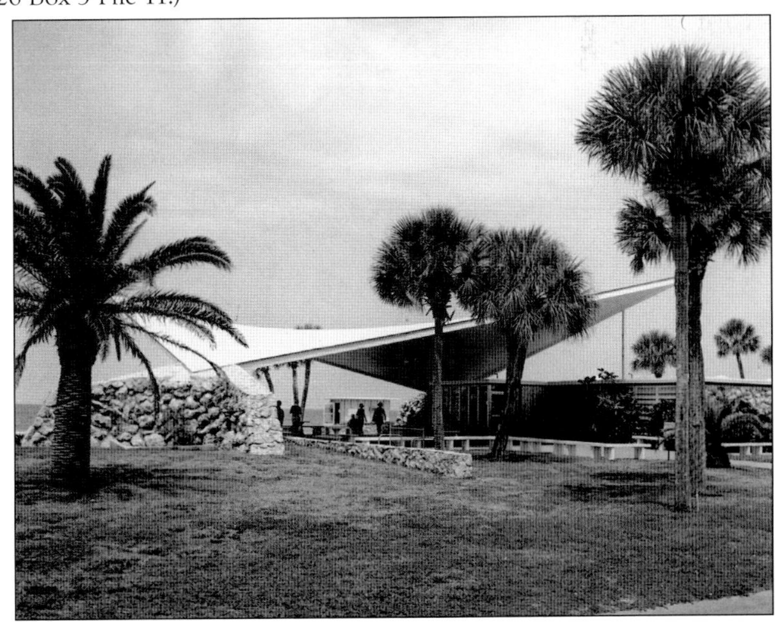

The third Beach Pavilion has lasted much longer than the two previous ones. It has a Mid-Century Modern look and a unique structure, with stone walls that elongate the view. The wings provide both structure and a lightheartedness. (MS26 Box 3 File 11.)

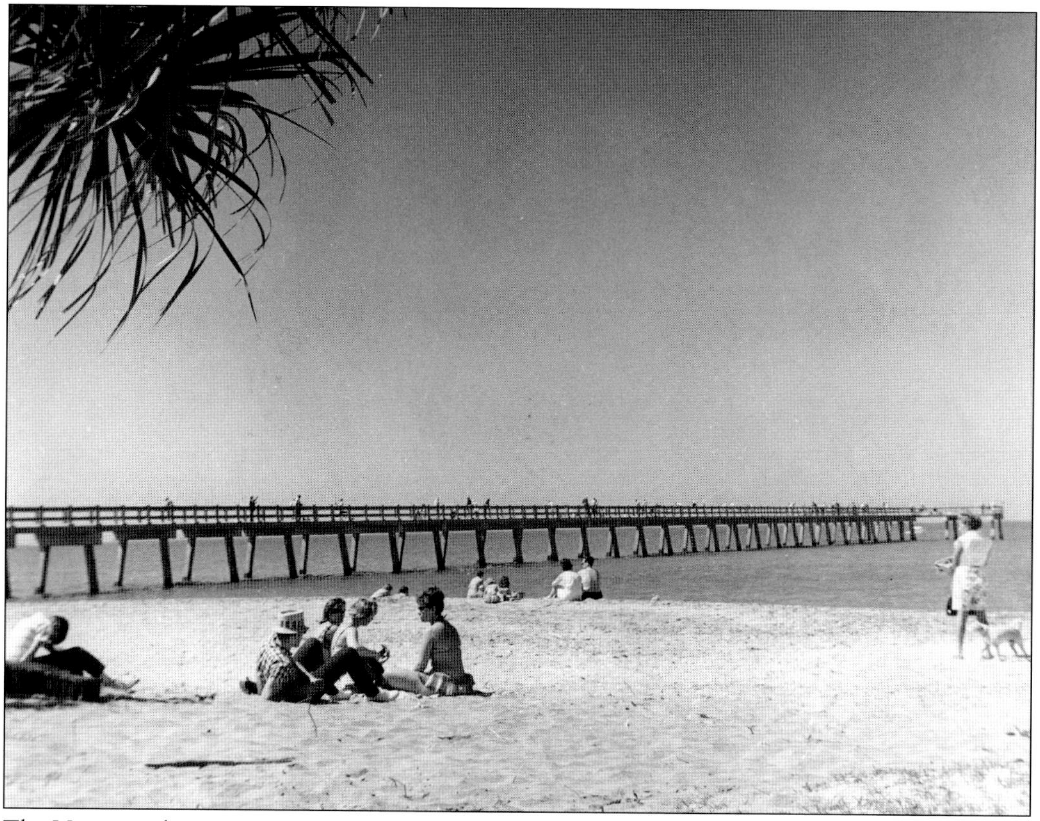

The Venice Fishing Pier is just north of Caspersen Beach. The original 1960s pier was 700 feet long, 12 feet high, and built of prestressed concrete. After a "No Name" storm in 1982, it was closed and then rebuilt in 1985 to be 20 feet longer. In 2004, it was again rebuilt to be 15 feet above the water. (NP0510.)

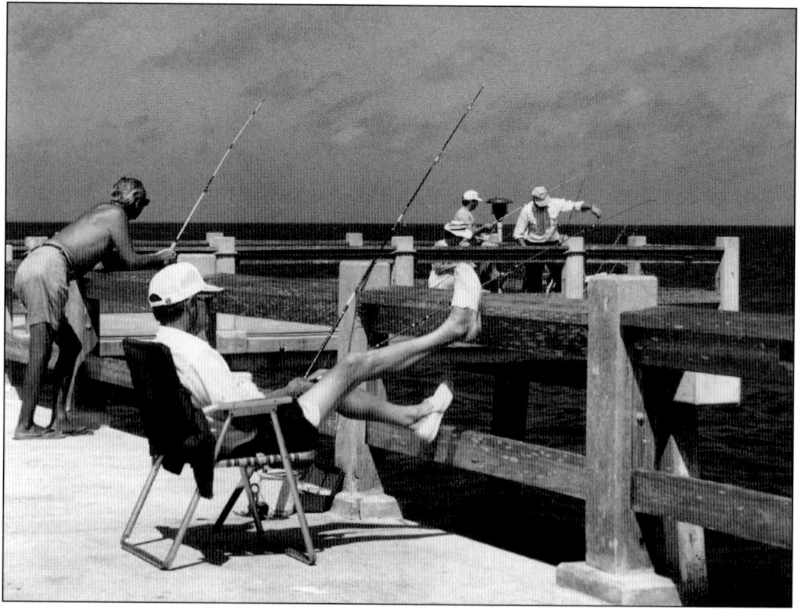

A walk out on the Venice Fishing Pier on a sunny day will make a visitor never want to leave Venice. People do not need a fishing license (at least in 2025) because the pier is owned by the city. The pier has been torn apart and closed for repairs several times due to storm damage but remains a popular site. (PH1.04.15.)

A child takes off running through the shallow waves, enjoying the moment without a care. With clear skies and sailboats, this scene is often repeated in Venice public relations brochures, newspapers, social media, and in real life. These photographs draw both tourists and property owners to the area. (PH01.32, Box 1.)

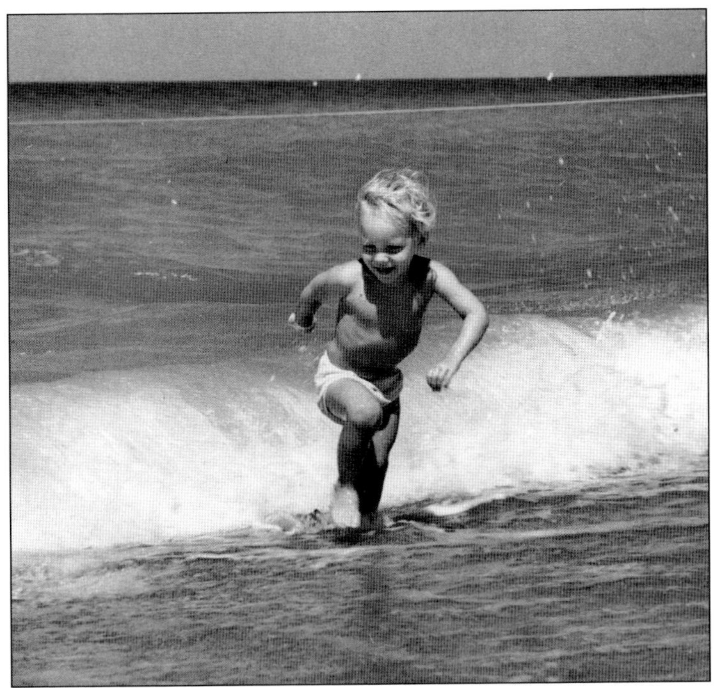

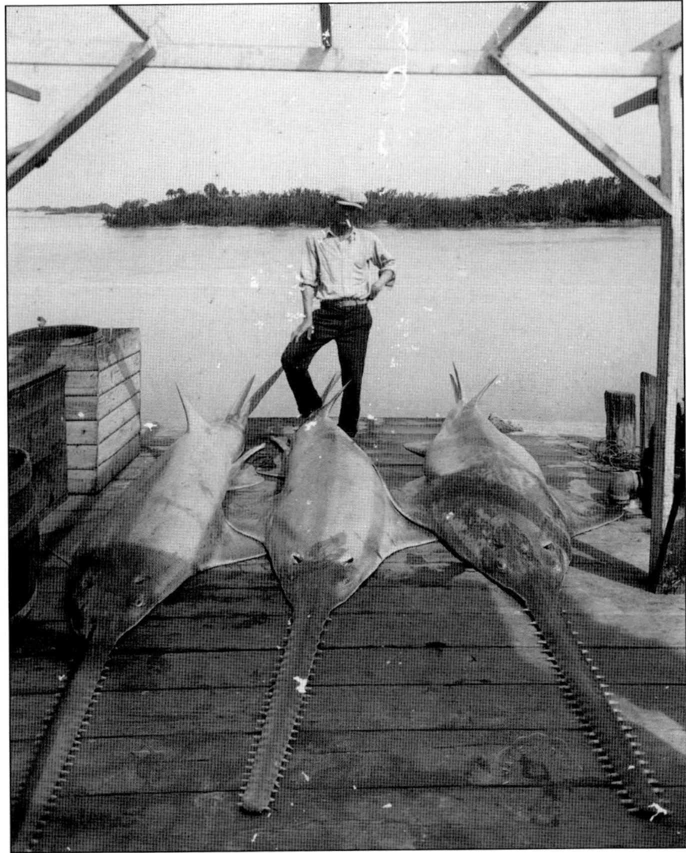

One fish often featured in older photographs is the smalltooth sawfish. Native to Florida, harvesting it has been prohibited since 1992. Since 2003, it has been on the Endangered Species List, and it has been protected from international trade since 2007. This c. 1926 image by Jay E. Brown of Elisha Turner features three sawfish, all larger versions than today's occasionally seen specimens. (NP0022.)

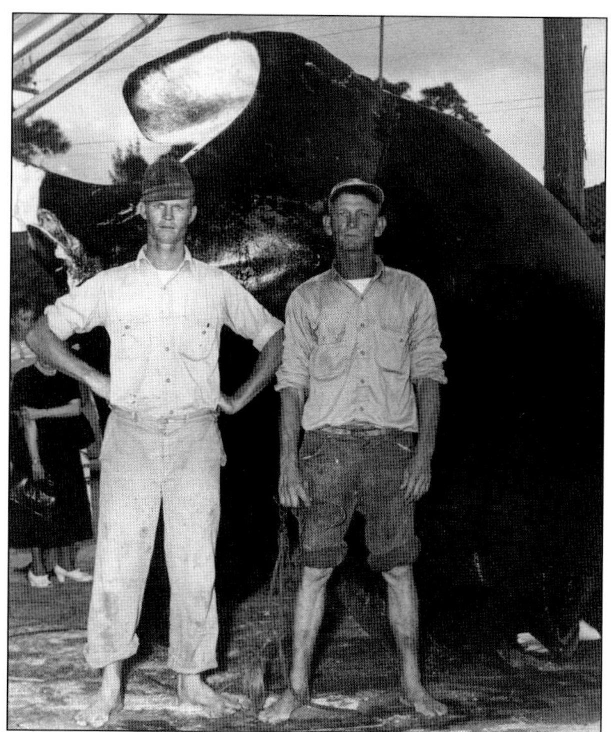

The manta ray also used to be sport fished. The underside of the sea creature is off white, while the top is almost black in color. Here, J.W. Moulton (left) and Earl Lewis are posing with Lewis's catch. Since 2018, when it was added to the US Endangered Species List, it has been illegal to capture, harass, or harm these gentle giants. (PH06.11.17.01.)

Earl Lewis looks exhausted and sweaty after landing this manta ray, possibly a *Mobula birostris*. Mantas eat zooplankton and sometimes small fish and can grow to 29 feet and 2,000 pounds. They are migratory, following warm waters, traveling in and out of the Gulf. (PH06.11.17.04.)

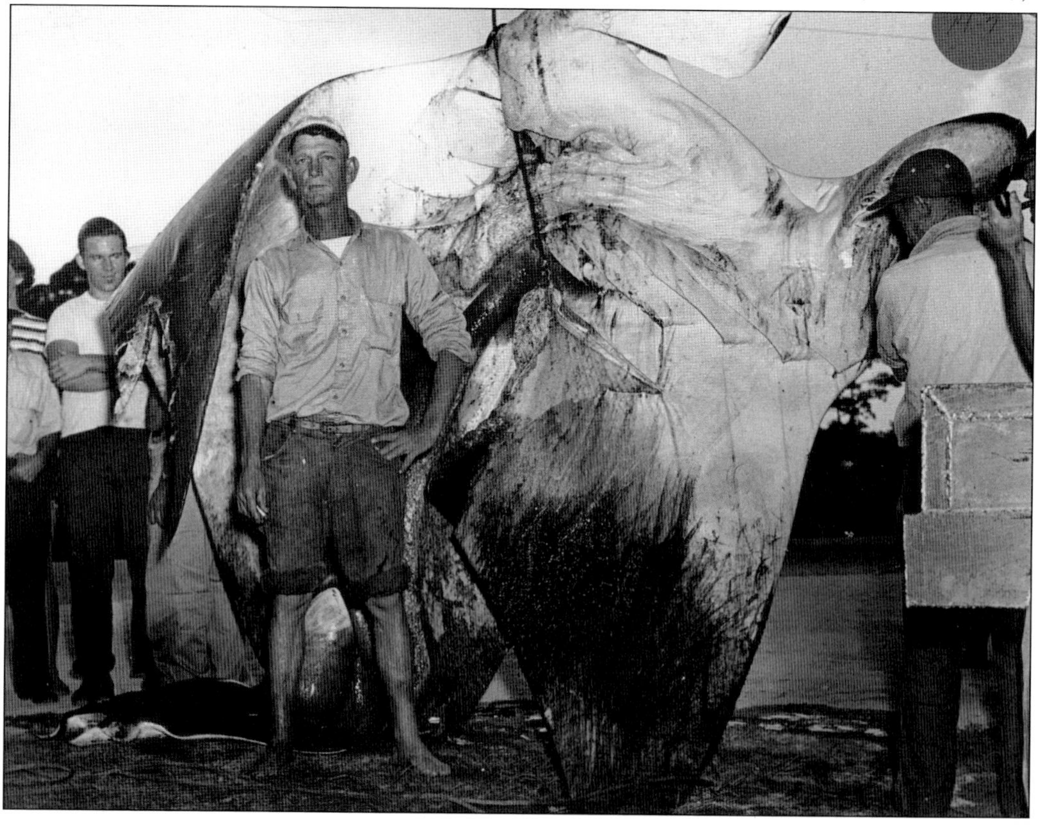

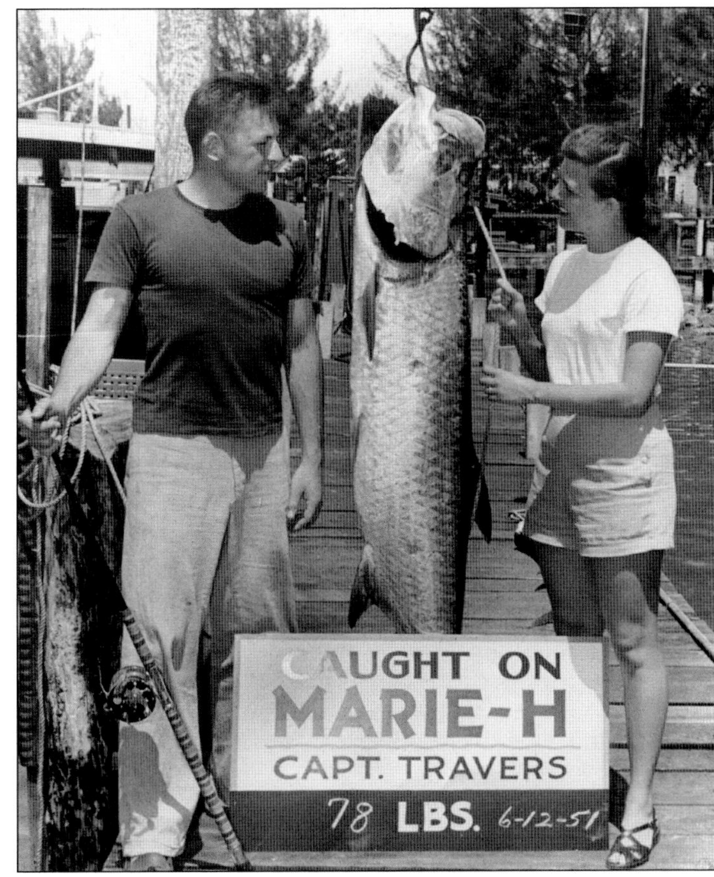

Tarpon often feed on vegetarian mullet fish in grassy areas. But overfishing, red tide, and polluted waters have decreased the numbers of tarpon caught and reduced their size. Since 2013, Florida state permits allow catch-and-release only on one tarpon tag per year. (PH06.11.21.09.)

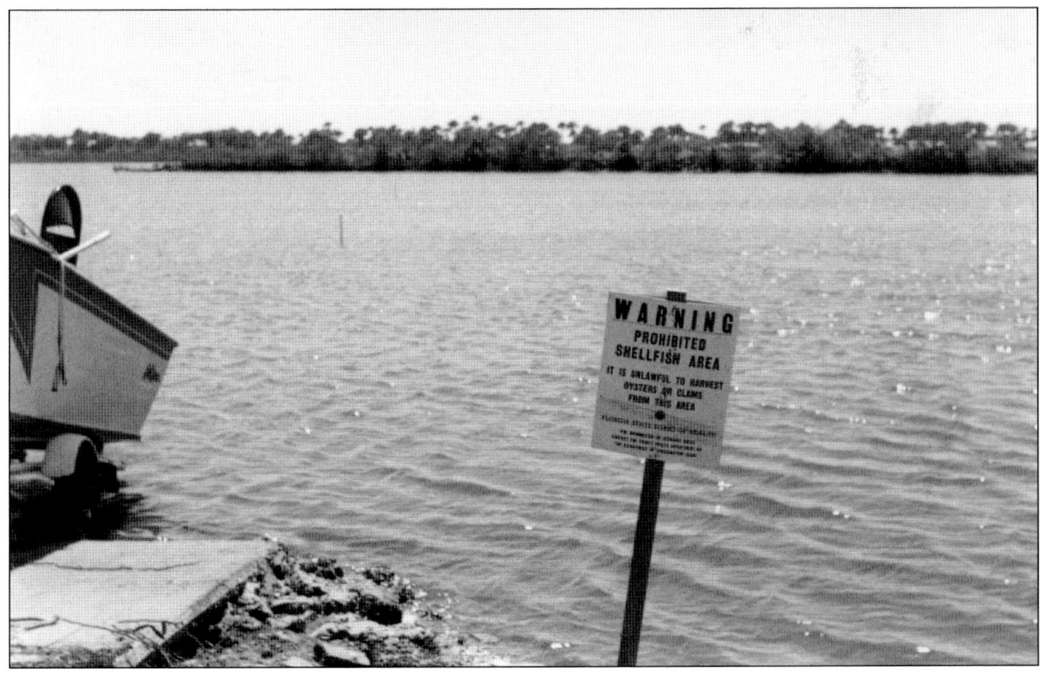

Even in 1966, sixty years ago, polluted waters dissuaded harvesting from once-plentiful clam and oyster beds. But early in the 1900s, county commissioners offered potential oyster beds for lease or sale, with the stipulation that beds be planted in the waterways and adjoining bays. Bertha Palmer had oysters off Eagle Point Resort, as did Joseph H. Lord near his Venice Groves. (PH03.01.08.)

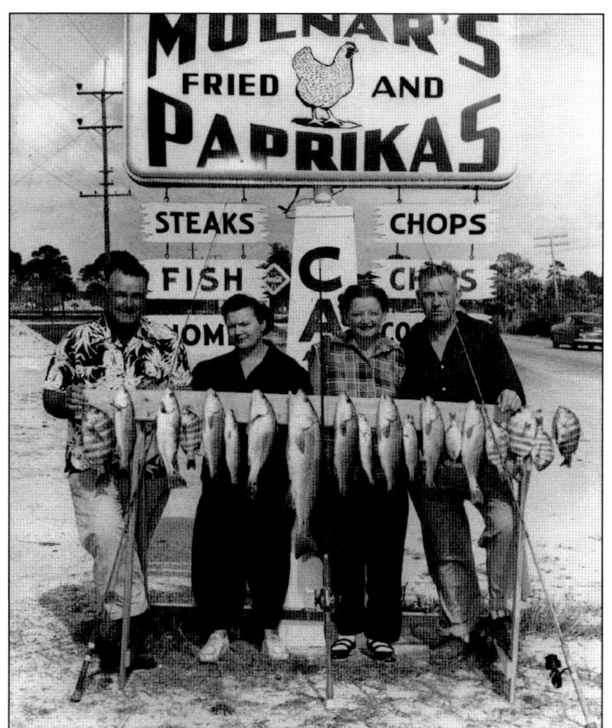

These days, most people practice catch-and-release, with the thrill of the catch most important. Plus, worries about polluted waters and red tide have dissuaded others. Years ago, many fishing charter boats were based in Roberts Bay, but no longer. Here in the 1950s, Charles and Margaret Molnar (left) of Molnar's Restaurant display catches by visitors Mr. and Mrs. Holler (right). (PH06.11.21.01.)

Years ago, almost everyone who lived in the area or who visited, famous or infamous, had their photograph taken. These were often of their family and friends displaying their catches, going fishing on a pier or boat, or participating in a fishing contest, as this 1950s image by Woody Thayer on Hatchett Creek demonstrates. (2008.21.076, image 10 of 46.)

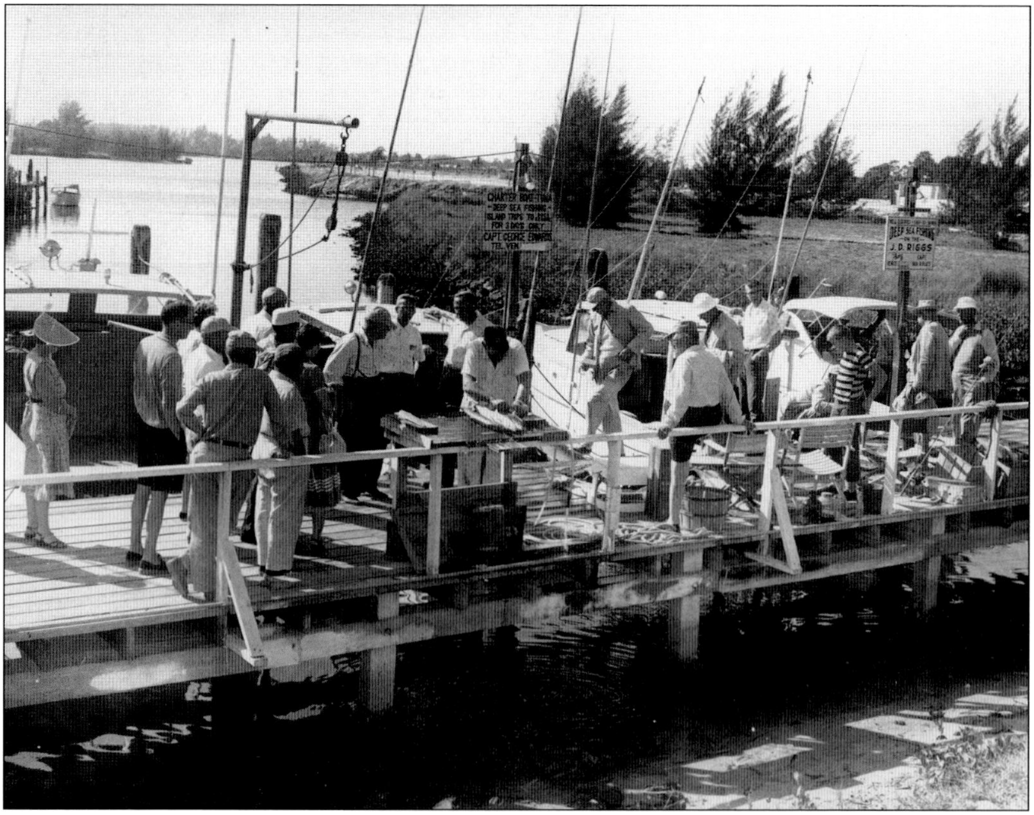

Two

Citrus Groves and J.H. Lord

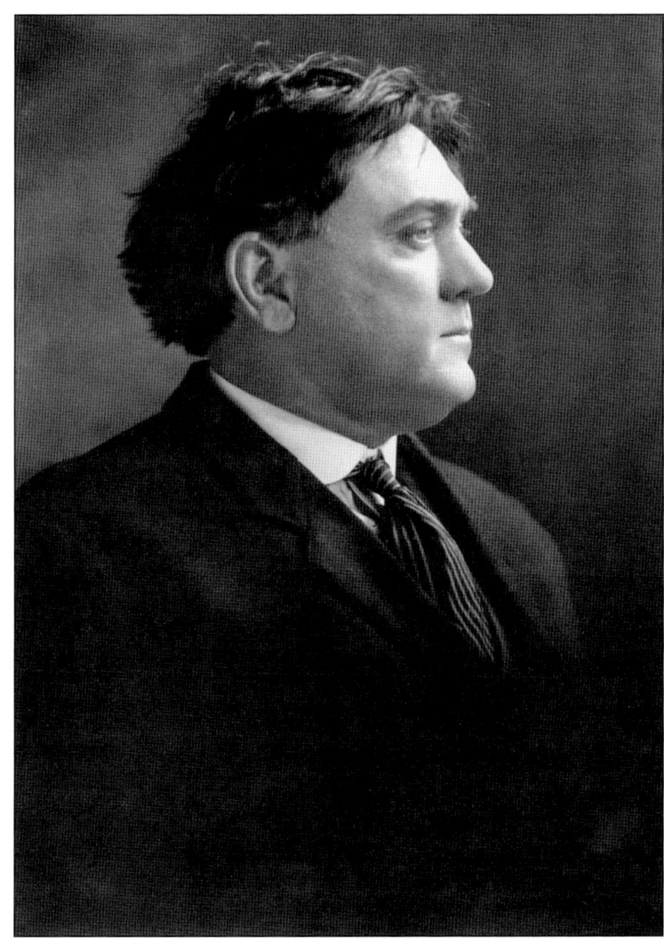

One of Joseph Haley Lord's legacies is his sturdy home in Venice, which has survived numerous storms and several moves. Now named the historic Lord-Higel House, it is the second-oldest house in Sarasota County. Lord was a lawyer, citrus grove developer, land speculator, real estate developer, and congressman. This image is from Chicago in 1910. (PH26.0593.)

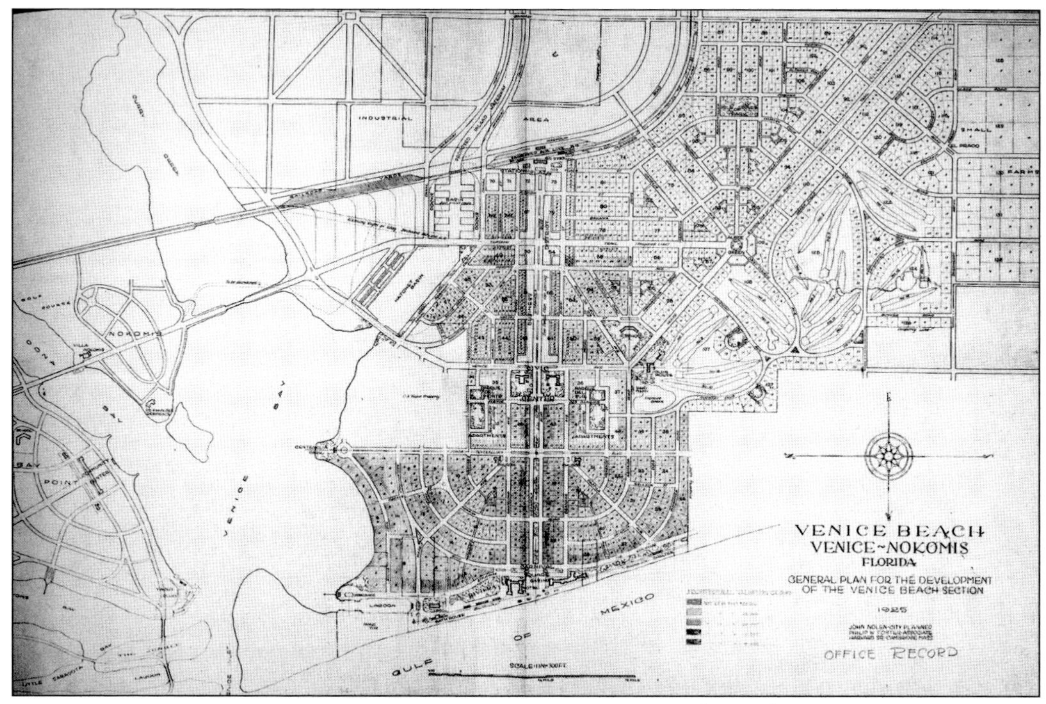

Since the citrus grove was never owned by the BLE, it was a blank, unlabeled area on the left side of the John Nolen Plan. With Lord's wife, Franc, and in-laws Sarah and Franklin Webber (Franklin was also a lawyer), Lord purchased or leased all or part of over 300 properties in old Manatee County from 1896 to 1930. (LIB 975.96 KOR.)

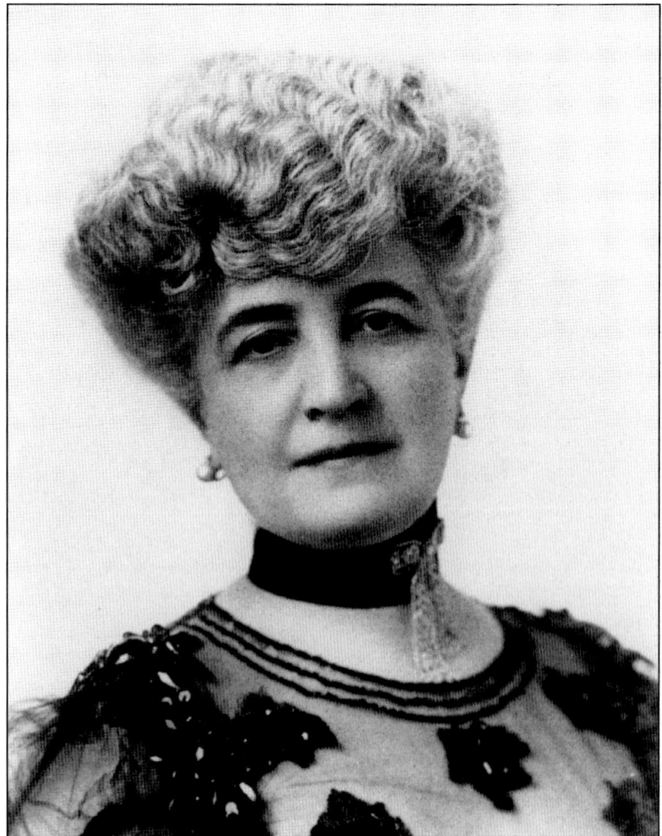

In 1910, Bertha Palmer's father, H.H. Honoré, and J.H. Lord both had their Chicago real estate offices in the Marquette Building, now in the National Register of Historic Places. This early steel-framed skyscraper is one of the best examples of the Chicago school of architecture. It is said that J.H. Lord encouraged Bertha Palmer's family to invest in Florida. (NP0643.)

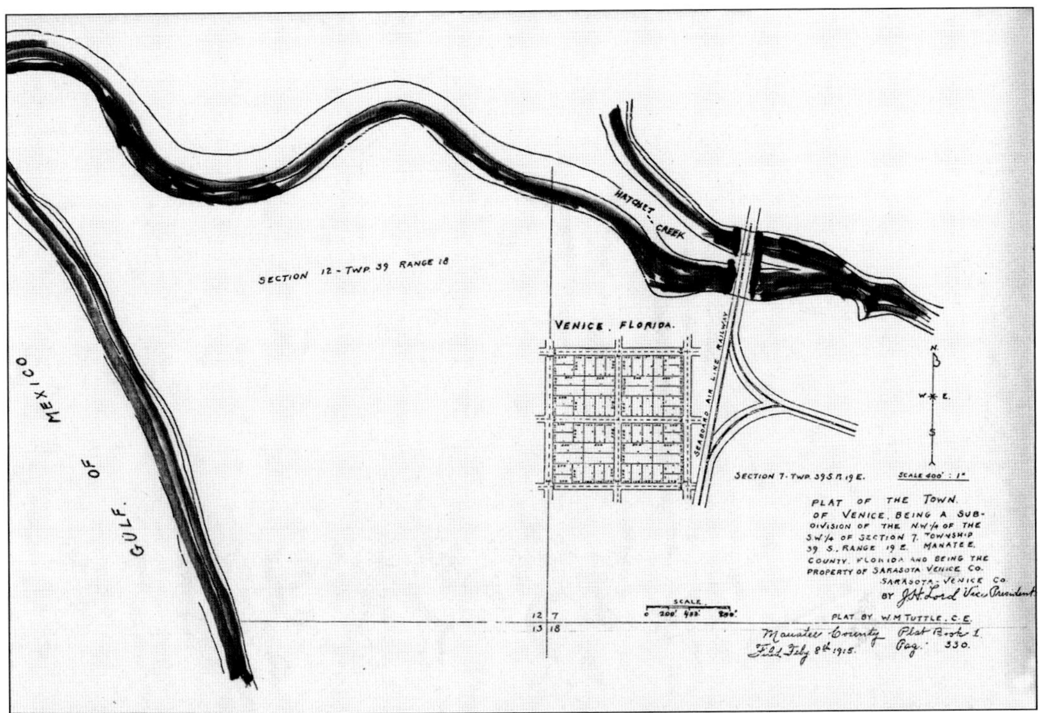

Lord was also vice president of the Honoré-Palmer firm, the Sarasota-Venice Company. He signed the first plat for Venice on July 19, 1915. It was located on the line separating Sections 7 and 12, Township 39 South, Range 19 East, in Manatee County, Florida. Sarasota County was formed in 1921. This image comes from *Manatee County Plat Book 1*, page 330. (CD119, 14 of 27.)

law and having an established place of business at Kittery, in the County of York and State of Maine, in consideration of the sum of one dollar paid by J. H. Lord of the County of Manatee and State of Florida, party of the second part;

W I T N E S S E T H;

That the said party of the first part for and in consideration of the sum of one dollar ($I.) in hand paid by the said party of the second part, the receipt whereof is hereby acknowledged has remised, released and quitclaimed, and by these presents does remise, release and quitclaim unto the said party of the second part, and his heirs and assigns forever, all the right, title interest, claim and demand which the said party of the first part has in and to the following described lots, pieces or parcels of land, towit:

The N-½, N-½ of the SE-¼, SE-¼ of the SE-¼, E-½ of the SW-¼ of the SE-¼, NW-¼ of the SW-¼ of the SE-¼, N-½ of the SW-¼, and the SW-¼ of the SW-¼ of Section I; N-½, SW-¼, S-½ of the SE-¼, and the NE-¼ of the SE-¼, of Section 2; Section 3; W-½, N-½ of the NE-¼, SW-¼ of the NE-¼, W-½ of the SE-¼ and the SE-¼ of the SE-¼ of Section 4; S-½ of theNE-¼, W-½ of the SE-¼ of the NW-¼, NW-¼ of the SE-¼, and the SW-¼ of the SE-¼ of Section 5; S-½ of the NE-¼, NW-¼of the NW-¼, and the SE-¼ of Section 8; Section 9; NE-¼, NE-¼ of the NW-¼, NE-¼ of the SE-¼, S-½ of the SE-¼, NW-¼ of the SW-¼, and the S-½ of the SW-¼ of Section I0; N-½, E-½ of the SE-¼ of Section II; E-½ of the NE-¼ of the NE-¼, the NW-¼ of the NE-¼ (Except the NW-¼ of the NW-¼ of the NE-¼); S-½ of the NE-¼, W-½ and the SE-¼ of Section I2;(N-½ of the NE-¼, N-½ of the SE-¼ of the NE-¼, W-½ of the SW-¼ of the NE-¼, N-½ of the NE-¼ of the NW-¼, NW-¼ of the SE-¼, S-½ of the SE-¼, SW-¼ of the NW-¼ (except NE-¼ of the SW-¼ of the NW-¼) and the SW-¼ of Section I3;) all of Section I4; all of Section I5 all of Section I6; N-½ of the NE-¼, E-½ of the SE-¼ of the NE-¼, the W-½ of the SW-¼ of the NE-¼, NW-¼ of the NW-¼, the S-½ of the NW-¼, and the S-½ (except the SW-¼ of the SW-¼ of the SW-¼) of Section I7; Lot I of Section I8, the NE-¼ of the NE-¼ and Lot 2 of Section 20; NE-¼, E-½ of the NW-¼, SW-¼ of the NW-¼, S-½ of the SE-¼, N-½ of the SW-¼ and the SE-¼ of the SW-¼ and the NW-¼ of the NW-¼ of Section 2I; E-½, and the E-½ of the NW-¼, the NW-¼ of the NW-¼, and the Ne-¼ of the SW-¼, and S-½ of the SW-¼ of Section 22; Section 23; Section 24; (except S-½ of the SW-¼ of the NE-¼); Section 25; Section 26; Section 27; N-½ of the NE-¼, SE-¼ of the SE-¼, of Section 28; N-½ of Lot I, of Section 33; all of Section 34, (except W-½ of the NW-¼ of the SW-¼, and the ...

This June 1910 deed, while hard to read, was for over 25,075 acres. Often with partners, Lord bought, sold, or leased over 100,000 acres of land for turpentine camps, phosphate mining, and potential railroad sites, plus resorts, farms, groves, and homesteads near Venice. In 1923, he was the Florida state representative for the newly formed Sarasota County after its separation from Manatee County. This information came from pages 264 and 265 of *Manatee County, Florida, Deed Book 19*. (MCHRL.)

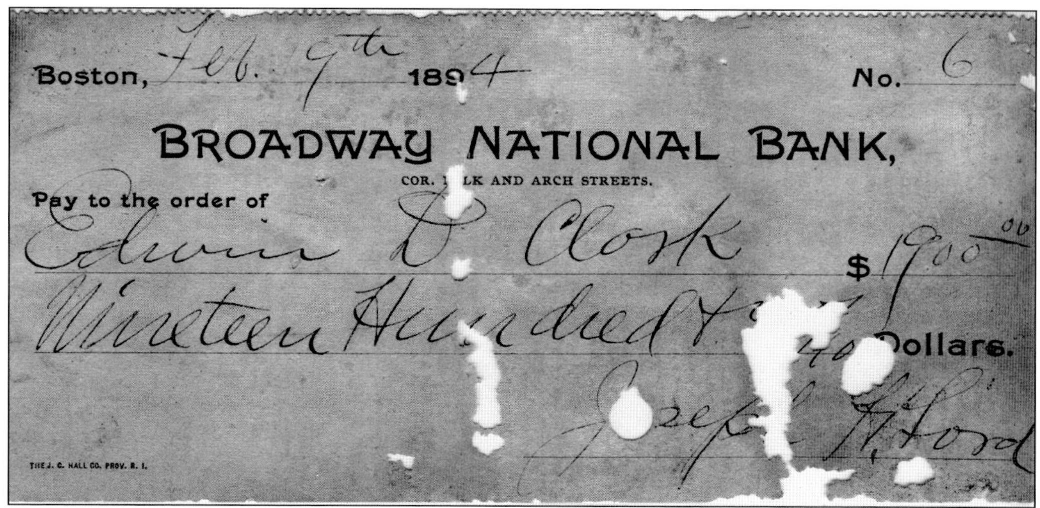

Boston, Feb. 9th 1894 No. 6

BROADWAY NATIONAL BANK,

COR. [illegible]LK AND ARCH STREETS.

Pay to the order of Edwin D. Clark $1900.00

Nineteen Hundred & [illegible] Dollars.

Joseph H. Lord

THE J. C. HALL CO. PROV. R. I.

Born in Maine, Lord attended Harvard University in 1884, graduated from Brown University in 1885, and attended Boston University in 1886. By 1894, he was a general manager for Northwestern Packing Company of Boston and had residences in Sioux Falls, South Dakota, and the Venice area in Florida. This check was found during renovations of the Florida home. (RG204 Box 1 Folder 4.)

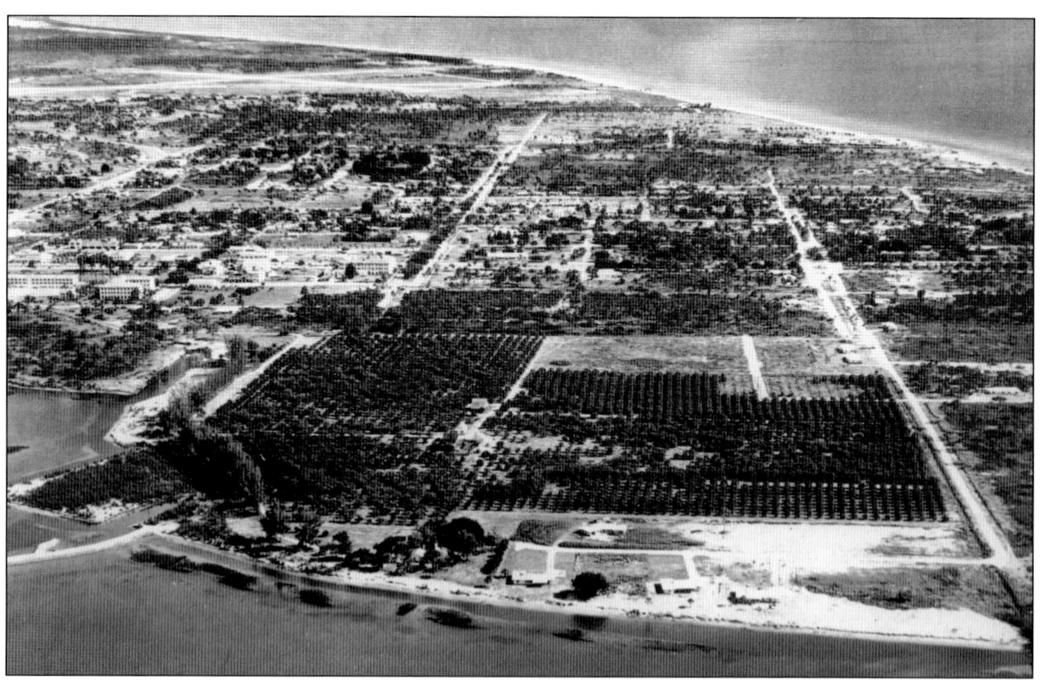

J.H. Lord, his wife, family, and in-laws first moved to Orlando. By May 1886, he was certified as an attorney and counselor at law in Florida. They then moved to Braidentown (now Bradenton) and later Venice. Looking south in this aerial, note the 90-acre grove on the south side of Roberts Bay. Park Boulevard runs from bottom right to top right. (2013.07.223.)

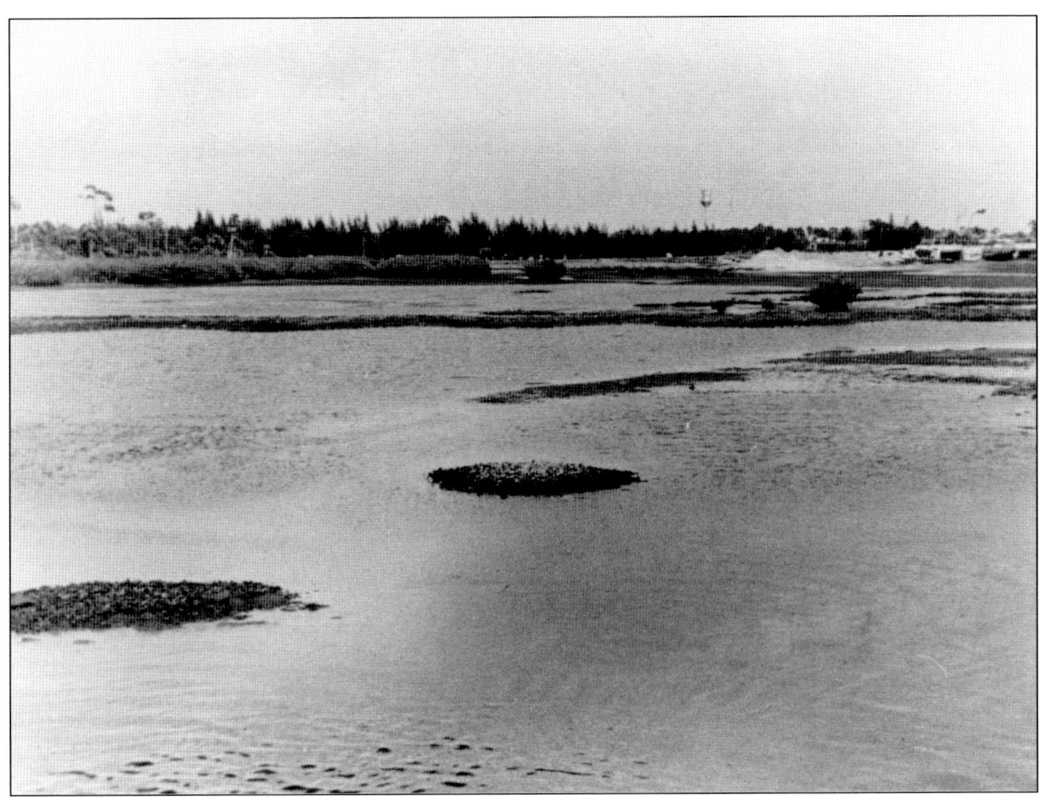

J.H. Lord, along with the Palmers, leased and planted oyster beds in Roberts Bay near his property and the Palmer-owned Eagle Point Resort, as well as the planned Venice Resort. This 1947 image shows just a few oyster beds remaining in Roberts Bay at low tide. (NP0185.)

In this 1912 deed, the Lord family is selling the oyster bed property, which was originally leased in 1907 to the Bertha Palmer family. But by 1965, many of the oyster beds no longer existed. They were killed by pollution or covered with dredged fill from the ICW. This information was found in *Manatee County, Florida, Deed Book 33* on page 343. (MCHRL.)

whereof is hereby acknowledged, has hereby assigned, transferred and set over, and by these presents does assign, transfer and set over to Bertha Honore' Palmer of the County of Cook and State of Illinois, her heirs and assigns, all of its right, title, interest, privileges and immunities of every kind whatsoever under and by virtue of a certain lease made by Sarah O. Webber to said Sarasota Fish & Oyster Company dated October 7th, 1907, said lease being for a term of twenty years, of a certain oyster grant made by the Board of County Commissioners of Manatee County, Florida to the said Sarah O. Webber, dated June 3rd, A. D. 1907 recorded in Deed Book 15, on page 467, public records of Manatee County, Florida and described as follows, to-wit: Beginning at a point midway of the public bridge crossing Dona Bay, running thence Southwesterly to the Northeast corner of the Northwest quarter of the Southeast quarter of Section 1, Township 39 South, Range 18 East, thence South 64 degrees and 26 minutes West to the Middle of the West boundary line of said Northwest quarter of the Southeast quarter, thence South 76 degrees 50 minutes, West 16.25 chains, thence South 8 degrees 30 minutes, West to a stake on the Southern margin of the entrance to Venice Bay, thence Eastwardly and Southwardly along said margin to its intersection with the South boundary line of the Northeast quarter of the Southwest quarter of said Section 1, thence East to the margin of said entrance on its Eastern shore, thence Northerly and easterly along the shore to the Southeast end of the public bridge before mentioned, thence Northwesterly along said bridge to place of beginning.

Also, all of the right, title and interest of the said Sarasota Fish & Oyster Company in and to a certain lease made by J. H. Lord to the said Sarasota Fish & Oyster Company, dated November 7th, 1907, said lease being for a term of twenty years to certain oyster grants made by the Board of County Commissioners of Manatee County, Florida to the said J. H. Lord on the 3rd day of June A. D. 1907 and recorded in Deed Book 15 on page 464 public records of Manatee County, Florida,

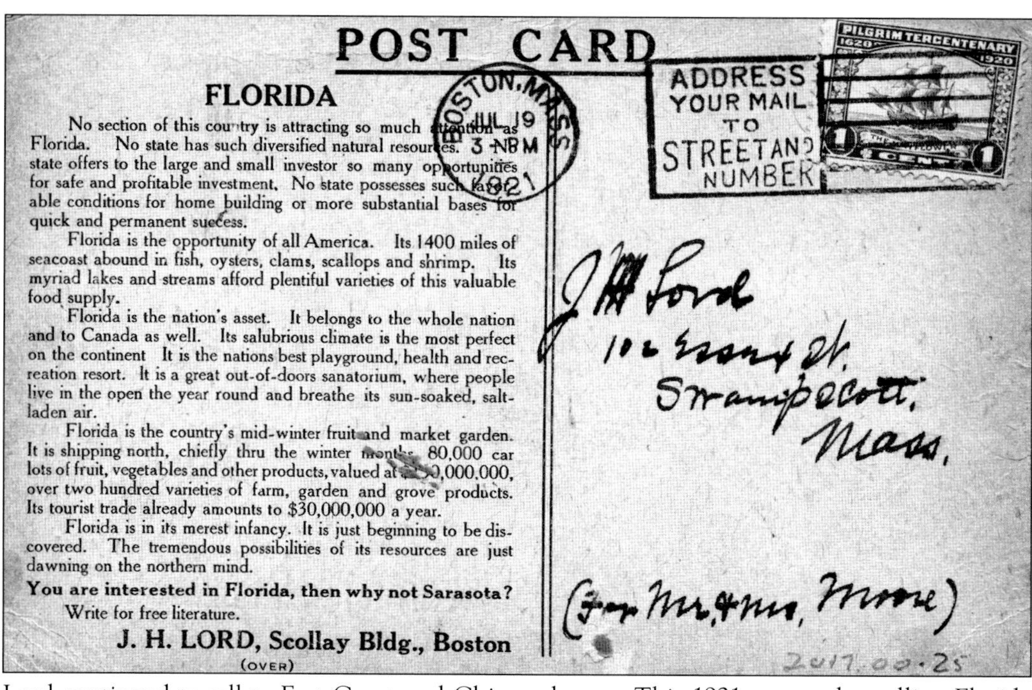
POST CARD

FLORIDA

No section of this country is attracting so much attention as Florida. No state has such diversified natural resources. No state offers to the large and small investor so many opportunities for safe and profitable investment. No state possesses such favorable conditions for home building or more substantial bases for quick and permanent success.

Florida is the opportunity of all America. Its 1400 miles of seacoast abound in fish, oysters, clams, scallops and shrimp. Its myriad lakes and streams afford plentiful varieties of this valuable food supply.

Florida is the nation's asset. It belongs to the whole nation and to Canada as well. Its salubrious climate is the most perfect on the continent It is the nations best playground, health and recreation resort. It is a great out-of-doors sanatorium, where people live in the open the year round and breathe its sun-soaked, salt-laden air.

Florida is the country's mid-winter fruit and market garden. It is shipping north, chiefly thru the winter months, 80,000 car lots of fruit, vegetables and other products, valued at [illegible],000,000, over two hundred varieties of farm, garden and grove products. Its tourist trade already amounts to $30,000,000 a year.

Florida is in its merest infancy. It is just beginning to be discovered. The tremendous possibilities of its resources are just dawning on the northern mind.

You are interested in Florida, then why not Sarasota?

Write for free literature.

J. H. LORD, Scollay Bldg., Boston

(OVER)

Lord continued to sell to East Coast and Chicago buyers. This 1921 postcard extolling Florida as an investment opportunity is an example. It was found during the restoration of Lord-Higel House. In 1905, Lord moved his family to Sarasota, probably for easier transportation and to be closer to Braidentown, the legal center, where the clerk's office and courts were located, plus his mother-in-law lived there. (Postcard 2017.00.25.)

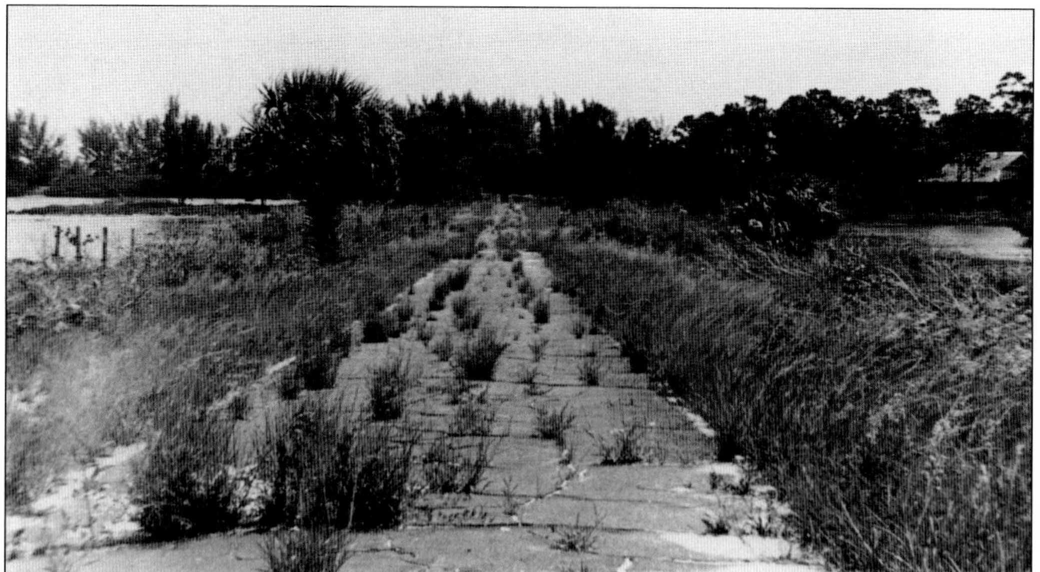

One of the first roads to Venice, and one used by the Lord family, was the nine-foot-wide sandy Sarasota-Venice Road. This image from 1947 by Woody Thayer shows the long-disused causeway looking east with Eagle Point in the background. It had been abandoned in the 1920s by the Brotherhood of Locomotive Engineers when the union moved both the railroad tracks and the road, US 41, farther east. (2008.21.076, image 29 of 41.)

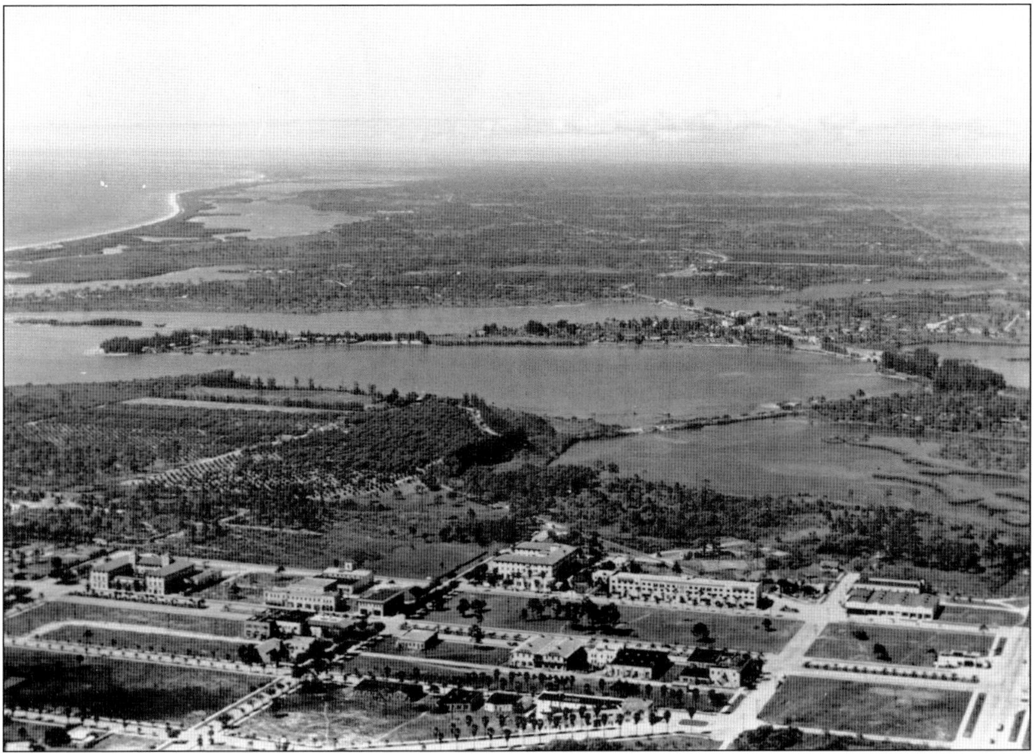

The old road had crossed the water from Eagle Point, and as seen in this 1940s aerial, it continued south (or left) through the citrus grove down onto what is now called West Bay Drive. There it turned left onto angled St. Augustine Avenue behind the old San Marco Hotel, then called the Kentucky Military Institute, in downtown Venice. (NP1183.)

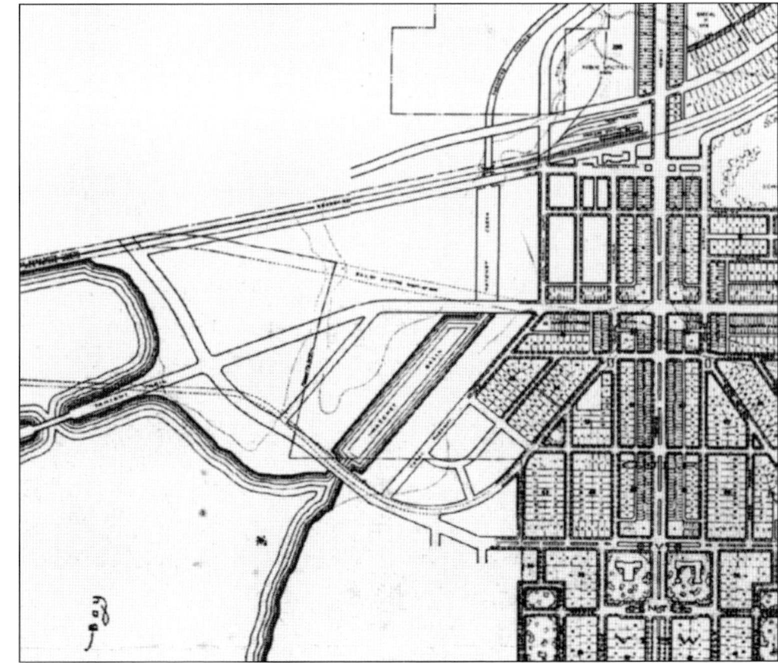

This 1925 John Nolen plan, drawn for Dr. Fred Albee and partially adopted by the BLE, is one of the few images showing both the old causeway and the current highway US 41. The grove, not labeled, is the blank area at the bottom center. (LIB 975-961 KOR.)

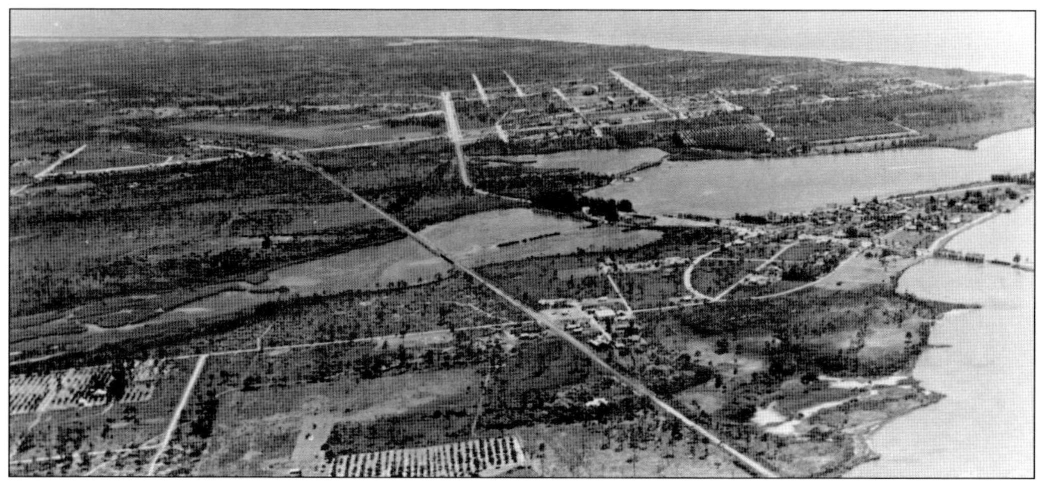

Citrus groves proliferated in early Venice, as seen in this aerial. Oranges, grapefruits, mangos, guavas, lychees, and bananas thrived. Robert Roberts's grove was in Venice. George Higel was the grove manager for the Lord Grove. John Webb of Osprey grew citrus and shipped it via his own boat to Key West. The railroad's arrival in 1911 in Nokomis and Venice in 1915 made shipping easier. (NP1185.)

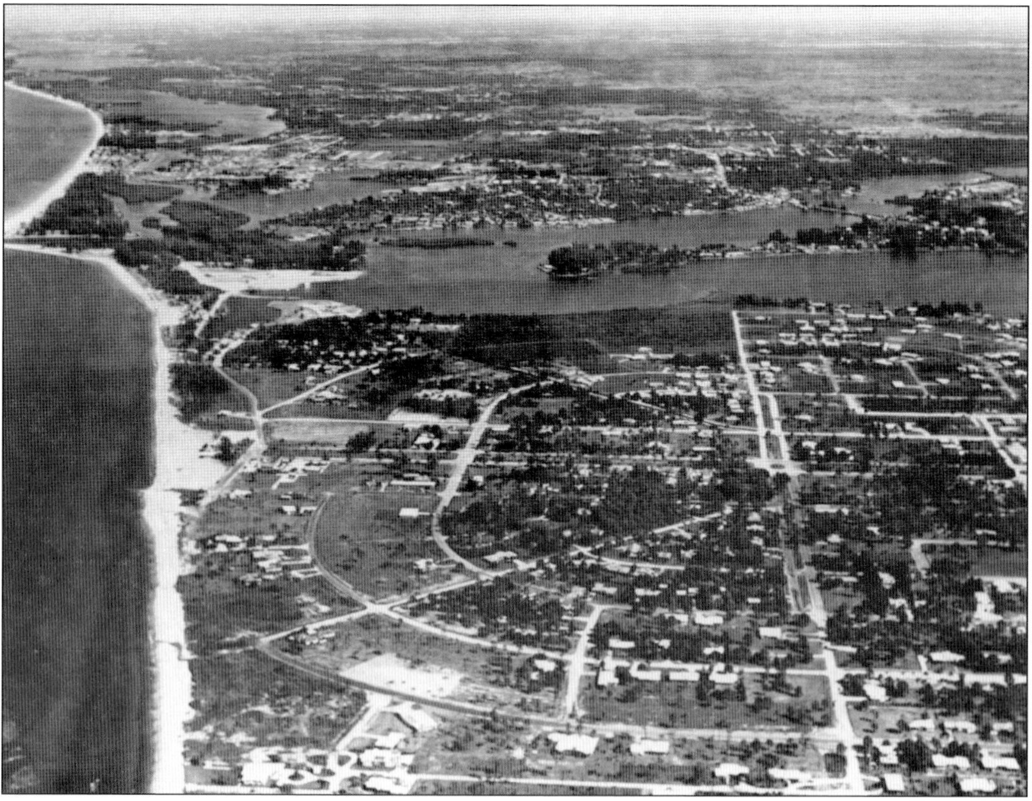

Lord retained his Venice citrus grove until 1919, when it was sold, eventually being purchased by the Stone family. Their property remained a citrus grove through the BLE era of 1925 to 1950. Purchased by developers, the 90 acres became Bayshore Estates, as partially seen in this 1958 aerial. (NP0940.)

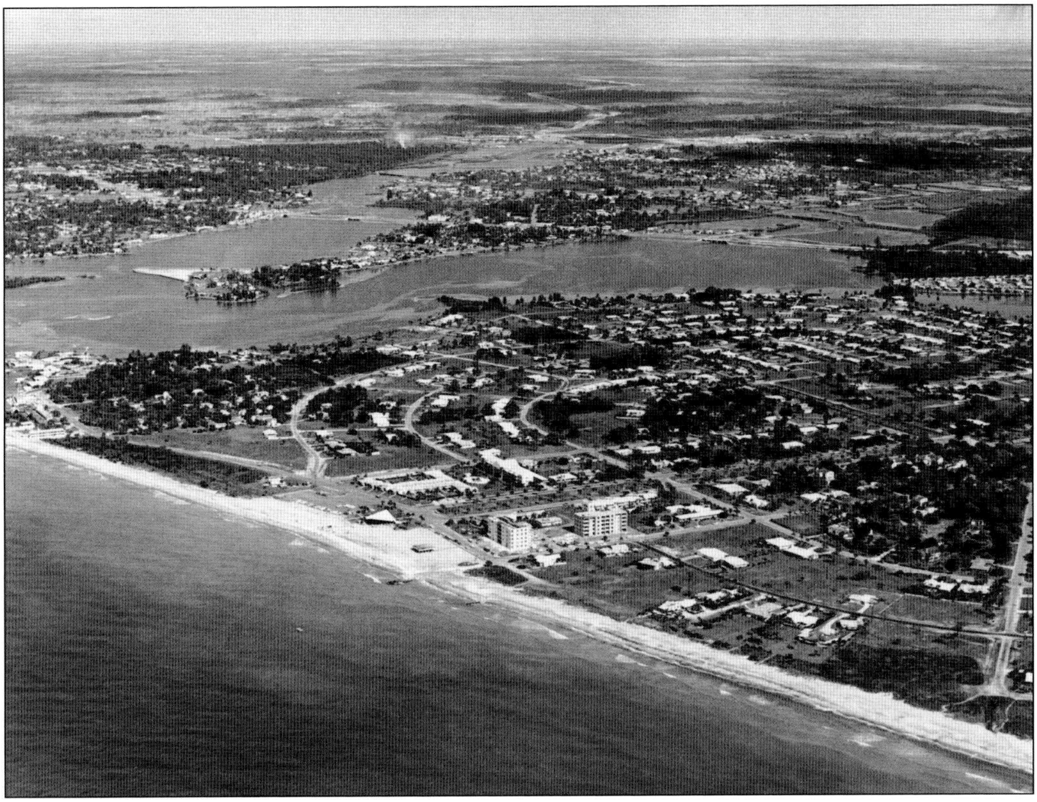

This aerial was taken seven years later in 1965 by Ted Turner, looking northeast. Bayshore Estates is almost built out, as are the surrounding areas in Venice and Nokomis. The causeway to the citrus grove is gone. Hatchett Creek is smaller, and the areas east of Nokomis and Venice have yet to be filled with subdivisions and housing. (1999.17.01, 7 of 11.)

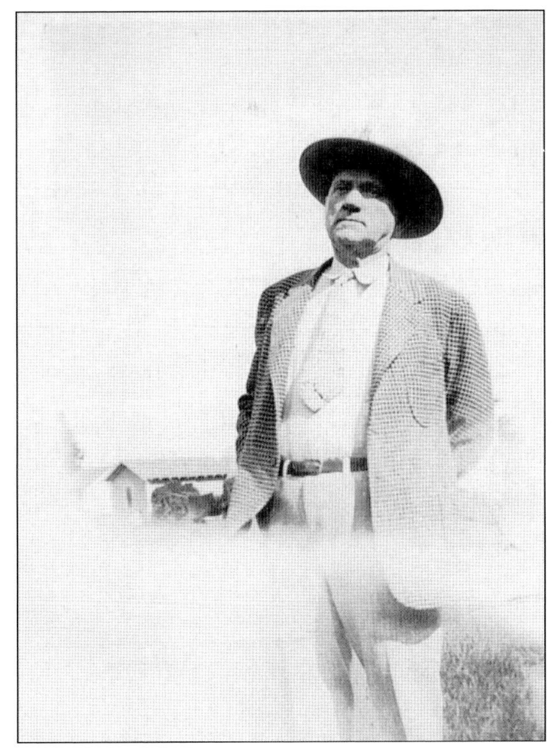

In 1930, as Florida land development declined, J.H. Lord and his wife, Franc, moved permanently to Chicago from Sarasota. He died at the age of 76 in 1936, and his obituary describes his occupation as "landlord." The family lived at 228 East Huron Street. That block is now part of Northwestern University's medical center. (2017.07.01.)

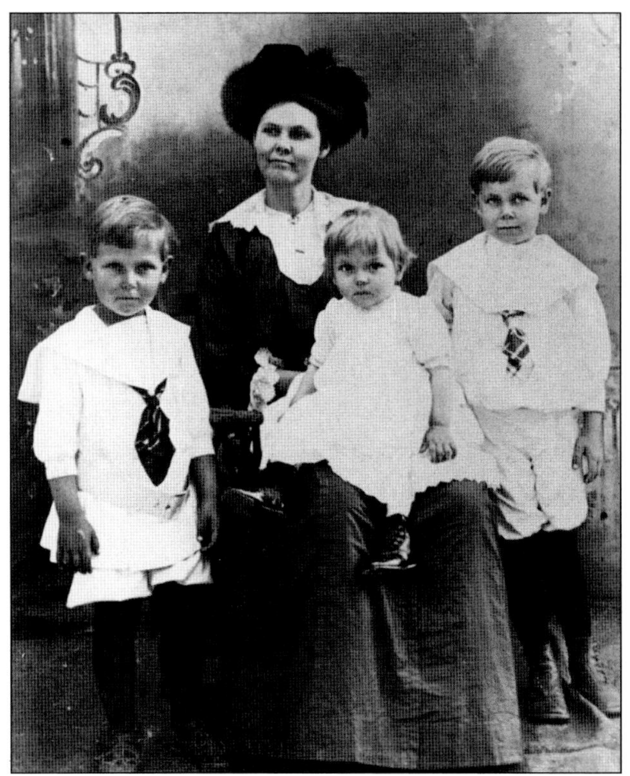

The Lord-Higel House has a fascinating history. It was built by J.H. Lord in the 1890s. After the Lords moved to Sarasota, their citrus grove manager, George Higel, moved into the house with his wife, Abbie, and six children. Abbie and three of the children are pictured here in 1914: from left to right are Donnally, George Jr., and Clyde. (NP0335.)

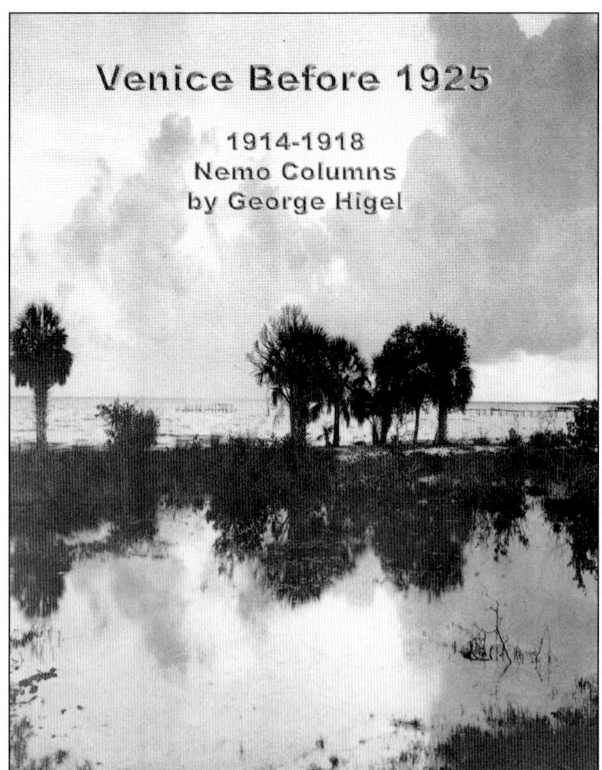

George Higel was a Venice postmaster and a newspaper commentator as well as the first Venice-area historian. His Nemo social commentary series was published in local newspapers from 1889 to 1923. Those columns have now been collected and published in three books at the Venice Museum & Archives. (LIB 975.041 VEN.)

The Lord Grove was sold in 1919, and the Higel family was forced to move. However, the old house, built by the Joseph Lord family, remained on the grove's property, where it was then known as the Stone Grove house, until 1950. (SCHR and SCHCP, CD067.)

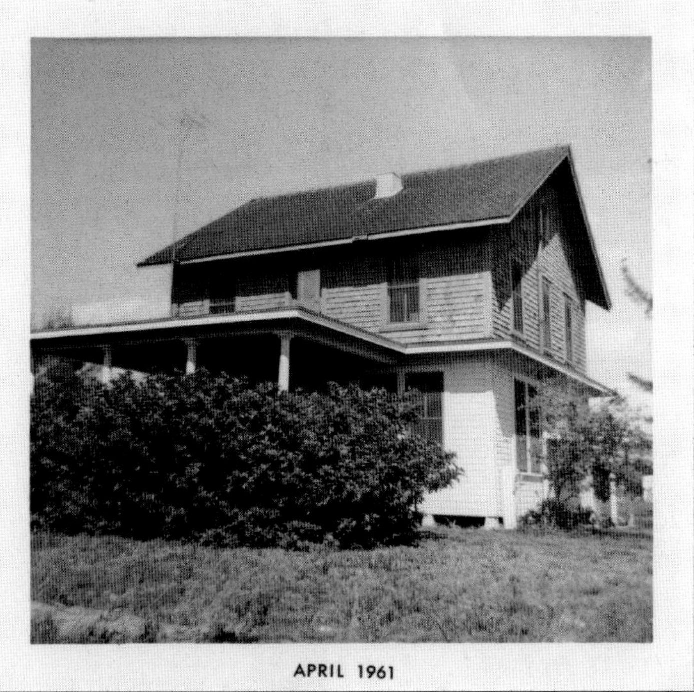

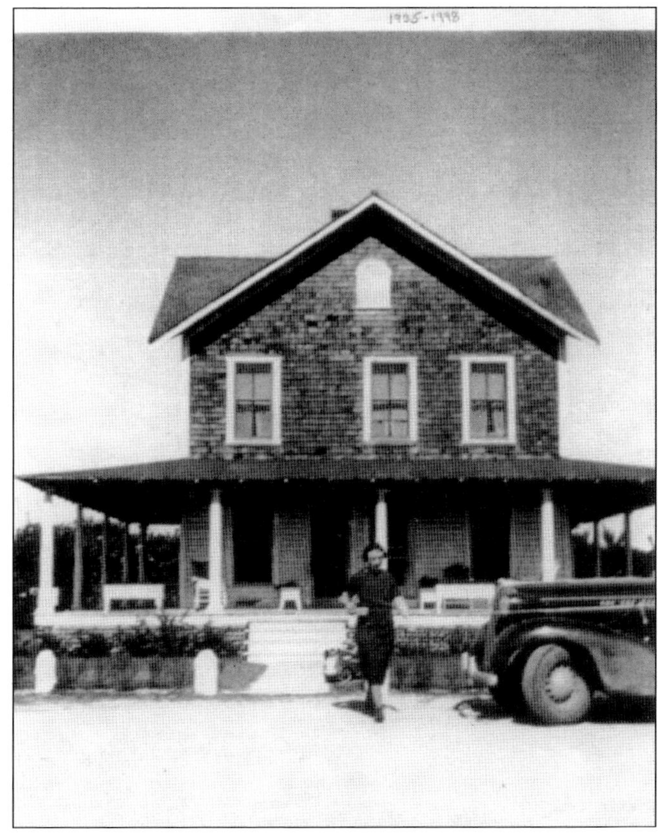

The house was saved from demolition in 1950 by George Higel Jr., who moved his childhood home to 811-813 Laguna Drive. It became a home for the Higels, then a rental property, then was subdivided into two rental apartments, and finally was converted back to a single-family home. (Street File Laguna Dr. 811.)

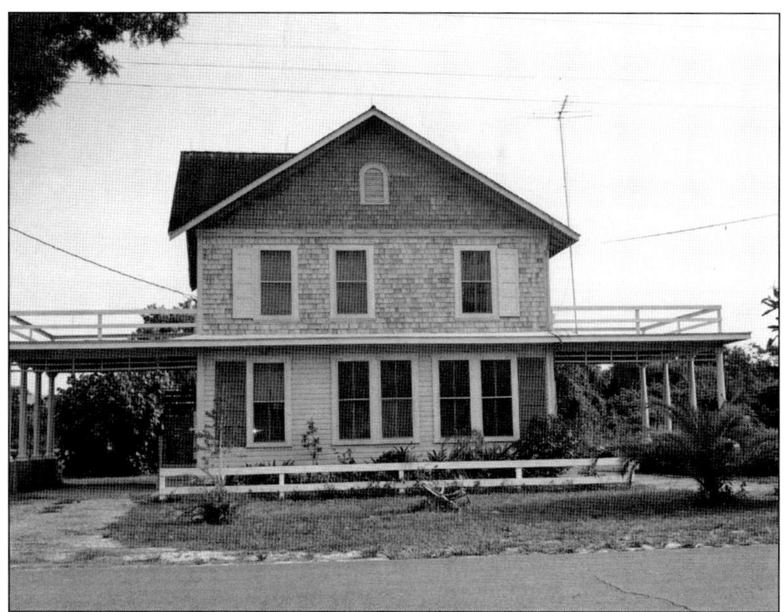

A look at the series of Lord-Higel House photographs shows numerous versions of the home. In this 1963 image, the house looks much the same. However, the distinctive porch and cypress columns had to be removed for both moves in 1950 and in 2005. They were sometimes modified but always reinstalled. (Street File Laguna Dr. 811.)

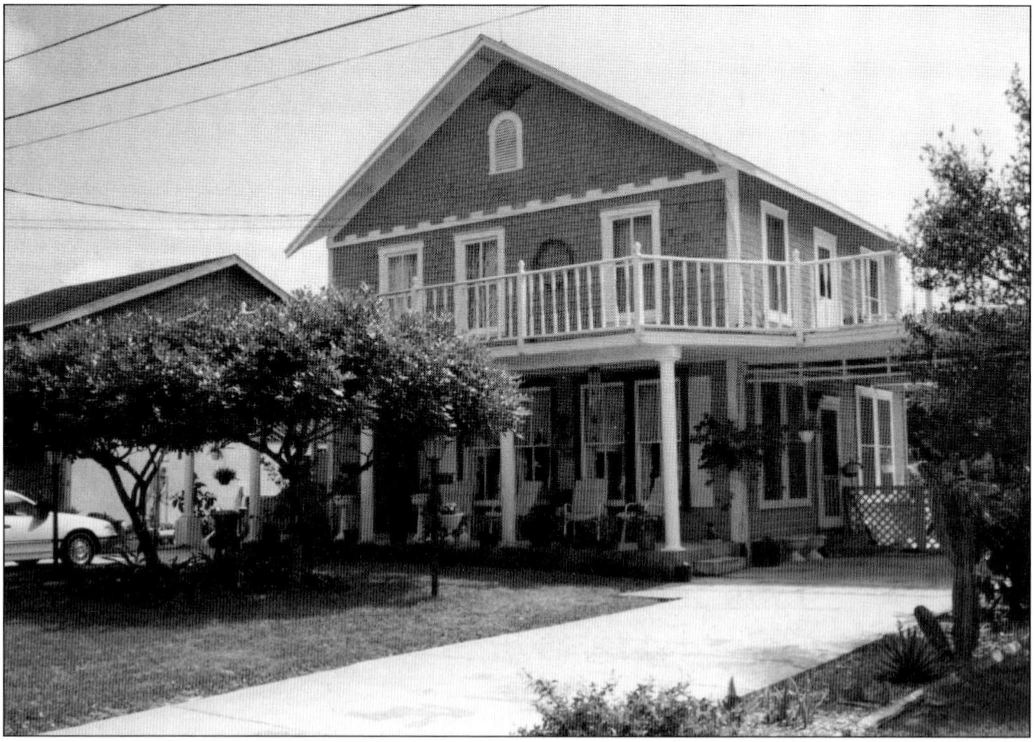

This photograph was taken in 1984. In 2005, the Historic Preservation Board and Commission persuaded the new owners to deed the building, which was scheduled for demolition, to the City of Venice. The city paid $89,000 for house movers, with city works, police and fire departments, and the utility companies participating in the move to 409 Granada Avenue, a city-owned lot. (Street File Laguna Dr. 811.)

Thus, on July 25, 2005, the house rested on steel beams with hard supports jacking up the building. Porches had again been removed, and utilities were disconnected. The interior, built from very dense fat-lighter pine, was solid and not affected by termites. The exterior porches would be added back once again. (DSC N0018, 37 of 54.)

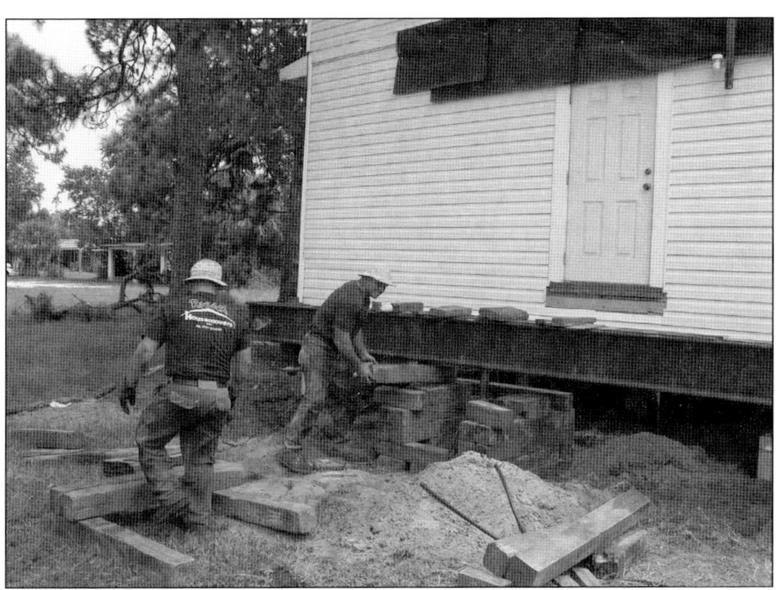

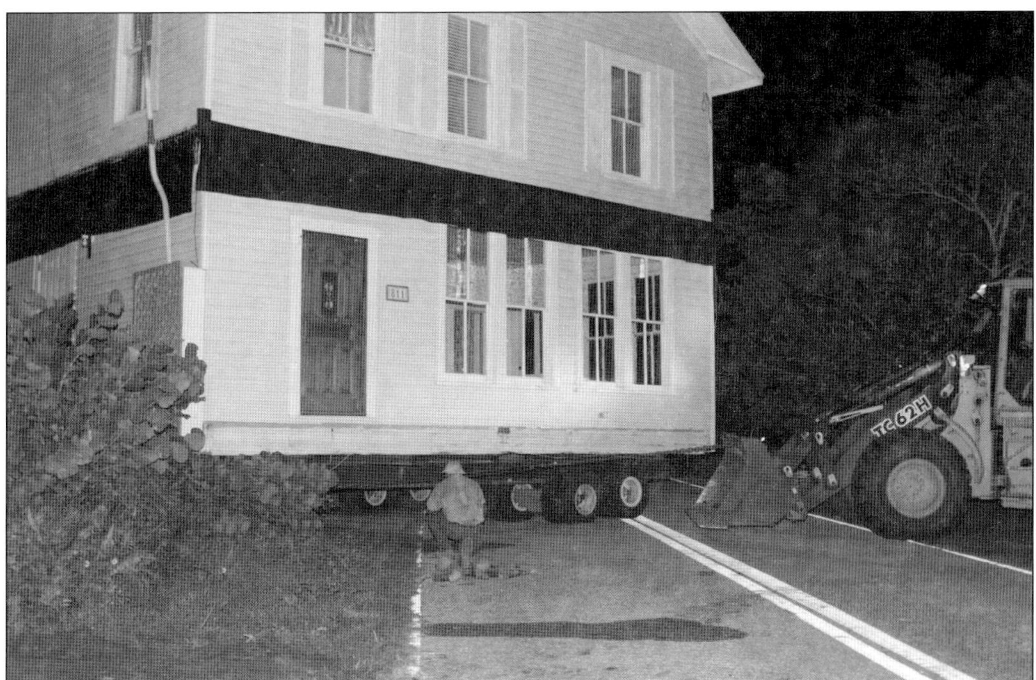

The now-named Lord-Higel House was jacked up and moved to its current location south of city hall with much excitement and ABC Channel 7 News media attention. The house is now on the Local Register of Historic Places and is the second-oldest building in Sarasota County. (CD 129, image 52 of 79, 2015.00.61.)

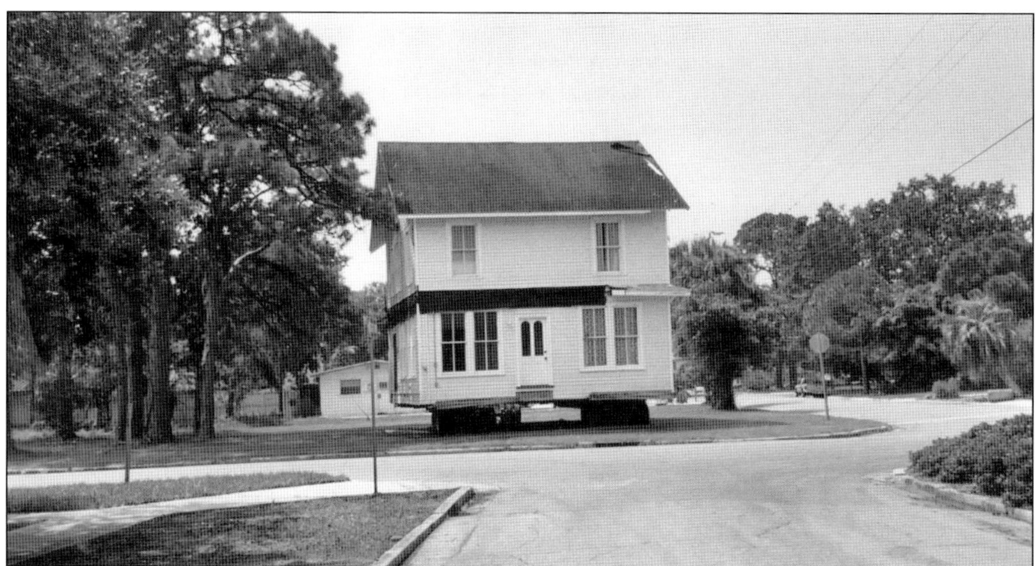

Here, the house-on-the-move is resting at Avenue Des Parques and Granada Avenue prior to its final alignment at 409 Granada Avenue. The building had undergone many, many changes in its 110-plus-year history. Restoration work proceeded slowly, with multiple individuals and volunteer groups raising funds and the city providing support. (MS255 Box 1, 2005.7.28.)

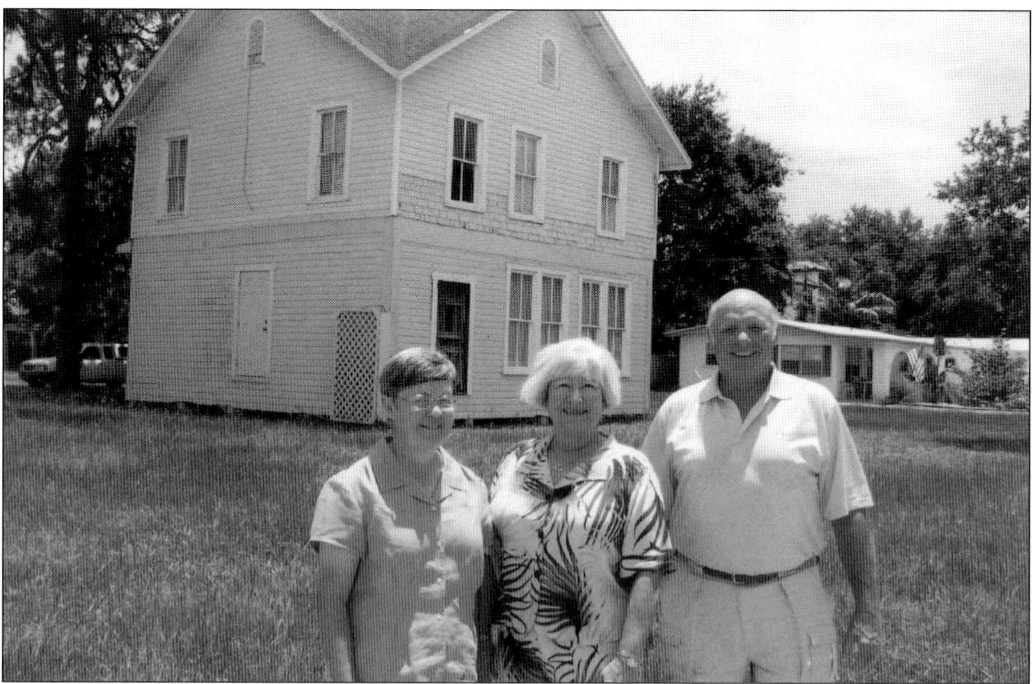

The Friends of the Lord-Higel House held its first organizational meeting in July 2008, and later it merged with Venice Heritage Inc. For over 15 years, founding director Dorothy Korwek (left), pictured here with Judie and Jack Bauer (right), and many other volunteers raised funds and directed the numerous contractors necessary to make the old home a museum. (MS255 Box 1 File 1.)

FRIENDS OF THE LORD-HIGEL HOUSE DIRECTORS ORGANIZING MEETING
MINUTES OF JULY 21, 2008

THE MEETING WAS CALLED TO ORDER BY INCORPORATING DIRECTOR JACK BAUER AT 7:10 P.M., AT THE CITY OF VENICE COMMUNITY HALL. JACK WELCOMED ALL IN ATTENDANCE AND THANKED EVERYONE FOR VOLUNTEERING THEIR INTEREST AND PARTICIPATION IN THIS VERY WORTHWHILE ENDEAVOR TO RESTORE THE OLDEST HOUSE IN VENICE, BUILT BY JOSEPH H. LORD IN 1896.

PRESENT AT THE ORGANIZING MEETING WERE: DOROTHY KORWEK; JACK BAUER; JUDIE BAUER; BETTY WALKER; DOT FUHRMEISTER; BETTY INTAGLIATA; FRAN VALENCIC; SUE CHAPMAN; ROBERT BROOKE; JACQUE' RING; JERRY TOWERY; MICHAEL REED; JOYCE NORTON; JIM MIDDLETON; JAMES HAGLER; CLAIRE SUTER; AND BARBARA DEIN.

In the restoration, first an era had to be decided upon. Then the interior needed to be completely rebuilt. Porches had to be added back. New codes required that a handicap entrance be installed. Restrooms had to be constructed in a separate building. It is hoped that with the city's support, the building will open to the public in 2025. (MS255 Box 1 File 11.)

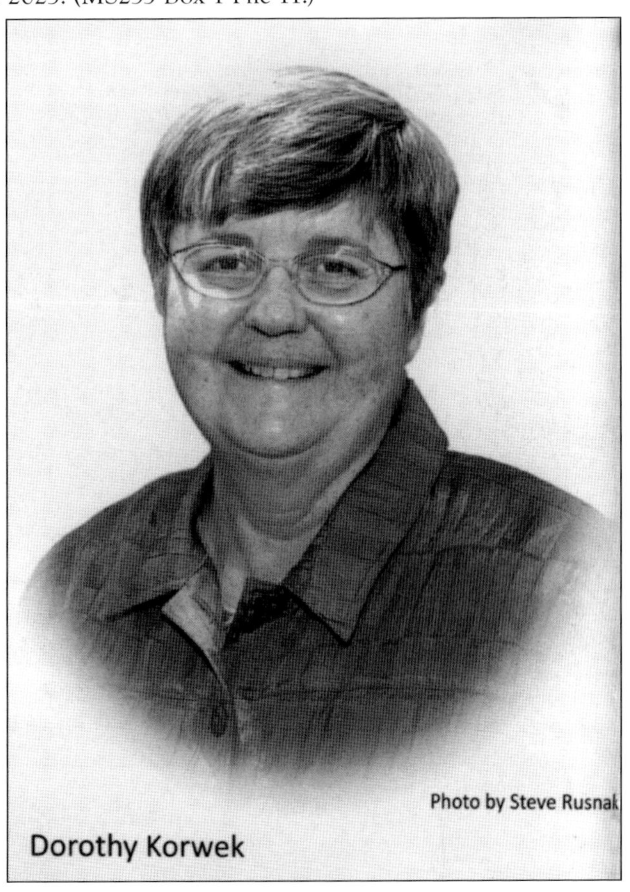

A quiet expert, Dorothy Korwek, as the second historical resources director, has received many awards for her persistence, knowledge of Venice-area history, and saving of historic buildings. She moved the Triangle Inn building to its current location, co-authored *John Nolen Plan for Venice*, compiled six booklets of *Venice Area Old Timers Stories*, edited the Nemo columns, and recently wrote *The Intracoastal Waterway*. (LIB 975.961 KOR.)

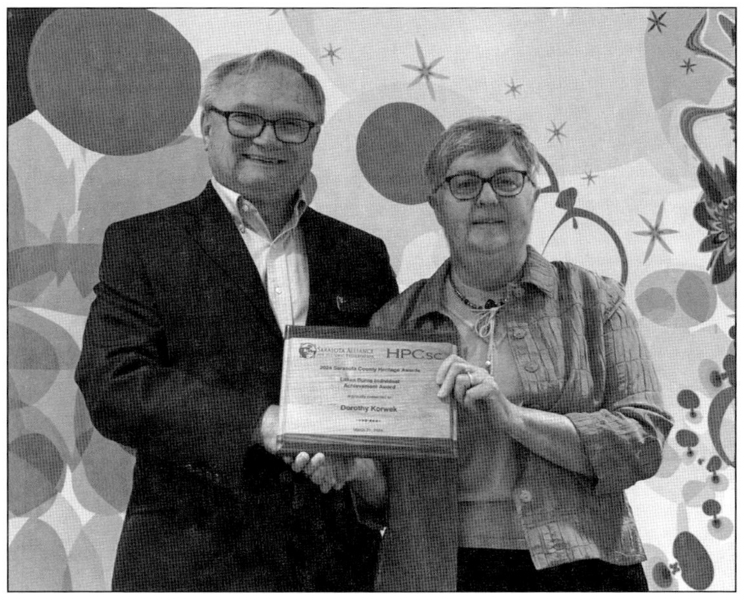

Dorothy Korwek constantly does research and fundraising for historical issues. Over the years, working through numerous friends organizations, including the Triangle Inn Association, Venice Heritage Inc., the Venice Museum & Archives, the Lord-Higel House Association, and others, she is a much-recognized treasure in Sarasota County, Florida, as this award presented by Dave Baber (left) to her indicates. (SAHP.)

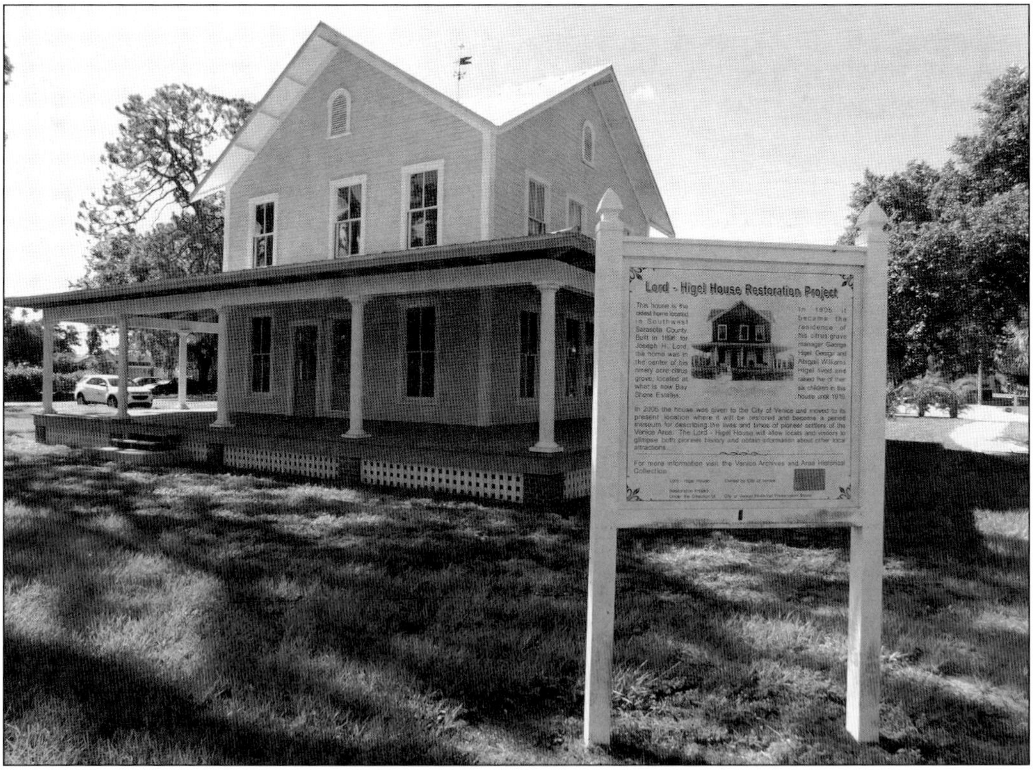

The Lord-Higel House, like the 1926 Old Betsy Fire Engine, is a reminder that, primarily through the efforts of neighbors and volunteers, historic Venice is being saved. Volunteers donate time, money, and numerous talents to educate residents and visitors and to maintain the historical heritage. Volunteers are welcomed and appreciated. (RGS 220 File 48.)

Three

A Man-Made Island, ICW, and Jetties

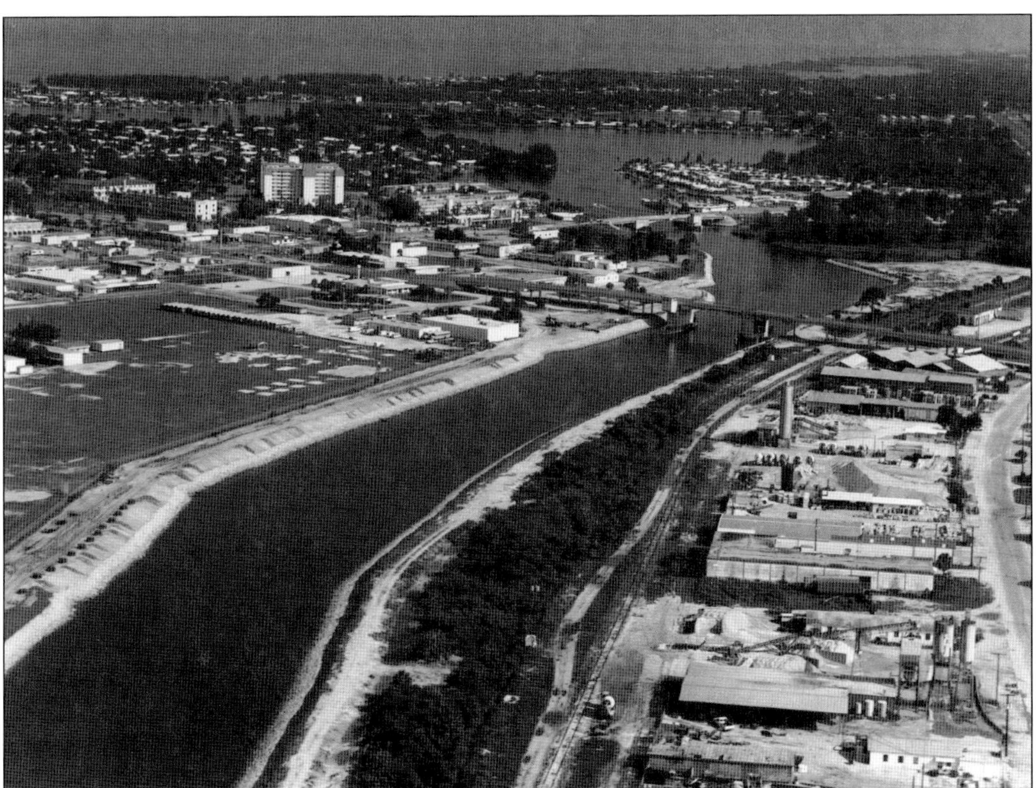

It is important to remember that Venice Island is not a natural island. It was man-made in 1967 as the result of the Intracoastal Waterway. From Boston to Texas, dredging has built commercial trading lanes sheltered from storms. Looking north, this late-1960s aerial shows both the North Bridge at the top and the Venice Avenue Bridge connecting the newly created Venice Island to the mainland. (PH01.01.06.)

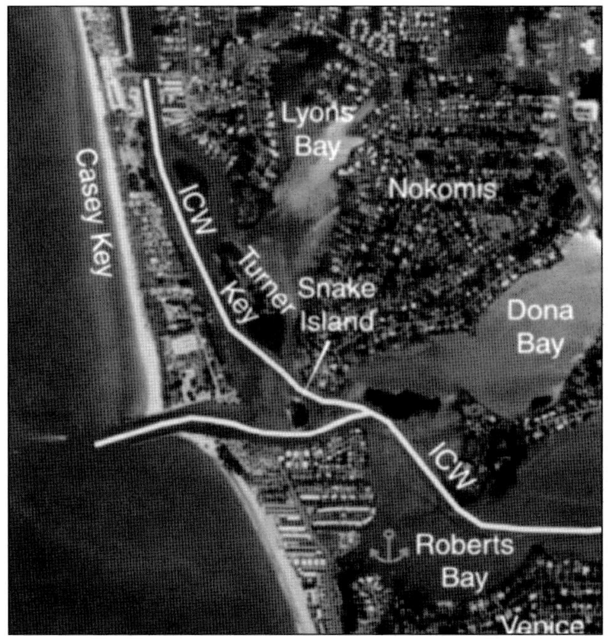

The US Congress's 1824 General Survey Act, plus the 1878 River and Harbors Act, provided federal control and money. Since approximately 1889, in southwest Florida, the US Army Corps of Engineers has conducted studies, proposed routes, and built dredged waterways to accommodate commercial shallow-draft sailboat traders and, later, steamships. This 1998 image is of the current-day ICW configuration, dredged in the 1960s. (LIB 629.048 ANT.)

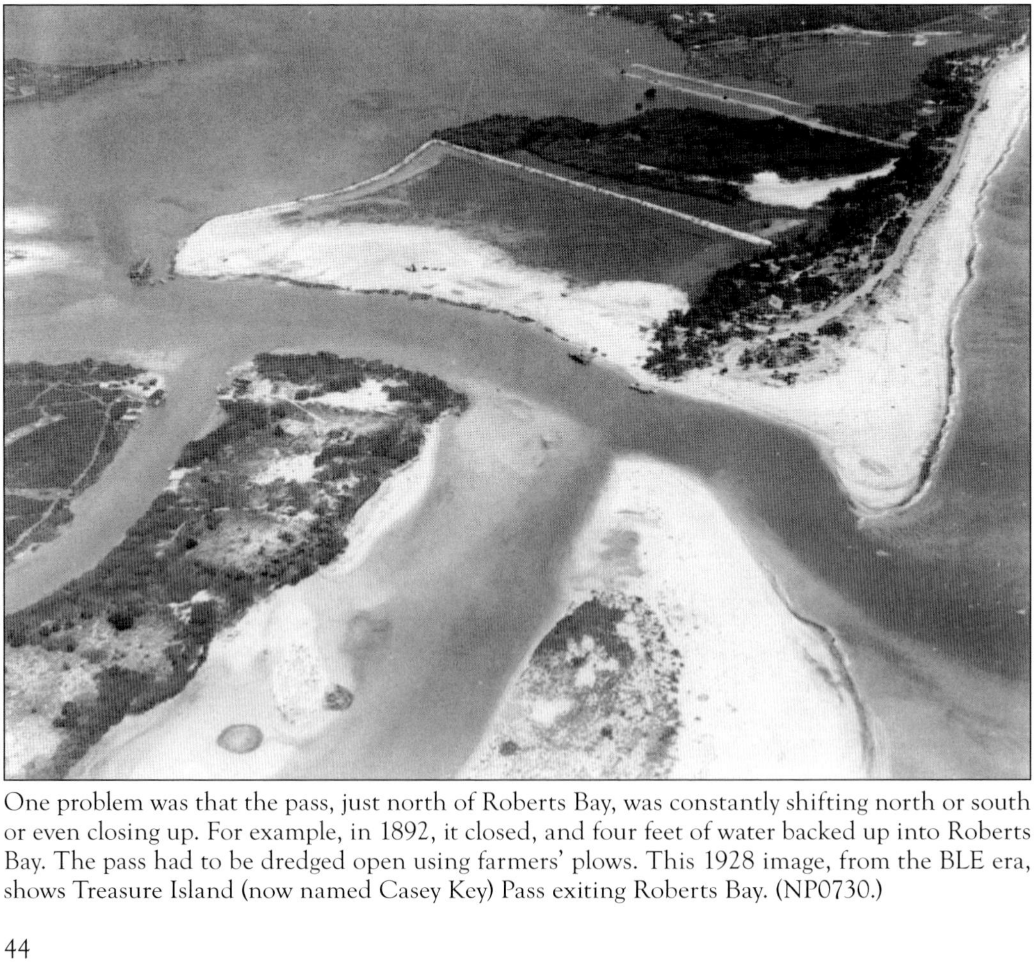

One problem was that the pass, just north of Roberts Bay, was constantly shifting north or south or even closing up. For example, in 1892, it closed, and four feet of water backed up into Roberts Bay. The pass had to be dredged open using farmers' plows. This 1928 image, from the BLE era, shows Treasure Island (now named Casey Key) Pass exiting Roberts Bay. (NP0730.)

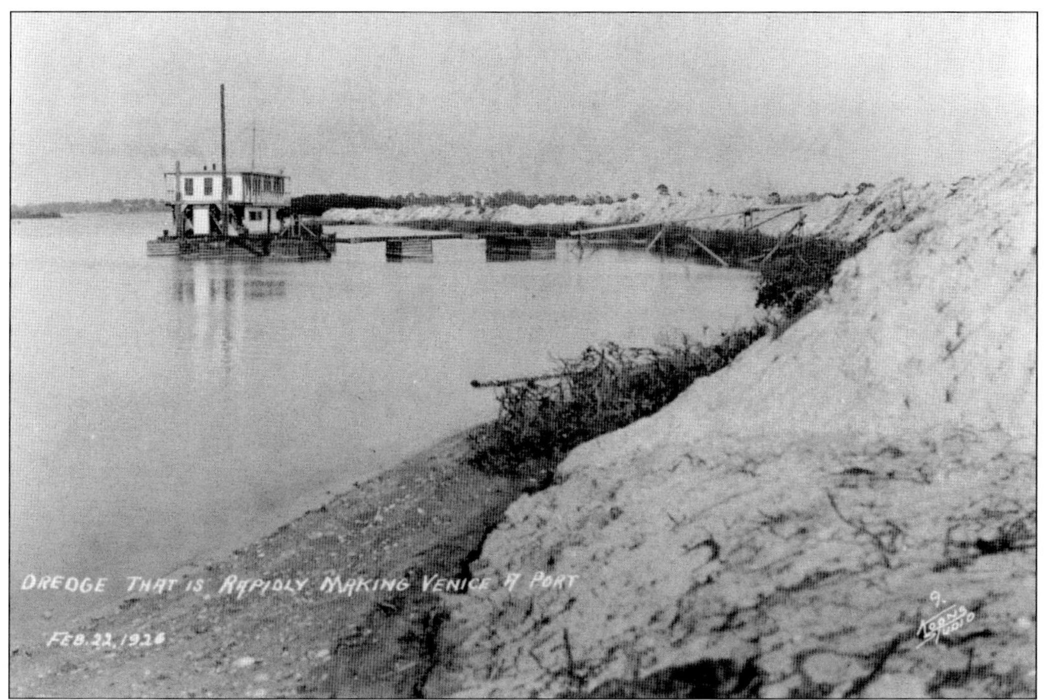

The jetties and Venice Inlet were not built by the Brotherhood of Locomotive Engineers, as is claimed by some. Yes, it did attempt to build a Port of Venice, as seen in this 1926 dredging image. However, the port and Hatchett Creek Basin were never completed; the union left town in 1929. The name "Harbor Drive" remains where the port would have been located. (NP0708.)

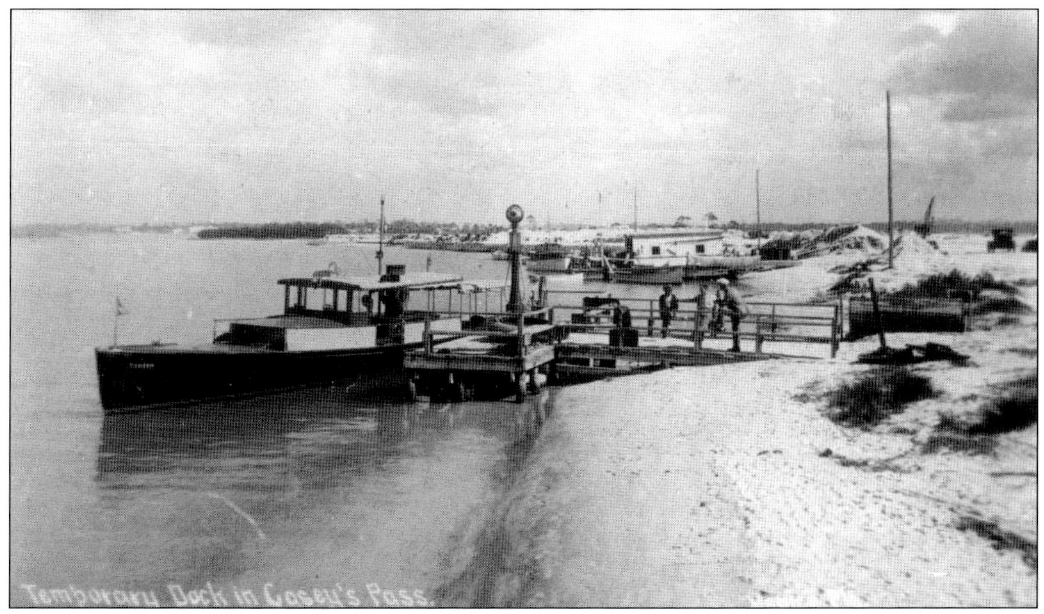

The steamship *Raven* is docked at the BLE's temporary dock on Treasure Island (Casey Key) Pass in 1927. As a promotional offer, for $5, one could travel from St. Petersburg on the *Raven* and spend a few days in the BLE's Venice. The BLE port exit is located in about the same location as the current-day Venice Inlet and two jetties. (NP0031.)

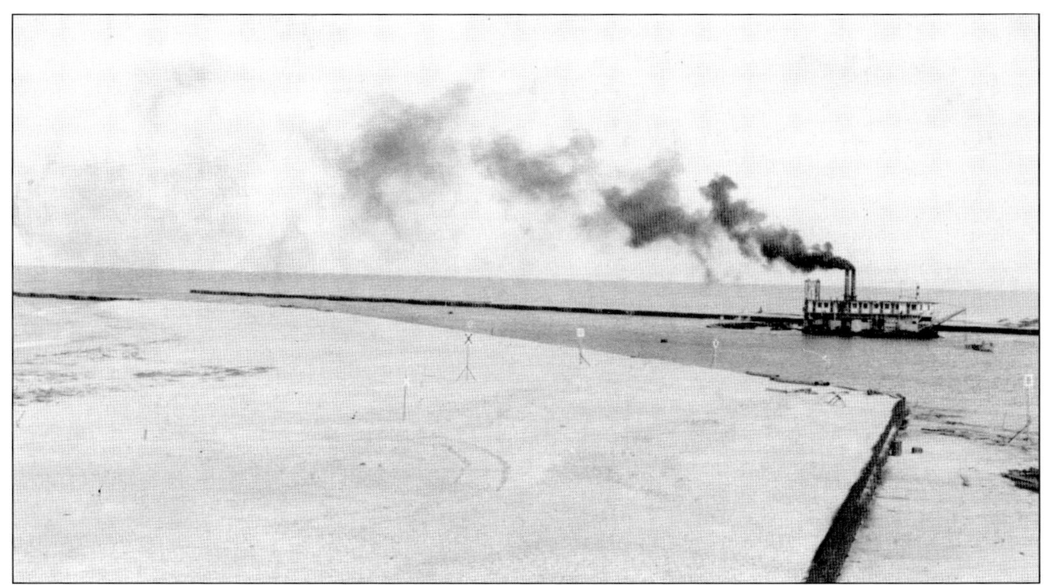

This 1936 image by Dr. Eugene Maier shows a dredger at work on the inlet. However, it was not until 1937 that the current Venice Inlet, from Roberts Bay, was created. At this time, it was the southern exit for the Intracoastal Waterway from Sarasota. The Venice Inlet channel was 100 feet wide and 8 feet deep. (PH26.0391.)

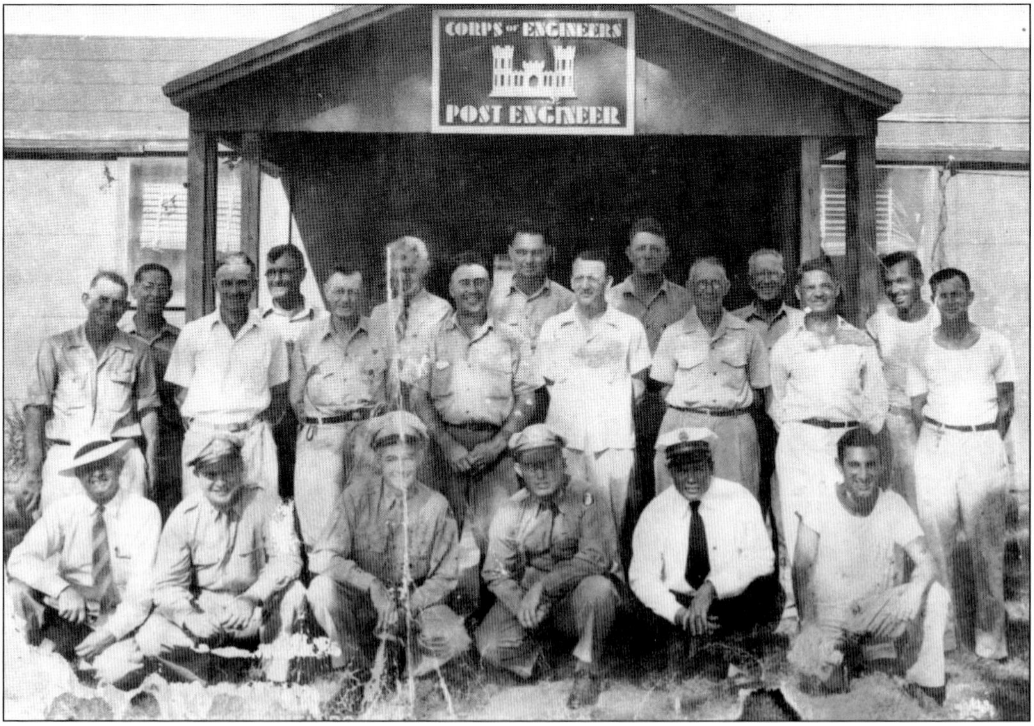

In 1937, four local workers were hired to help the Army Corps of Engineers build the jetties. In the third row, fifth from the left, is Pete Edge, and at the far left is Kenneth Higel. Joseph Jossart is fourth from the left in the second row, and Tom LaByer is somewhere in the first row. The others in the image are unidentified. (NP0763.)

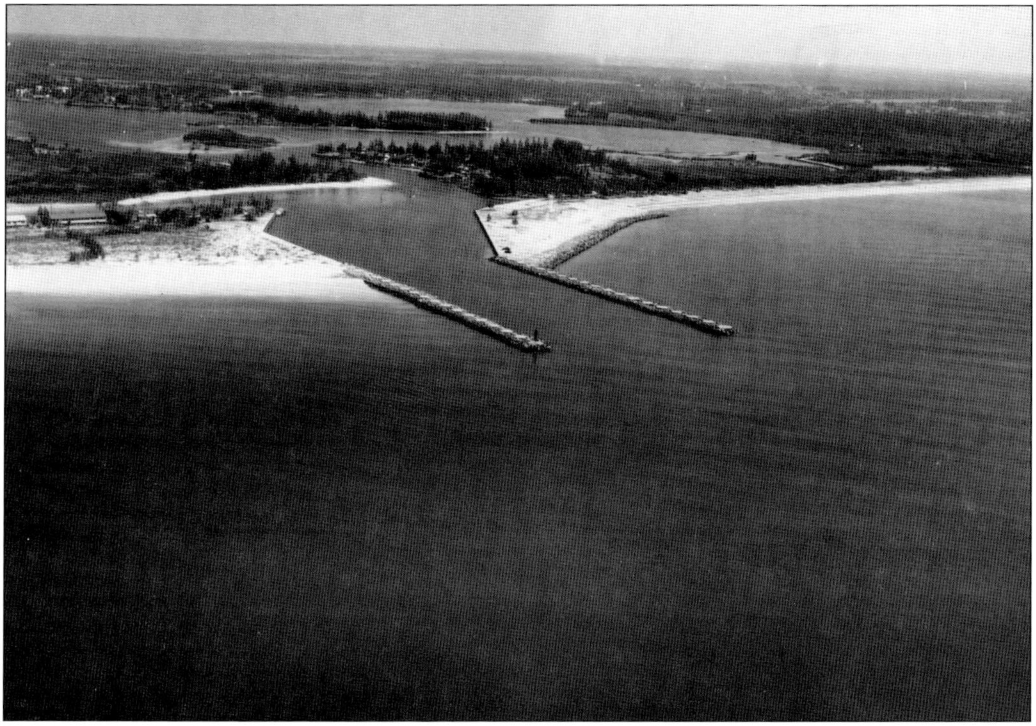

In this 1944 image, both jetties extended out 659 feet. The North Jetty is in Nokomis, and the South Jetty, at what is now called Humphris Park, is in Venice. Note how open the land was in 1944, prior to the building phases of the 1950s and 1960s. (NP0084.)

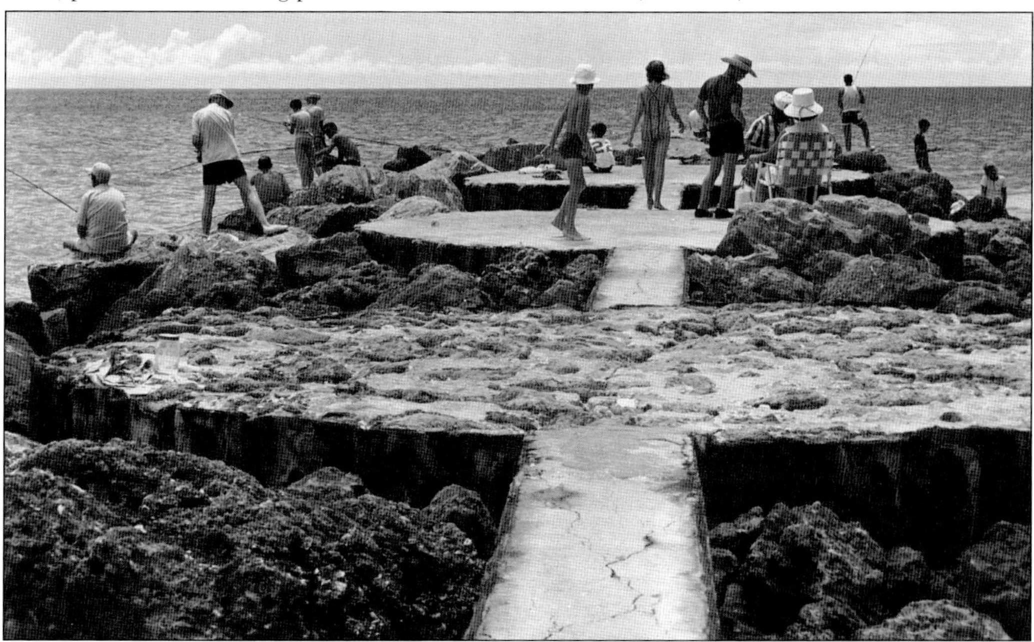

The two jetties have an interesting structure. The foundation of large metal "cans" is filled with rocks or concrete. They are linked by a narrow concrete path, which was later widened and covered by asphalt. (PH01.04.27, image 1 of 2.)

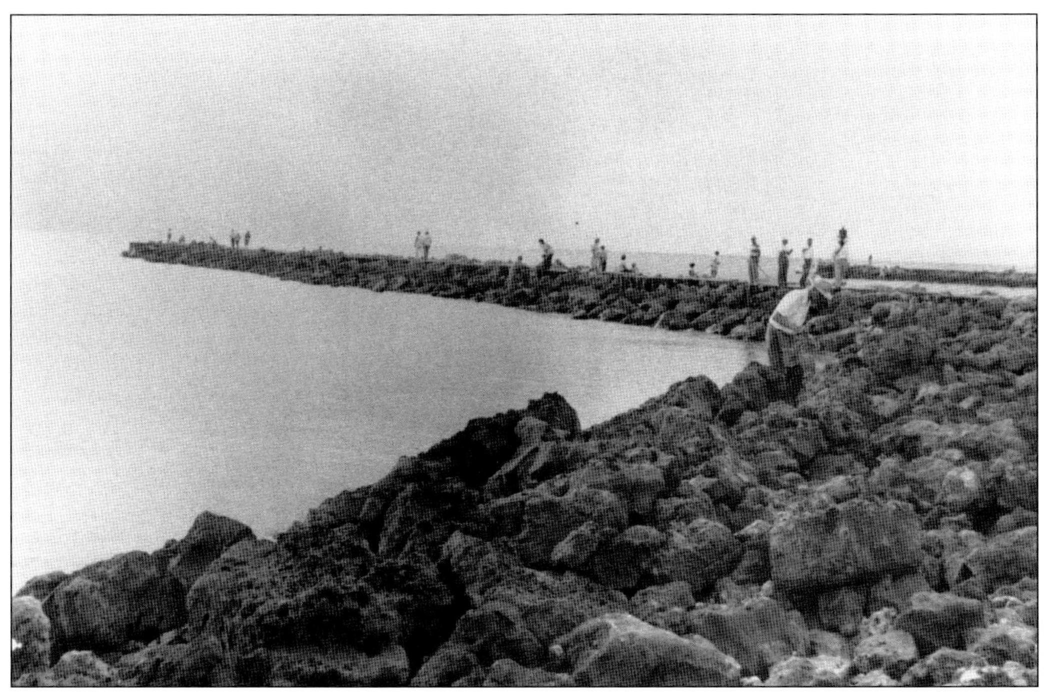

Large rocks formed the seawalls, but routine storms or surges from direct- or indirect-hit hurricanes result in extensive (and expensive) damage. In August 2023, Hurricane Idelia, which came inland 250 miles north of Venice, resulted in the closure of the jetties for a year. (NP1247.)

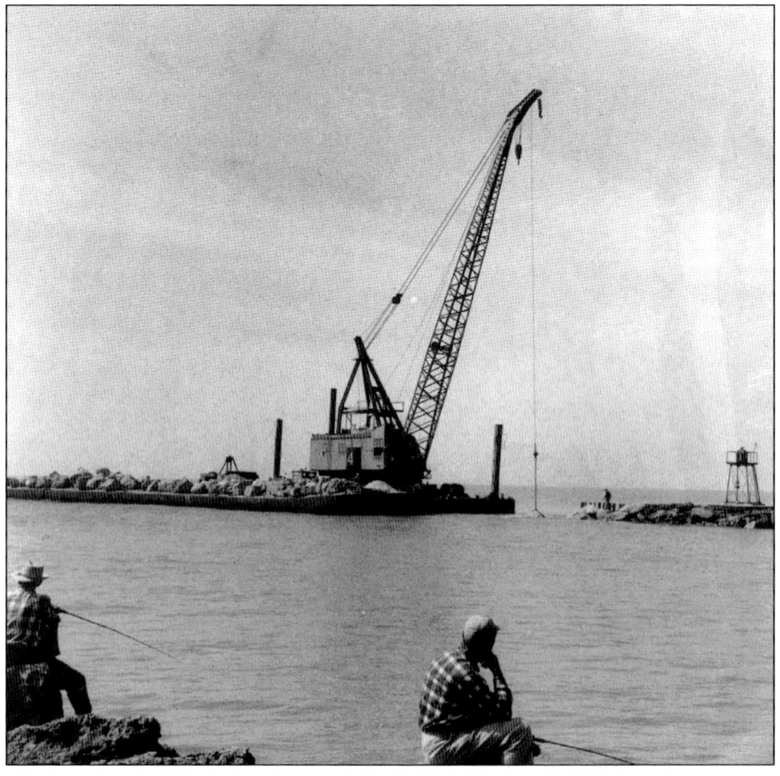

The West Coast Inland Navigation District (WCIND) has worked with the City of Venice to correct storm damage many times over the years. Here, in 1962, a crane is working to repair damage on the jetty while fishermen watch. (MS215.)

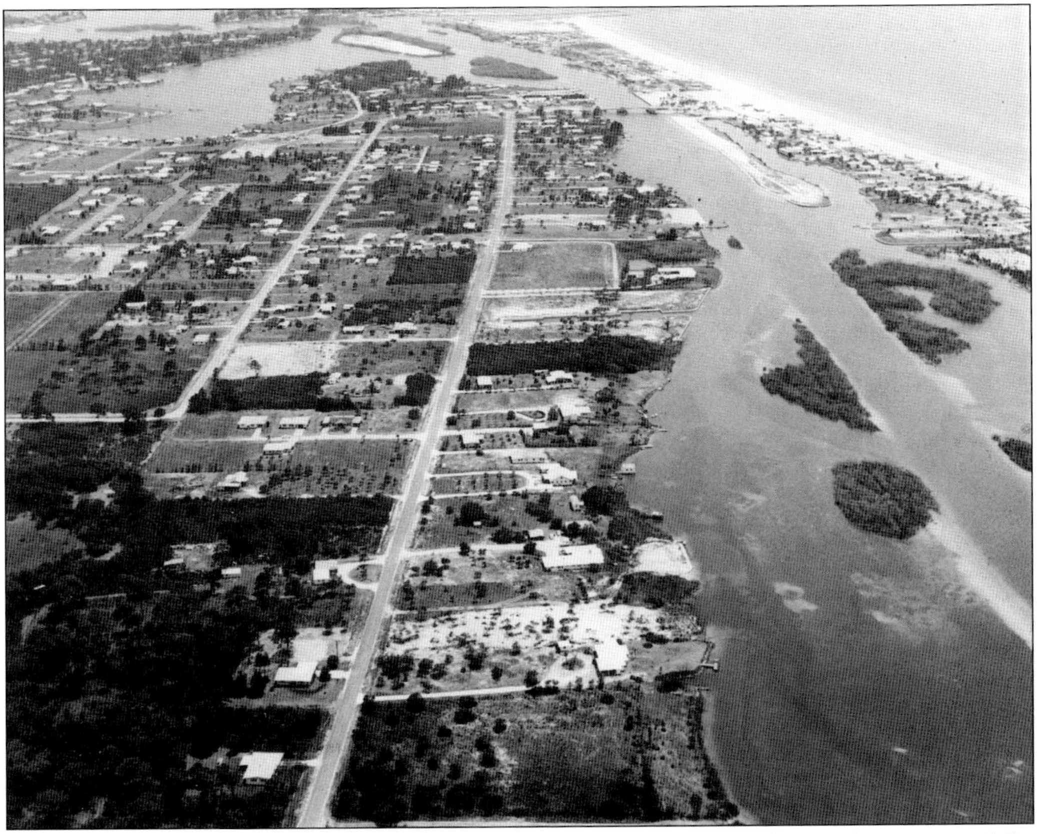

The Venice Inlet is navigable water and thus are dredged on a routine basis. This section of the ICW extends south from Tampa Bay all the way down to Charlotte Harbor. One can see in this 1962 image by Albert Erickson, looking south, how dredging has broken some islands in two, an east side and a west side, separated by the ICW. (PH26.0001, 12 of 48.)

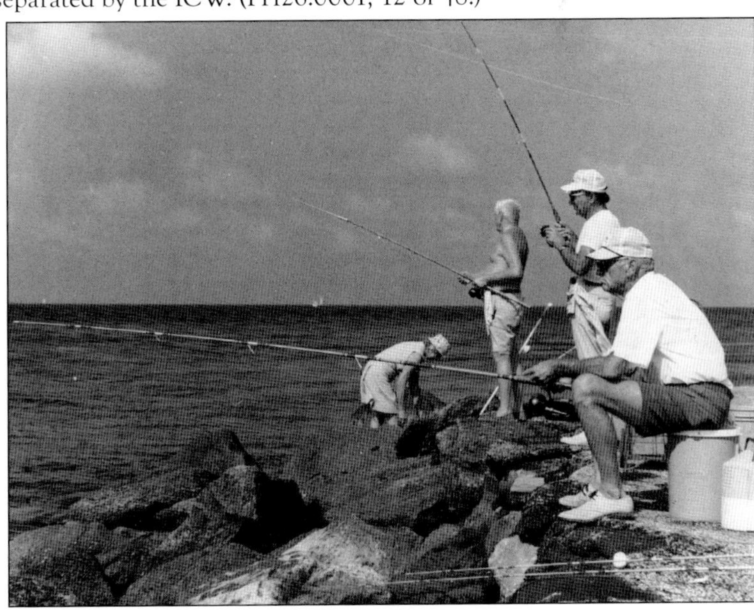

As shown in this 1970s image, the Venice Inlet Jetties are still a favored fishing spot for both dolphins and humans. The inlet today remains an outlet to the Gulf for sailboats and motor boats from the Intracoastal Waterway and nearby marinas. (PH01.04.27.)

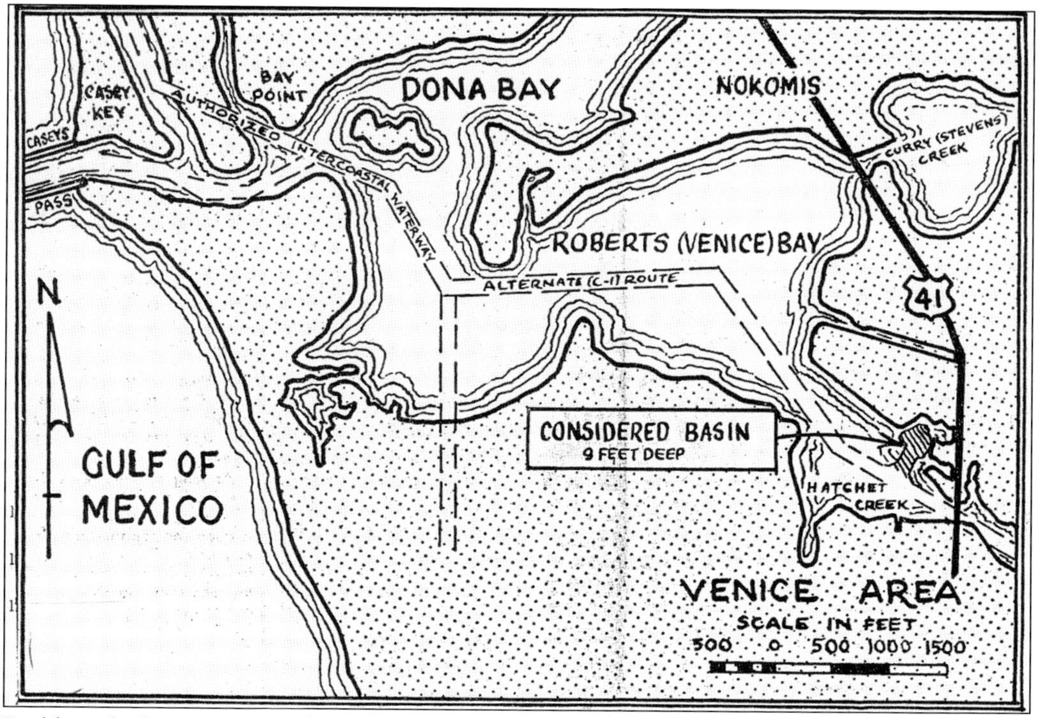

Building the last portion of the Intracoastal Waterway took 29 years, beginning in 1939. The US Congress in 1945 authorized a larger channel, 9 feet deep and 100 feet wide, but, due to World War II, funds were not released until 1948. Then, after much haggling by proponents of different routes and much controversy in the city council, the ICW was built. (LAT4D3.)

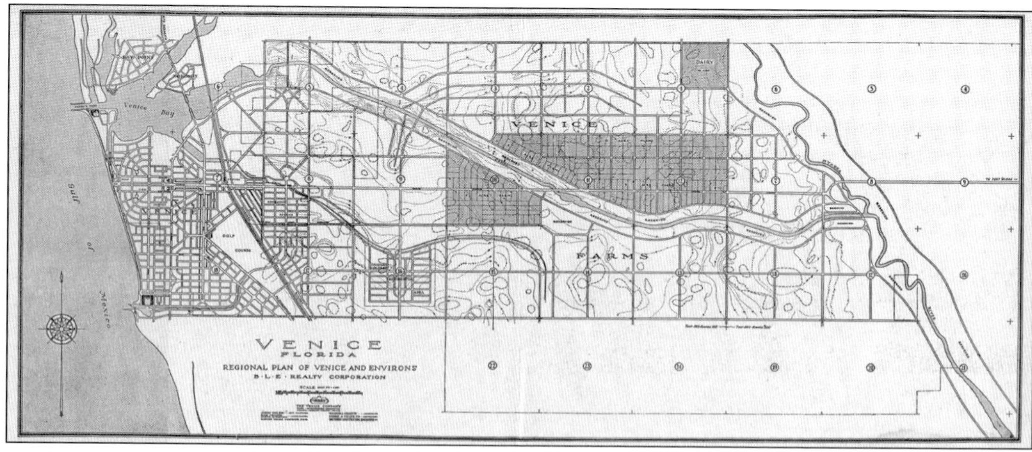

One route, the C-1 Alternative or Seaboard Route, ran parallel to the railroad tracks. Another route proposed in 1949, called Route 2, was also nicknamed the "Higel Route" as it ran down Park Boulevard, past the new city hall. It was finally disapproved, only after court cases and resolutions, in February 1951. John Nolen had also proposed a canal that siphoned water from the Myakka River. (LIB 975.901 KOR.)

Hatchett Creek was initially a low-lying, twisting estuary. In this 1965 aerial view, the Hatchett Creek Bridge (later known as the North Bridge and now called the KMI Bridge) is being replaced. There are many aerials that include this bridge. On the left is a bit of the newly dug Intracoastal approaching from the Venice Avenue Bridge on the south. (1996.17.01, image 3 of 11.)

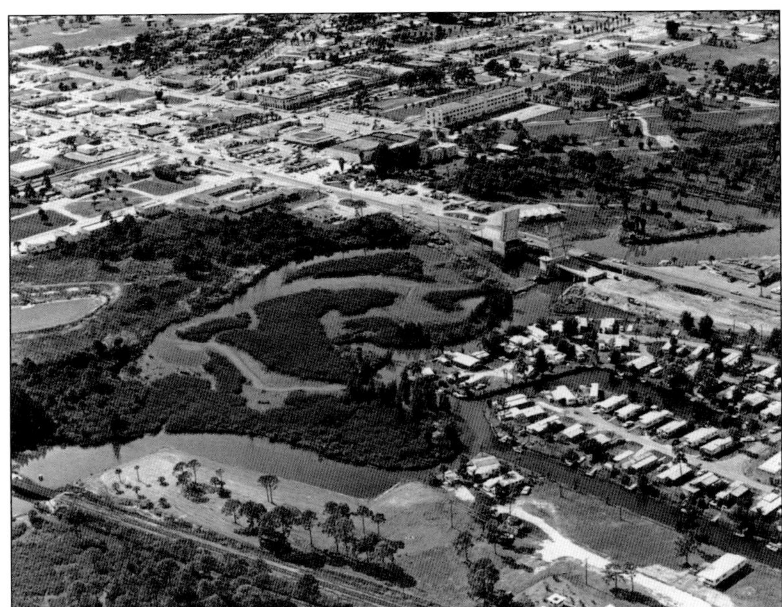

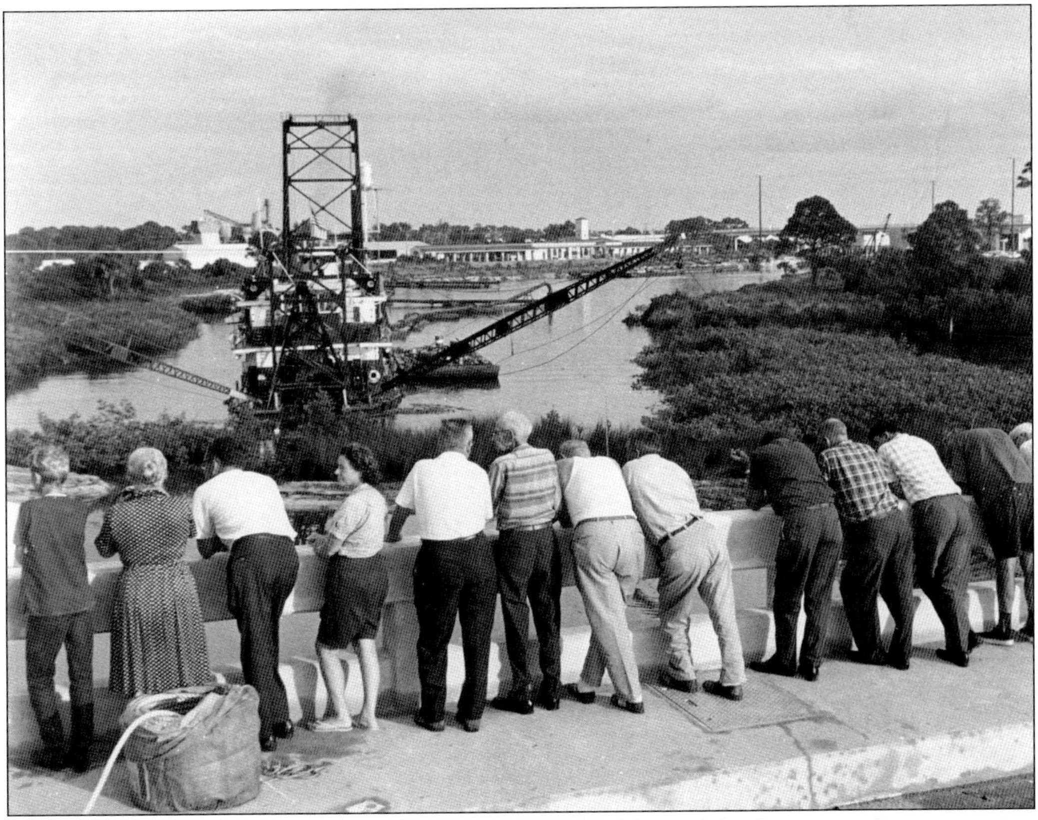

Standing on a bridge to watch dredging and bridge building of the Intracoastal was a routine pastime in the 1960s in Venice. Here, on the Hatchett Creek Bridge looking south toward the railroad depot and the industrial park, a crowd gathers to watch a dredger cut through Hatchett Creek. This was prior to the Venice Avenue Bridge being built. (MS199.)

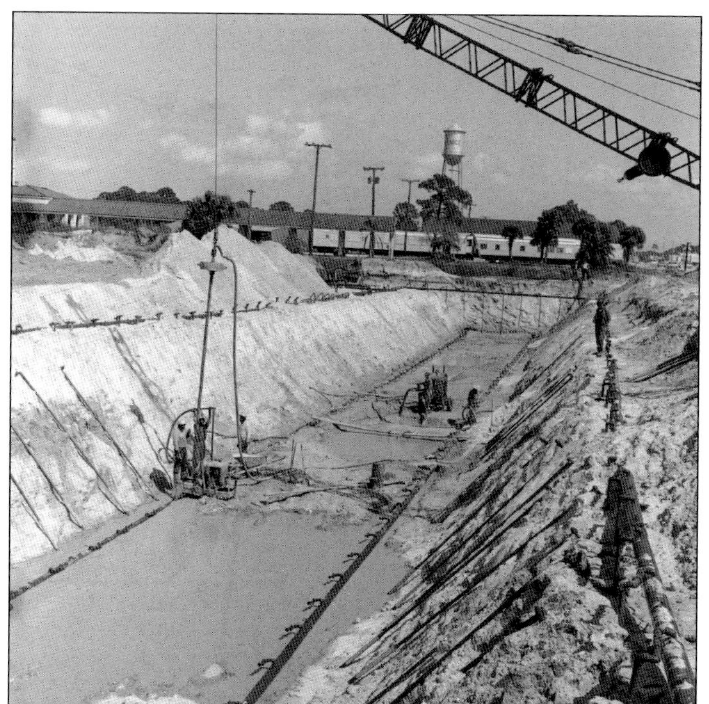

In 1965, just west of the Hatchett Creek bridge looking toward the train depot, was a clear, narrow strip of land in the path of the ICW. This is an image of initial construction after digging through this strip. Once utilities were placed, it was widened to the dimensions of the canal that is seen today. (PH26.0089.)

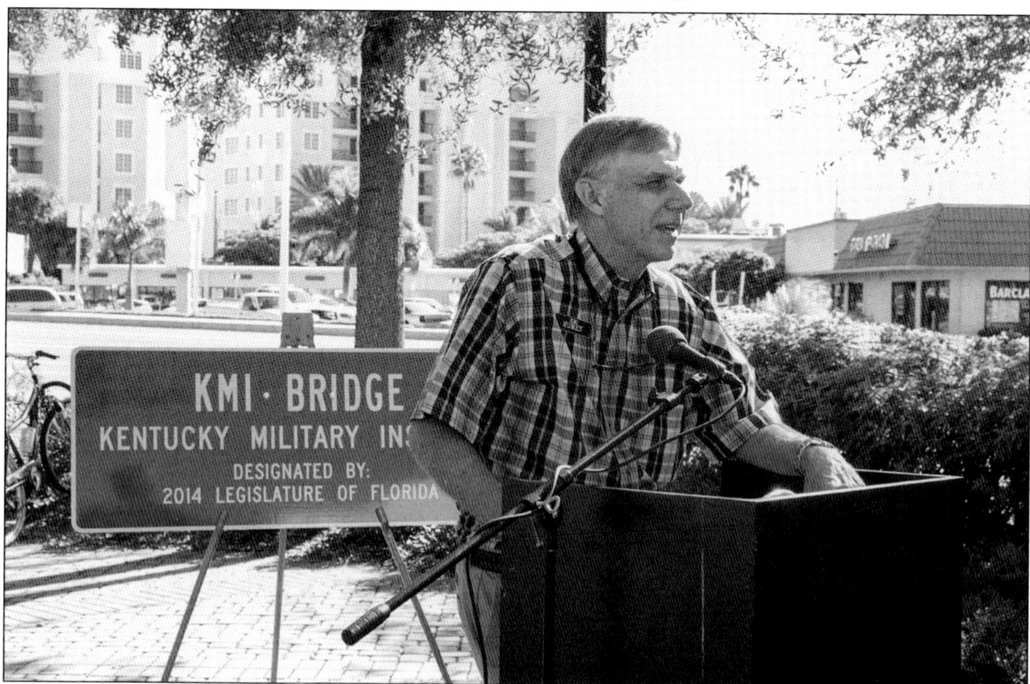

Later, the Hatchett Creek Bridge became part of Business US 41 coming into town. Sometimes called the North Bridge, it was rebuilt in 1998, 2003, and 2004 with four lanes. Then, on October 17, 2014, it was renamed the KMI Bridge for the Kentucky Military Institute. Larry Humes, of the *Venice Gondolier* newspaper, had been a KMI cadet and provided history at the event. (2014.00.57 CD image 2 of 5.)

With a view looking northwest from the Venice Avenue Bridge out to Roberts Bay, the ICW is now almost ready to open. The old North or Hatchett Creek Bridge has been removed, and one span of the new Hatchett Creek (now KMI) Bridge is complete. In this image, utility lines are now being dredged out, and support equipment remains on the water. (MS199 Box 1 File 8.)

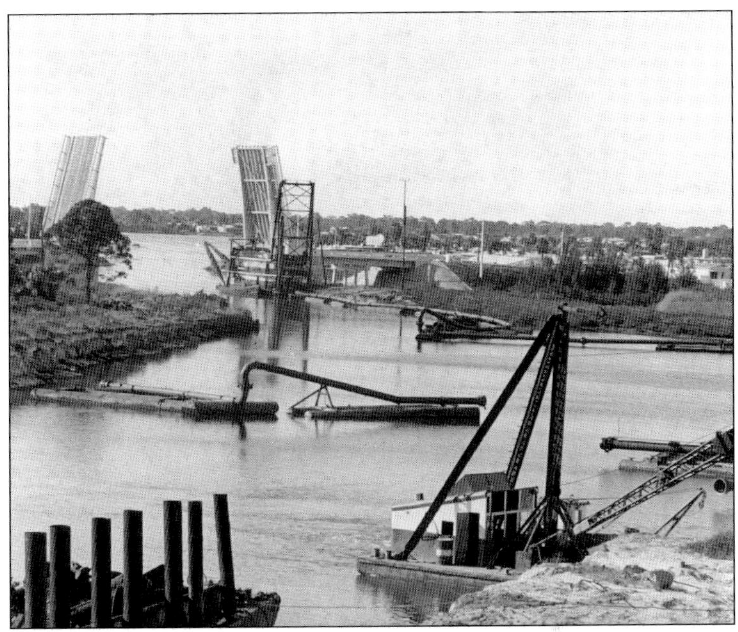

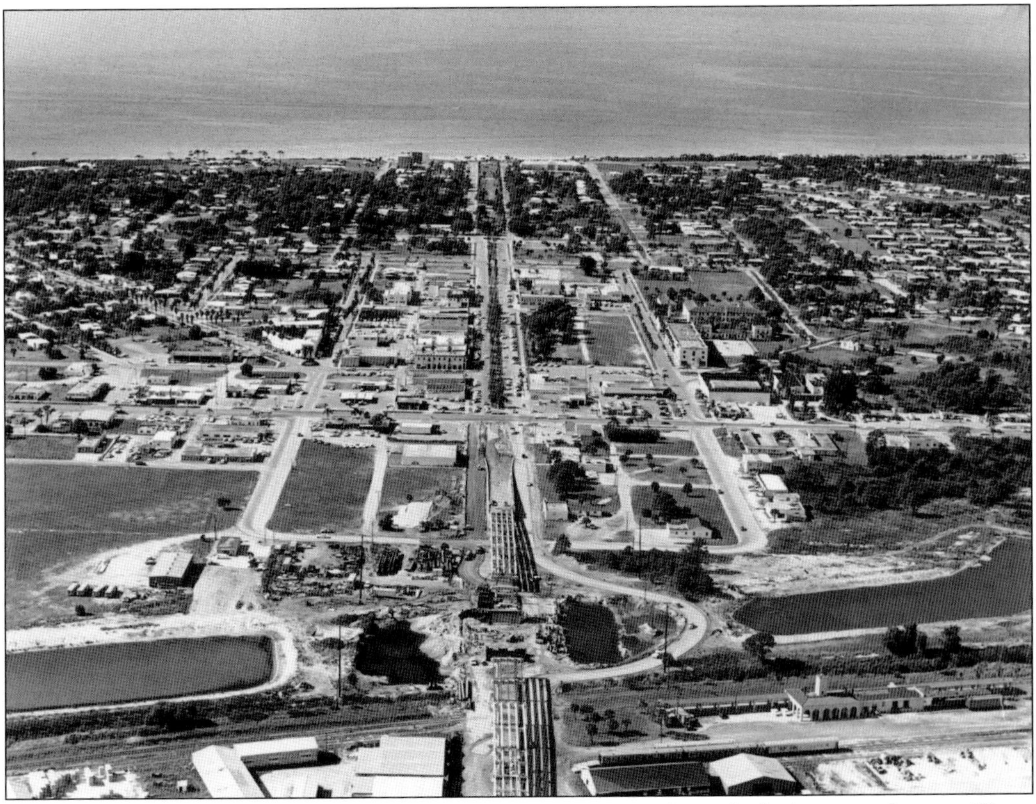

In the 1926 Nolen plan, Venice Avenue, shown here, ran west through the business district. There was, of course, no bridge before the advent of the Intracoastal. Seen here are the two legs of the ICW on either side of Venice Avenue waiting to be connected as the bridge is being constructed. To the left, an empty space awaits the eventual development of Venice Middle School. (1999.17.01.)

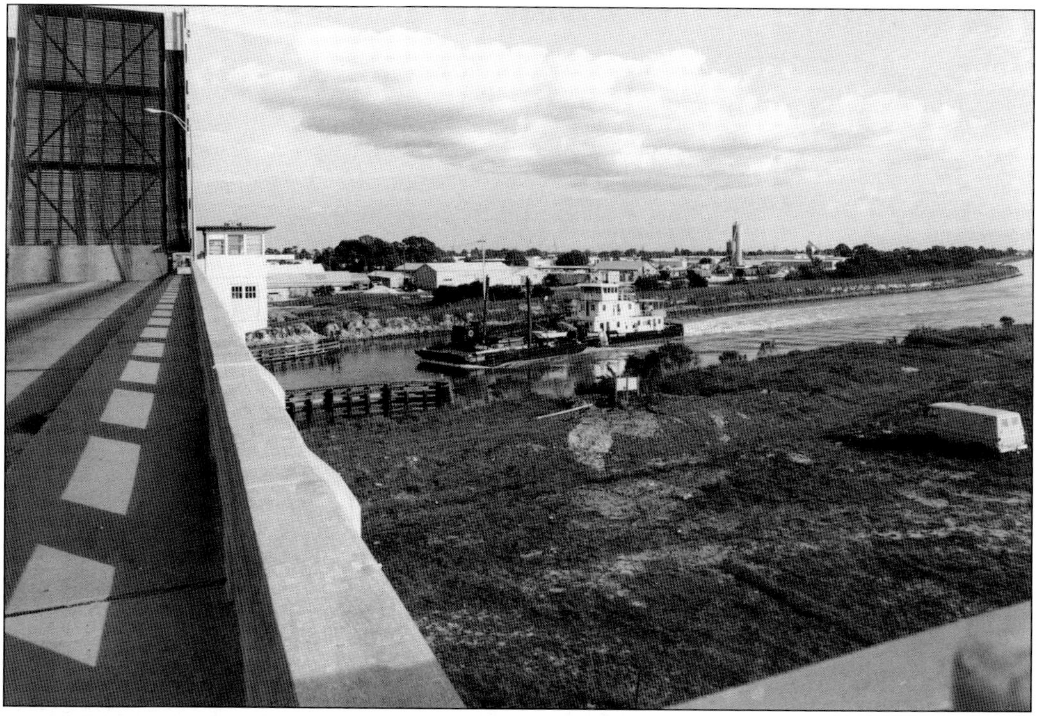

On the south side of the Venice Avenue Bridge, looking east toward the industrial park, one can see that the bridge tender tower's roof has not yet been modified with the angular tile roof it now has. This would not occur until 2004. (PH01.06.31, image 1 of 3.)

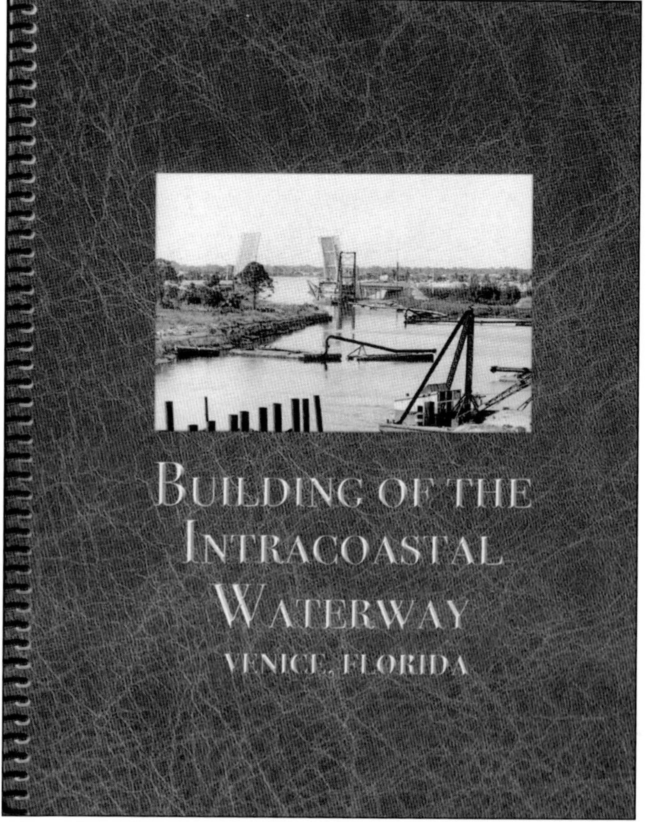

This book on the Intracoastal Waterway by Dorothy Korwek is an excellent one-subject book and provides many details and photographs on the development and building of the ICW in Venice. It focuses on the concepts of why a canal was needed for Venice, the planning process, and the construction. (LIB 975 KOR.)

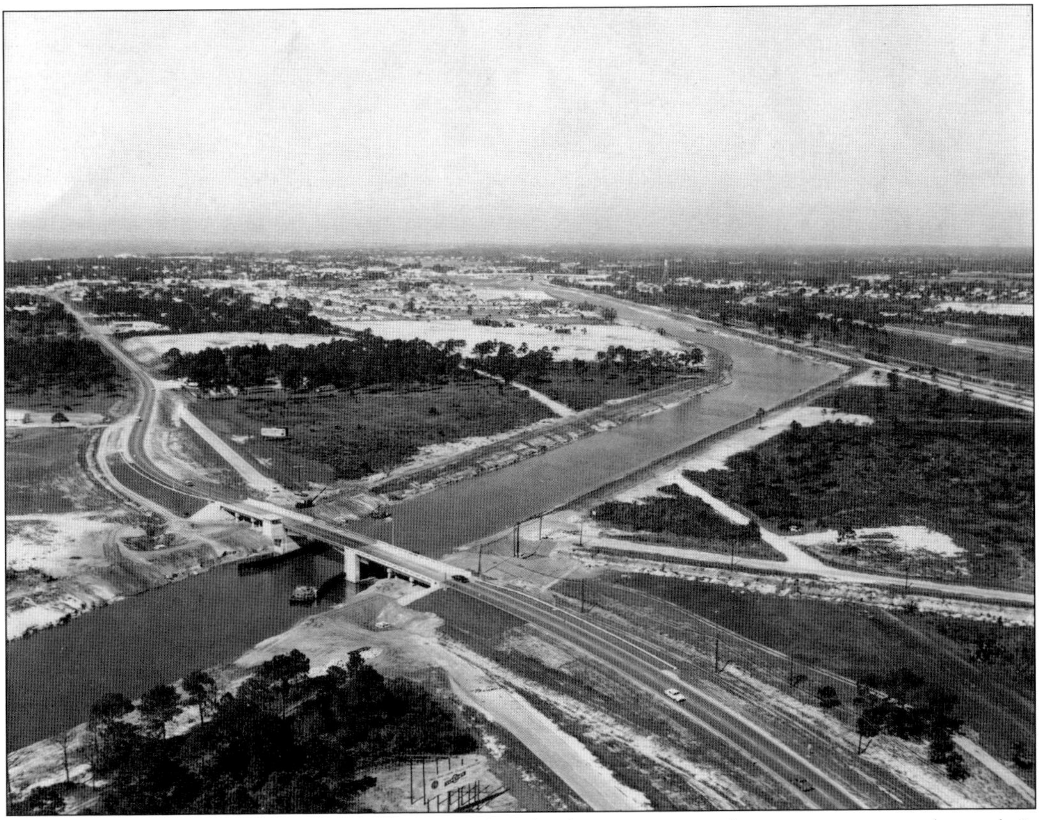

South Bridge was initially built as a single drawbridge span over the new intracoastal canal. It provided an easier traffic route through Venice as an island and also easier access to and from South Venice, Englewood, Manasota Key, and North Port on the new Business US 41. (NP0415.)

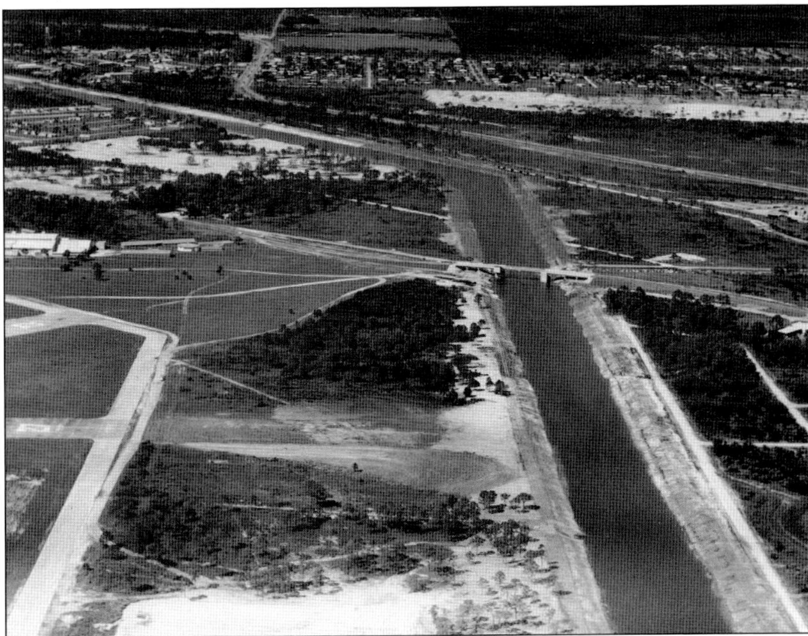

In 1965, looking north, part of the airport is on the left, including the circus arena and its buildings. The ICW makes a sudden turn near what would become a small industrial park on the right. These broad open areas await development in 1965. (MS26 Box 3 File 3.)

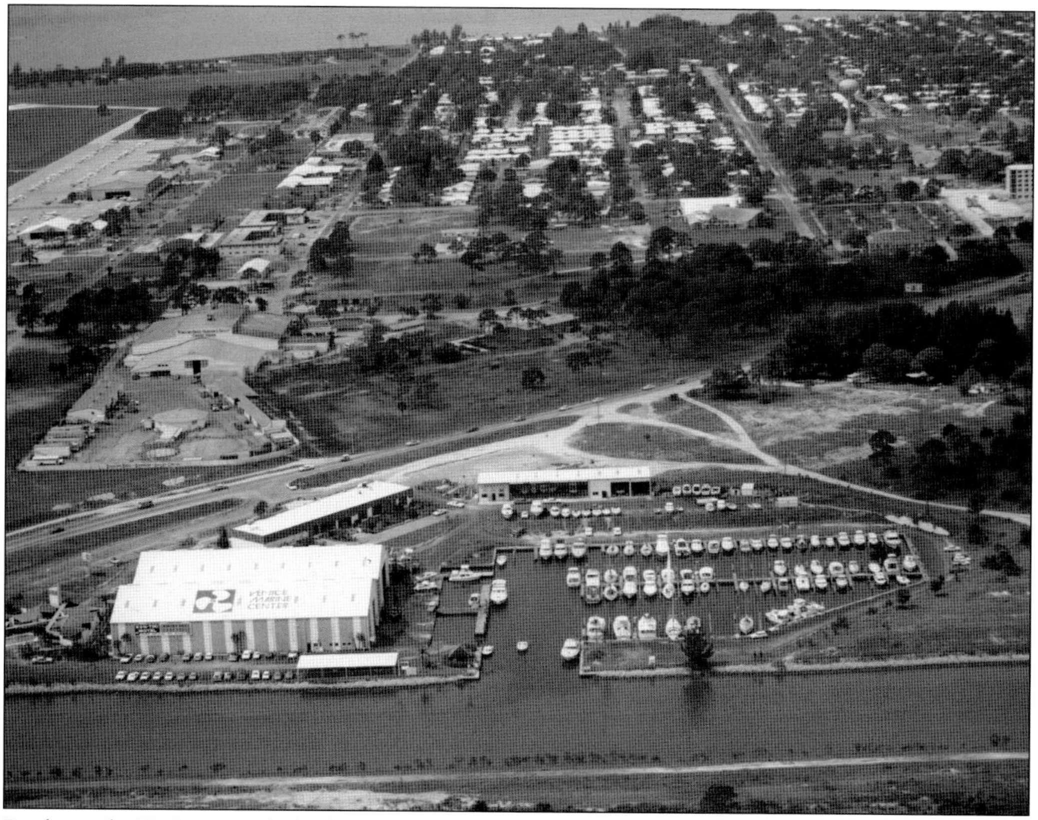

By the early 1970s, a newly built marina was located just north and west of South Bridge and the circus property. Note the circus arena and animal quarters in the middle left. A second Venice railroad station was added at Center Road, convenient for the circus. (MS43 Box 2 Folder 3.)

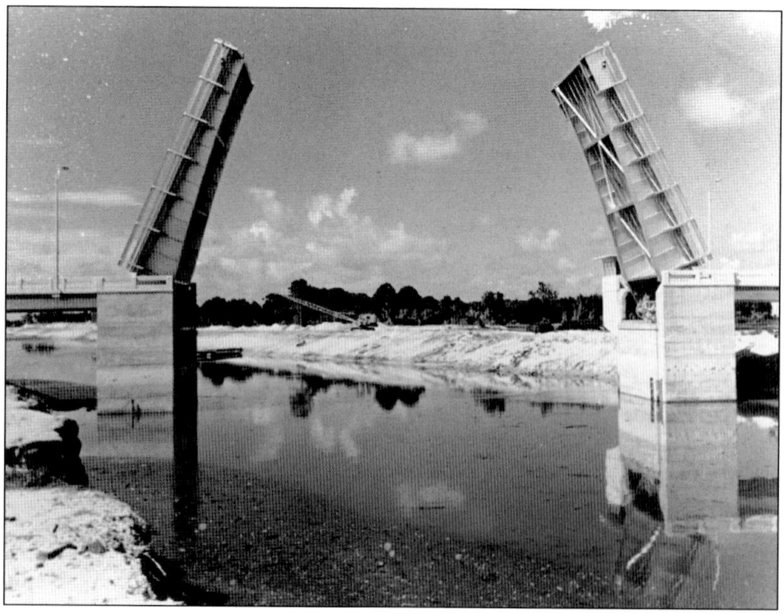

Much of the ICW's course around the island of Venice, from Roberts Bay to Lemon Bay, though planned for defense and/or commercial shipping, is now maintained for recreational purposes. Initially, South Bridge was only a two-lane drawbridge; then, in the early 2000s, another two-lane bridge was added to accommodate the increasing traffic. (NP0857.)

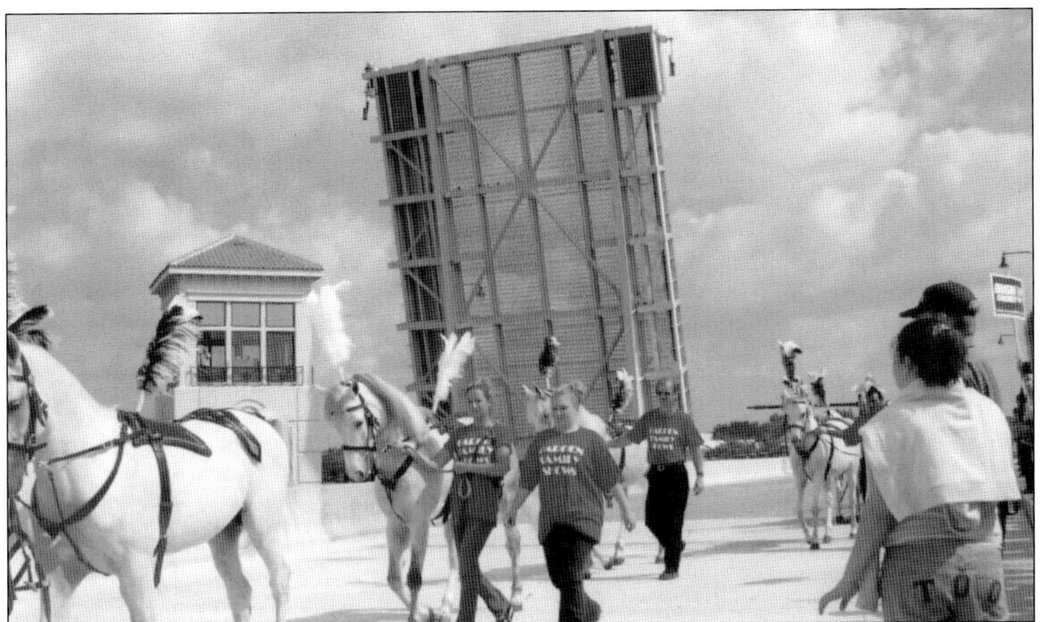

South Bridge was renamed Circus Bridge in 2004, after the Ringling Bros. and Barnum & Bailey Circus. Its winter headquarters and arena were adjacent for over 30 years (until 1992). Note the distinctive roof on the watch tower added to the new South/Circus Bridge. (PH26.0235, SCHRC.)

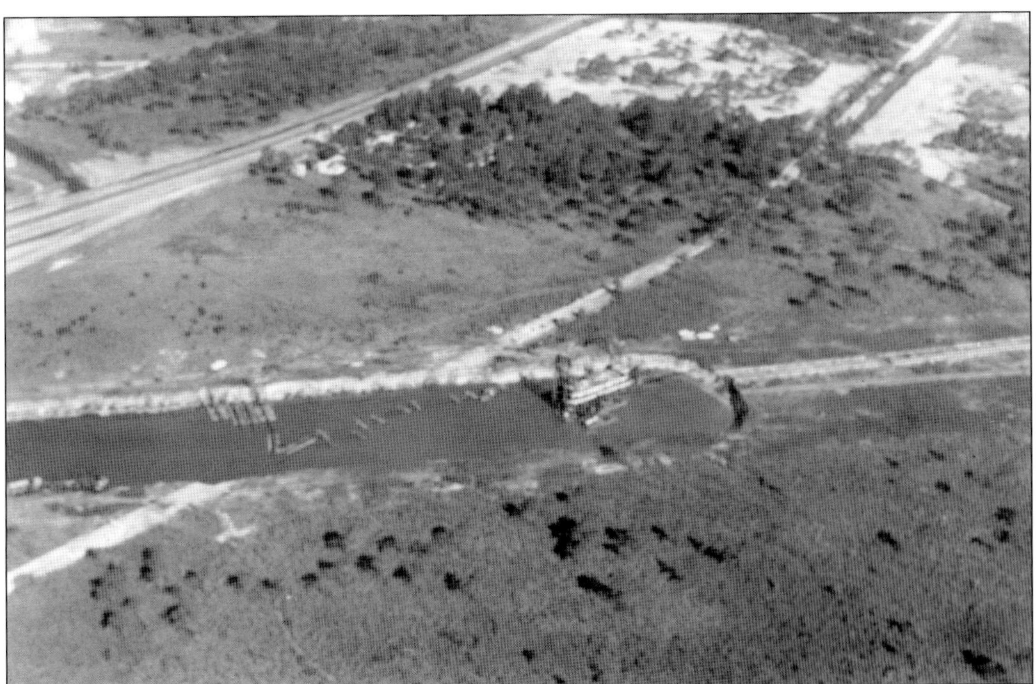

Plowing through a straight stretch of Florida landscape without homes or businesses was less complicated. This fuzzy image was shot by a local resident pilot and amateur photographer. It shows a dredger floating in a pool, methodically digging the Intracoastal Waterway south of Circus Bridge. (PH03.01.07.)

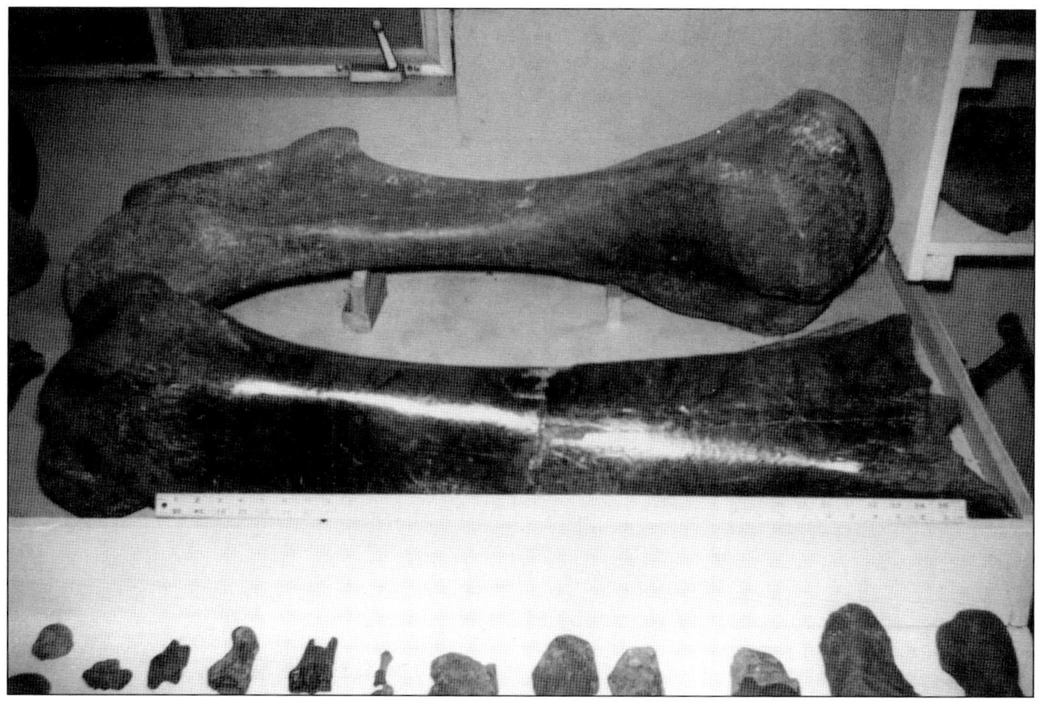

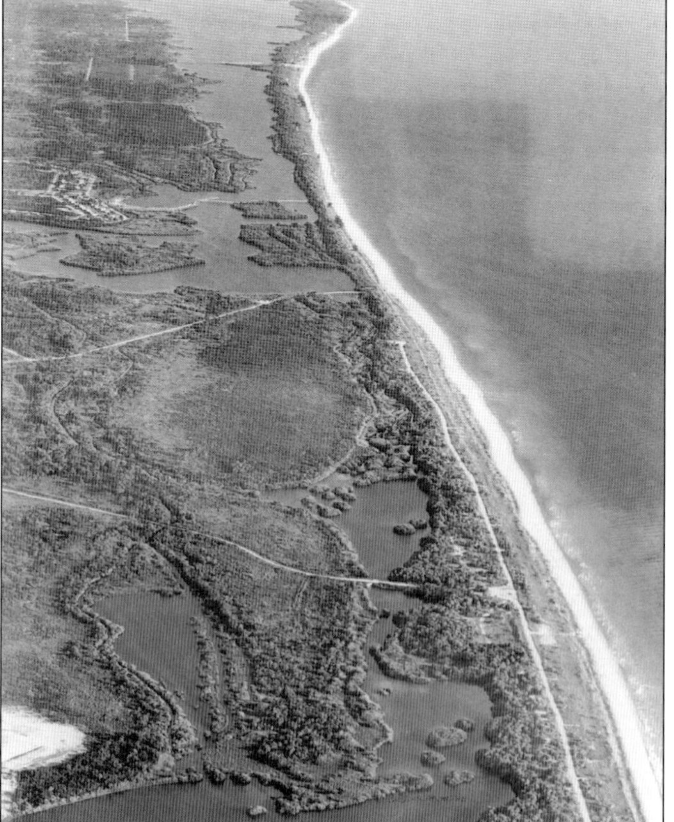

In the spring of 1965, while exploring in the southern portion of the ICW, two teenage amateur archeologists found shark teeth, projectile points (such as arrowheads), and animal bones, as shown here. Terry and Randy Owens donated their finds to the Florida Museum of Natural History at the University of Florida in Gainesville. (LAT 1D.)

The southern end of the Venice Intracoastal Waterway now goes behind Caspersen Beach past South Venice, into Lemon Bay, and then Charlotte Harbor. But, as shown in this 1953 aerial, the area was originally a series of ponds, one of which was named Buzzard Lake but has now been renamed Red Lake. (PH26.0161.)

In this 1970 aerial, the land looks completely different. The ICW is turning south down a narrow passage toward Lemon Bay. The white areas are dredged sand fills where previously old lakes or swampy land had been located. This created the new property that would become South Venice. (PH26.0456.)

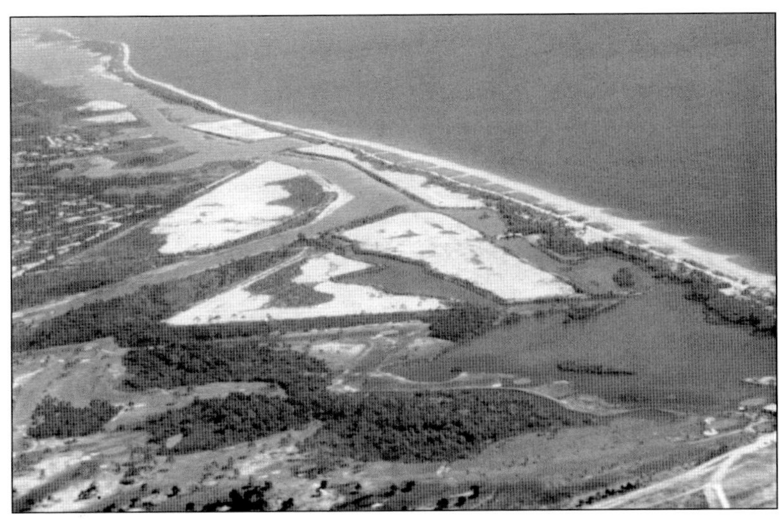

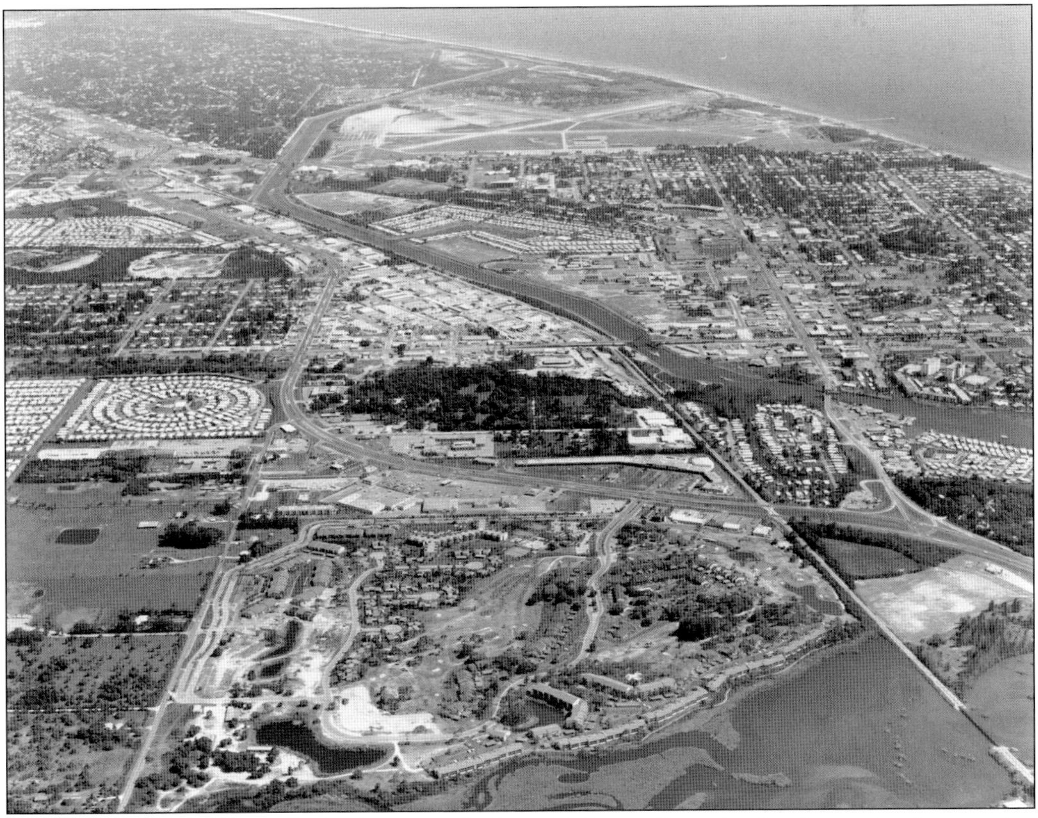

Taken in 1980, this aerial, looking south from Roberts Bay, clearly shows the burgeoning development of Venice. Also note the three drawbridges over the ICW. The then-still-active railroad tracks (which have now become the Legacy Trail) can be seen coming in at the lower right corner. (PH26.0469, 1 of 13.)

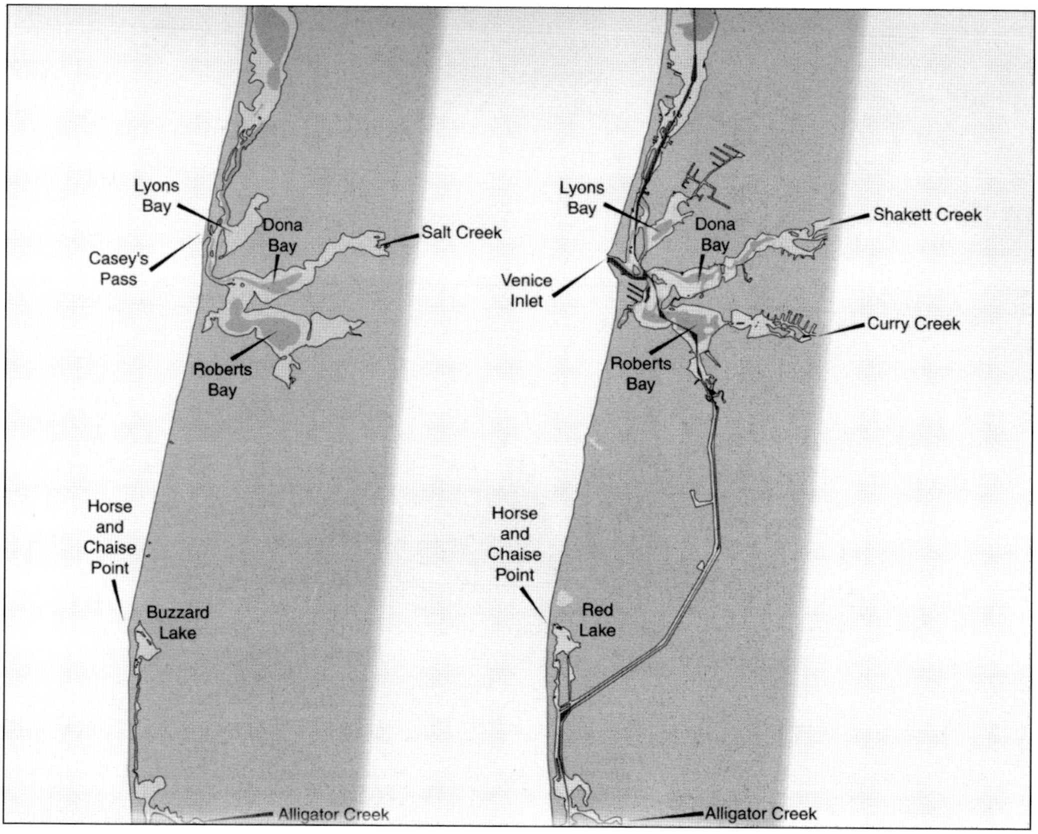

This map compares the 75 years between 1892 and 1967. Note the changes in Dona Bay, Salt Creek, Shakett Creek, Curry Creek, and Roberts Bay. Treasure Island (Casey Key) Pass, which had been a constantly shifting outlet into the Gulf, was permanently closed in 1937 with the construction of a new opening called the Venice Inlet and Jetties. (LIB 629.048 ANT.)

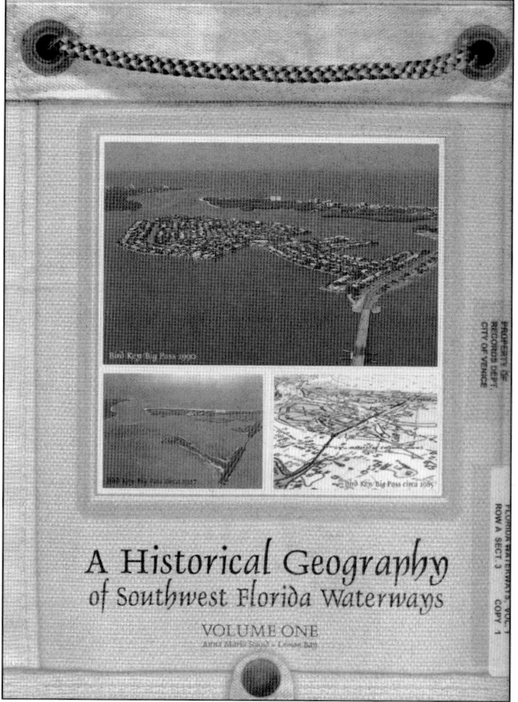

After the Intracoastal Waterway was extended in 1967, Venice became an island. Buzzard Lake took the more pleasant name of Red Lake. The map at the top of the page is from *A Historical Geography of Southwest Florida Waterways, Volume 1*, as well as online, but it is also available at the Venice Historical Resources Archives in the Julia Cousins-Laning and Dale Laning Archives Resource Center (CLARC) building. (LIB 629.048 ANT.)

Four

Promoters and Resorts

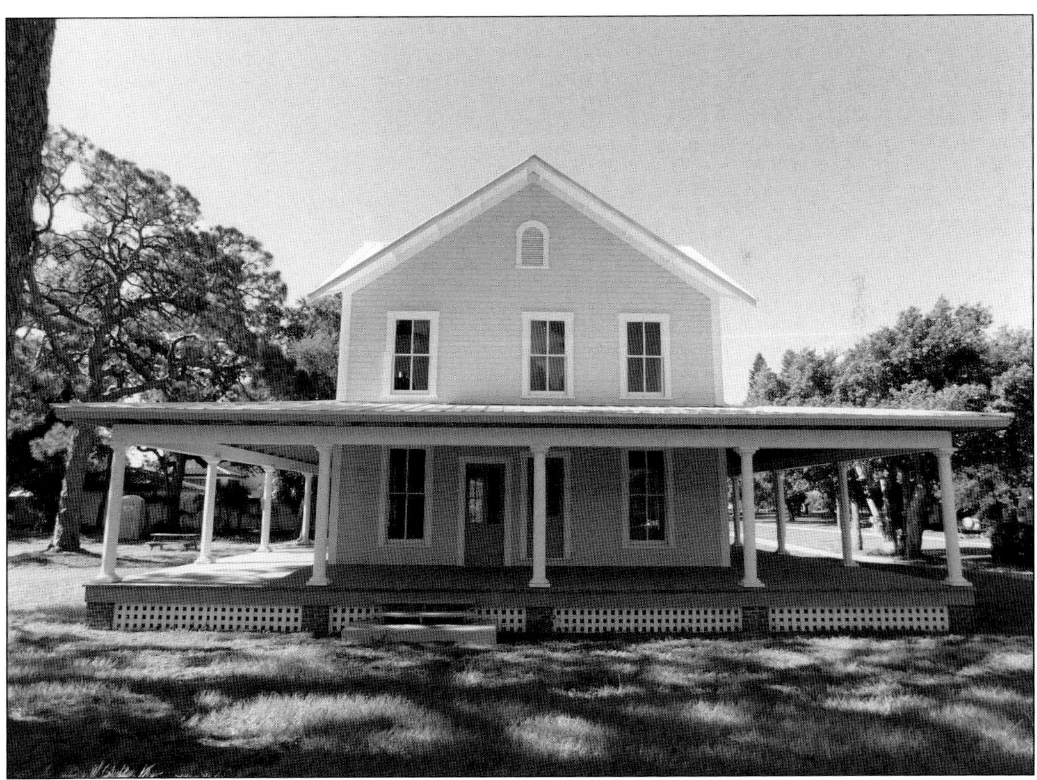

The first successful Venice-area promoter was Joseph Haley Lord, who established a citrus grove along Roberts Bay. He built the Lord-Higel House, the second oldest house in south Sarasota County, and made numerous real estate investments in lumber, turpentine, oysters, citrus groves, and housing in the area. (RG 204.)

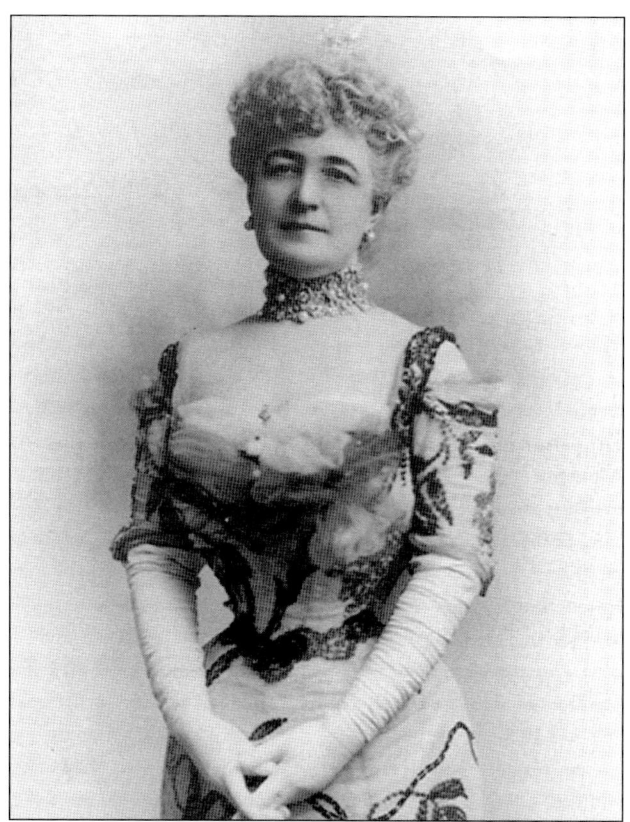

Winter resorts were the norm when Bertha Honoré Palmer invested in Venice. A socialite, philanthropist, and rich widow, she was encouraged by Joseph H. Lord. His Chicago real estate firm was in the same office building as her father, H.H. Honoré's firm. The Honoré and Palmer families' Sarasota-Venice Company eventually purchased thousands of acres in what was then a much larger Manatee County. (NP1378.)

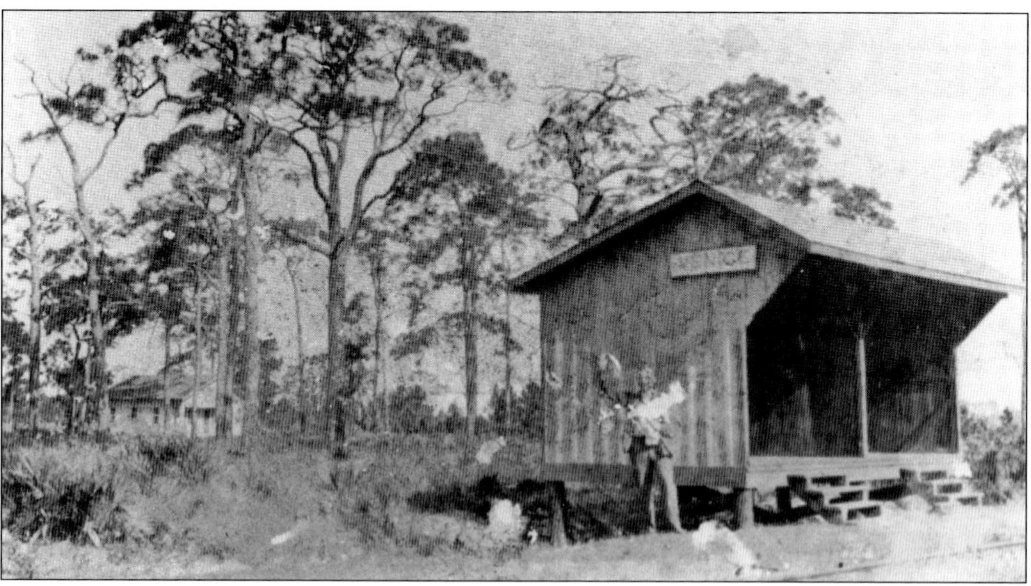

By 1915, the Palmers had encouraged the Seaboard Air Line Railroad (the first Venice station, shown above, was north of Roberts Bay in the now-named Nokomis) to extend its tracks from Nokomis to a new Venice, where at least two Palmer resorts were planned. The Palmers platted Venice in 1915, with the Eagle Point Resort started in 1916. But when the Palmer resort plans proved too expensive, they subsequently sold their Venice property to the Albees. (NP0775.)

The next resort promoters in the Venice area were Dr. Fred H. Albee and his wife, Louella, pictured here in the 1930s. They moved to Nokomis in 1917. Dr. Albee was a rich man, an orthopedic surgeon from New York who was famous for his innovative bone grafting techniques before and during World War I. (NP1318.)

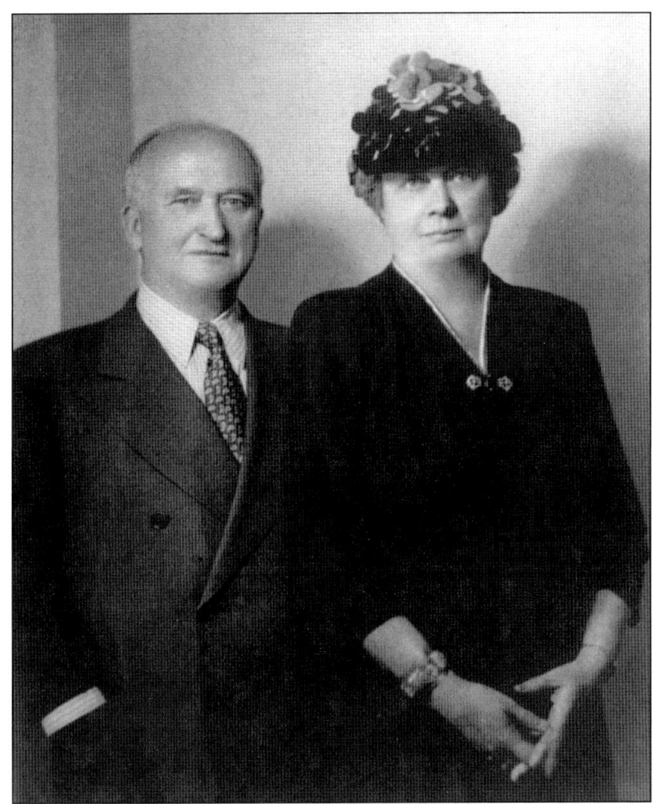

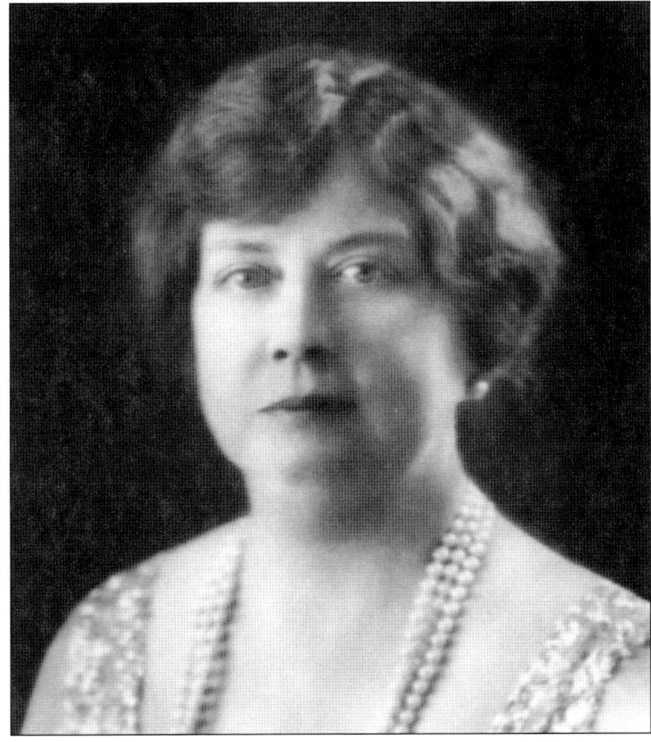

Louella Albee, in her book *The Doctor and I*, described her husband as a "whirlwind." They both made numerous contributions to the Venice area for over 30 years. Louella was founder of the Venice-Nokomis Woman's Club and established Venice's first library. (NP1317.)

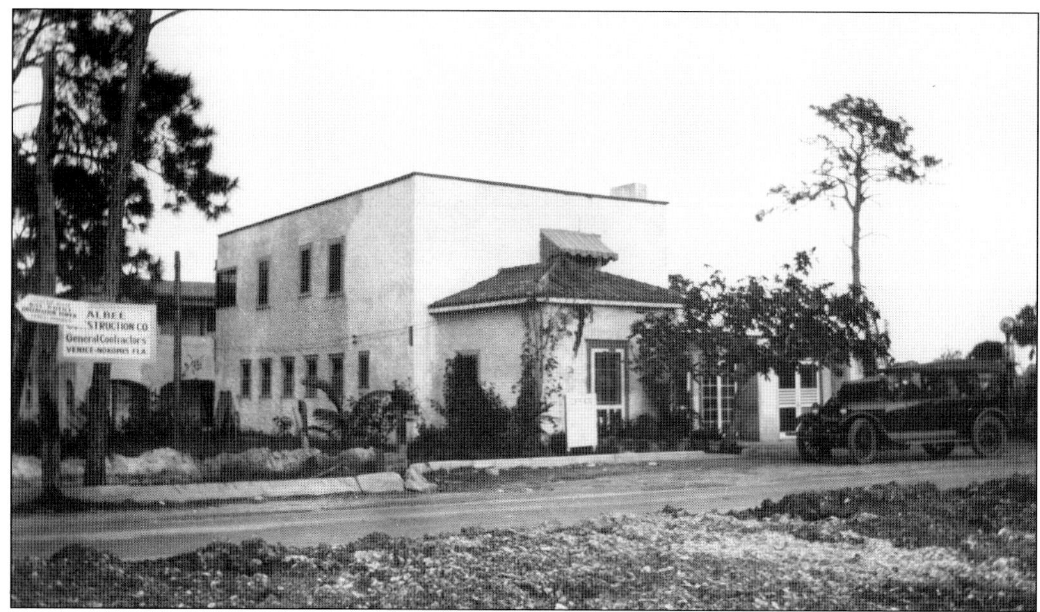

Dr. Albee initially invested in turpentine and lumber lands. He then began his Albee General Construction Company, pictured here. In 1922, he built the first resort hotel in the area, the Villa Pocono, then Villa Nokomis, on the site of his old turpentine camp. It was on the shore of Roberts Bay. In 1923, it was renamed the Pollyanna Inn. (NP0348.)

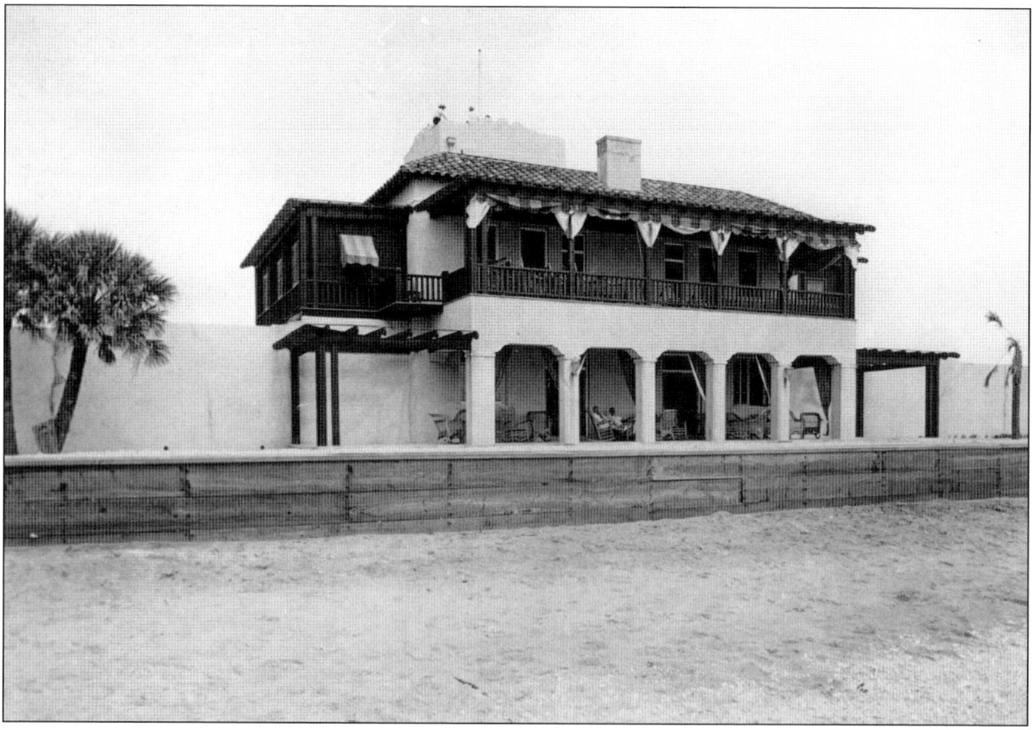

In 1922, Dr. Albee built the first Beach House in Venice, located at 811 The Esplanade, seen here in 1925. He further expanded his Venice-area housing and resort plans in 1925 with the purchase of 1,500 acres from the Palmer family's Sarasota-Venice Company. (NP0704.)

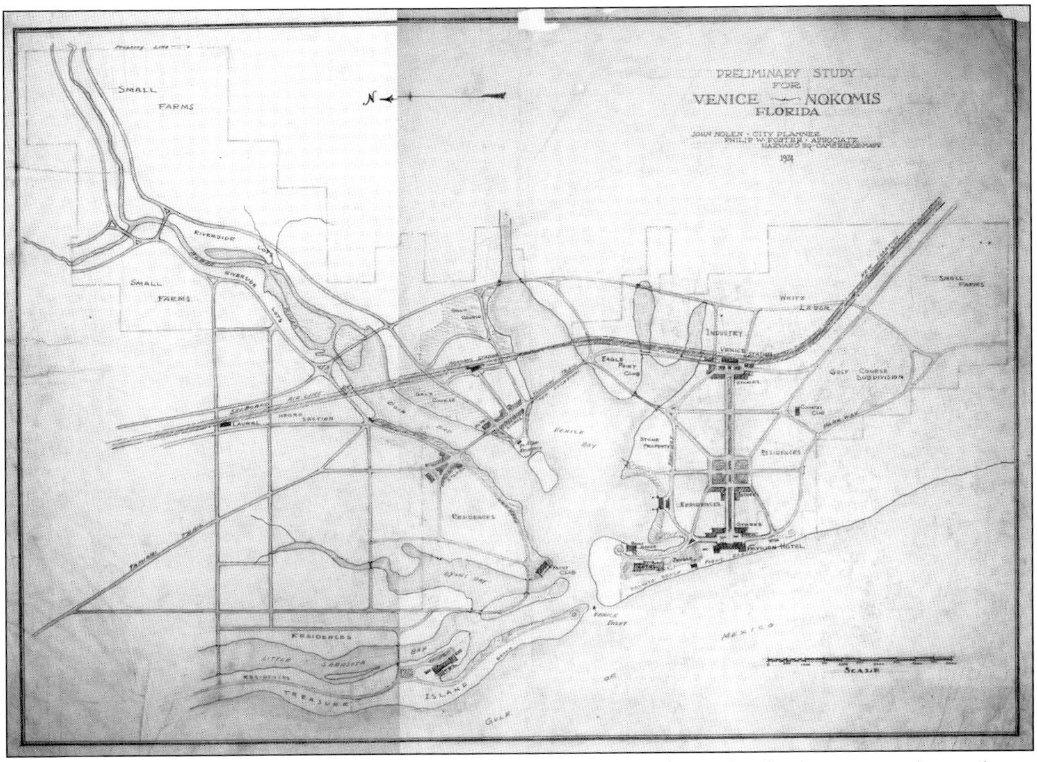

Dr. Albee soon hired John Nolen, the noted city planner, to draw the draft concept shown here. But realizing that the resort was too expensive for him to build, Albee negotiated a quick sale of his property that same year to the Brotherhood of Locomotive Engineers. The BLE also retained Nolen and purchased more land, all the way to the Myakka River. (LIB 975.961 KOR.)

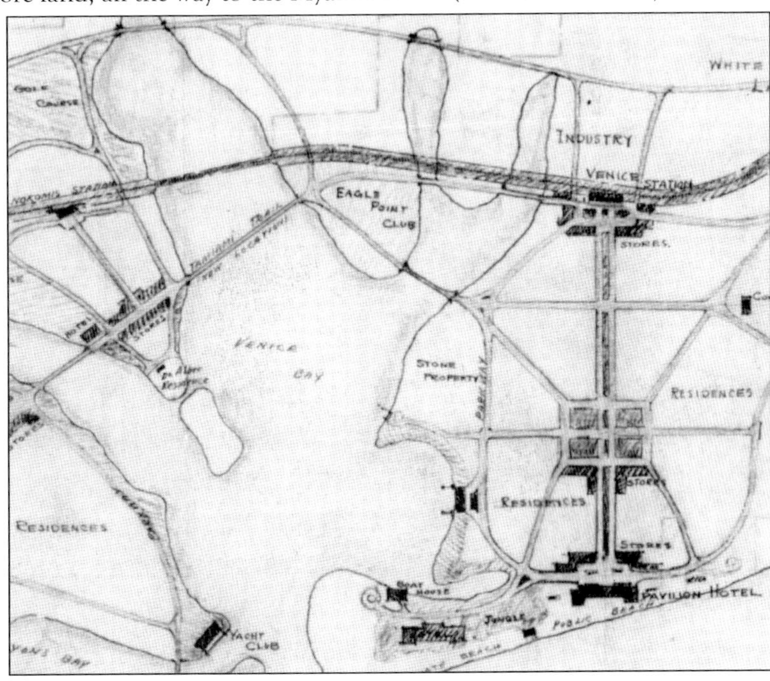

This version of the 1924 Albee and BLE plan, looking closely, includes both the old 1915 Palmer Venice Plat Map, signed by J.H. Lord, and Nolen's proposed changes. The railroad tracks would be moved farther east. The Tamiami Trail would move east, with businesses gathered around the train depot. (LIB 975-961KOR; OS60.)

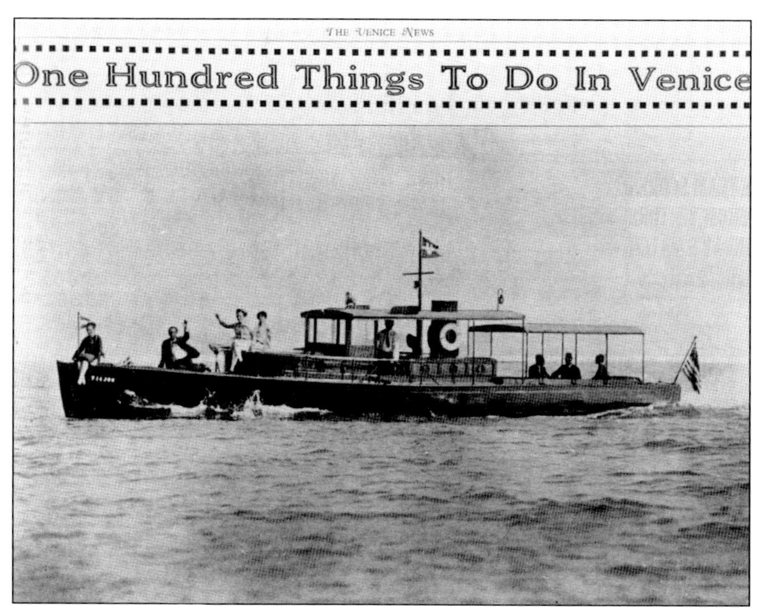

The BLE was the next resort and housing promoter. From 1925 through 1928, it built a community with an attractive and vibrant downtown, civic areas, housing at various income levels (including homes, apartments, and farms), and hotels. Greg Turner's *Venice in the 1920s* provides numerous details on John Nolen, his plans for Venice, and the BLE, including "One Hundred Things to Do in Venice." (LIB 975.961 and NP0966.)

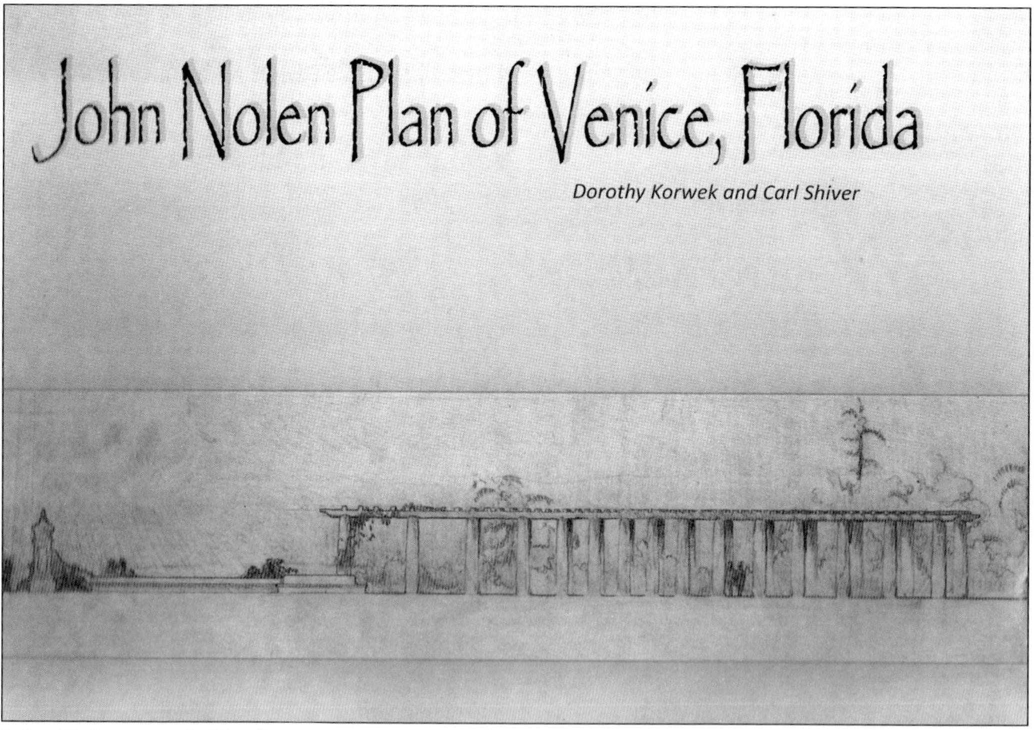

John Nolen is probably the reason many people still move here. They travel down Venice Avenue through the historic business district to a widened street median with huge trees and a meandering walkway to the beach. It was like heaven. To understand this impact, refer to Dorothy Korwek and Carl Shiver's book, *John Nolen Plan of Venice, Florida*. (LIB 975.961KOR.)

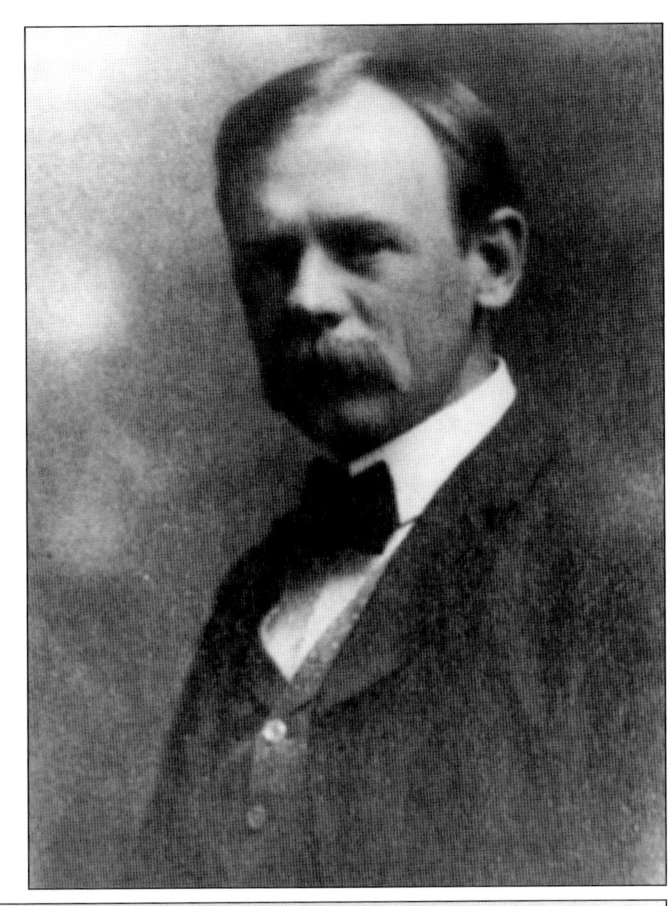

John Nolen (1869–1937) had been orphaned as a child but self-enrolled in Harvard, graduating in 1905. His innovative city-garden concepts, described in *John Nolen Plan of Venice, Florida*, are known for their livability. In Venice, he created a beautiful self-sustaining community for people of all incomes and lifestyles. (LIB 975.961KOR.)

Prentiss French, also a Harvard-trained landscape architect, brought livability by implementing Nolen's city-garden concepts. His staff of 30 installed over 300 varieties of plants from a 40-acre BLE nursery. Many of his planting concepts are still followed in Venice. Prentiss French Park is located on Avenue Des Parques North, with its twin, John Nolen Park, on Avenue Des Parques South. (DDC2008.21.079, image 37 of 39.)

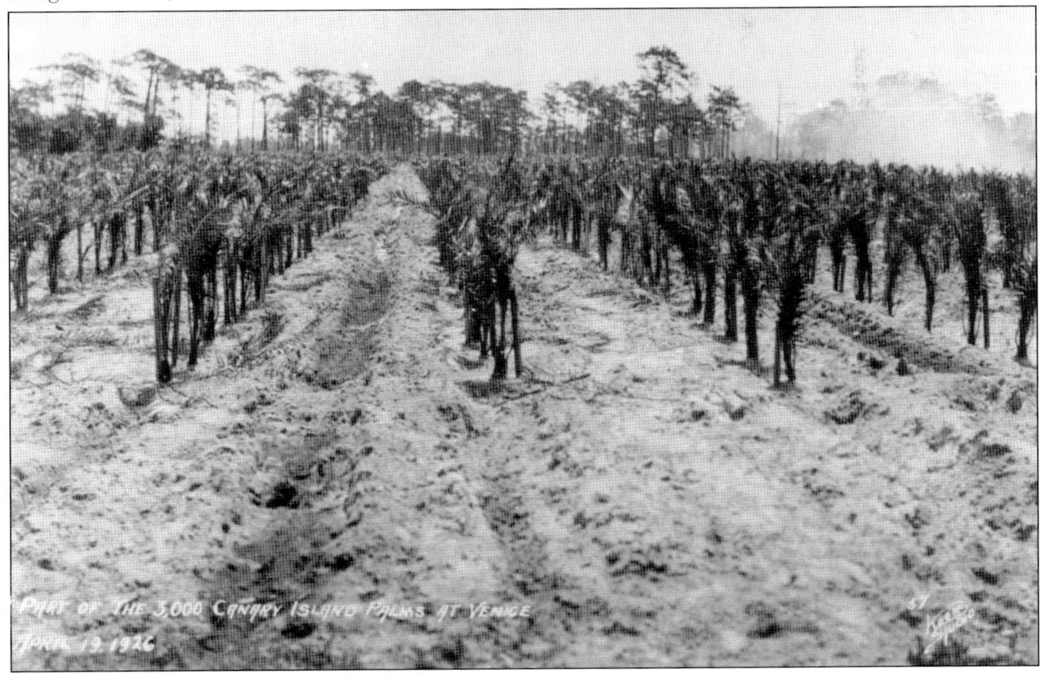

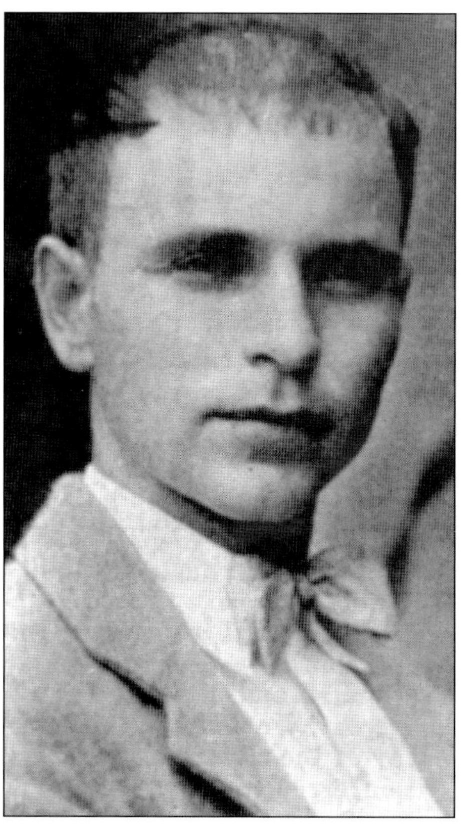

Prentiss French, born in Chicago, was the son of William M.R. French, founding director of the Art Institute of Chicago and founder of the American Association (now Alliance) of Museums. Prentiss was the nephew of the prolific sculptor Daniel Chester French, creator of the Lincoln Memorial in Washington, DC. French's family in the United States dates back to the 1630s. (NP0961.)

Shown here boating in 1928 on the Myakka River are, from left to right, Robert Boggess; Prentiss French; his wife, Helen B. Douglass, who was also a prolific and well-known architect; and a river guide. The articles that Prentiss wrote for the *Venice News* are very informative on Nolen, his landscape theories, and inspirational public relations tools. (NP0946.)

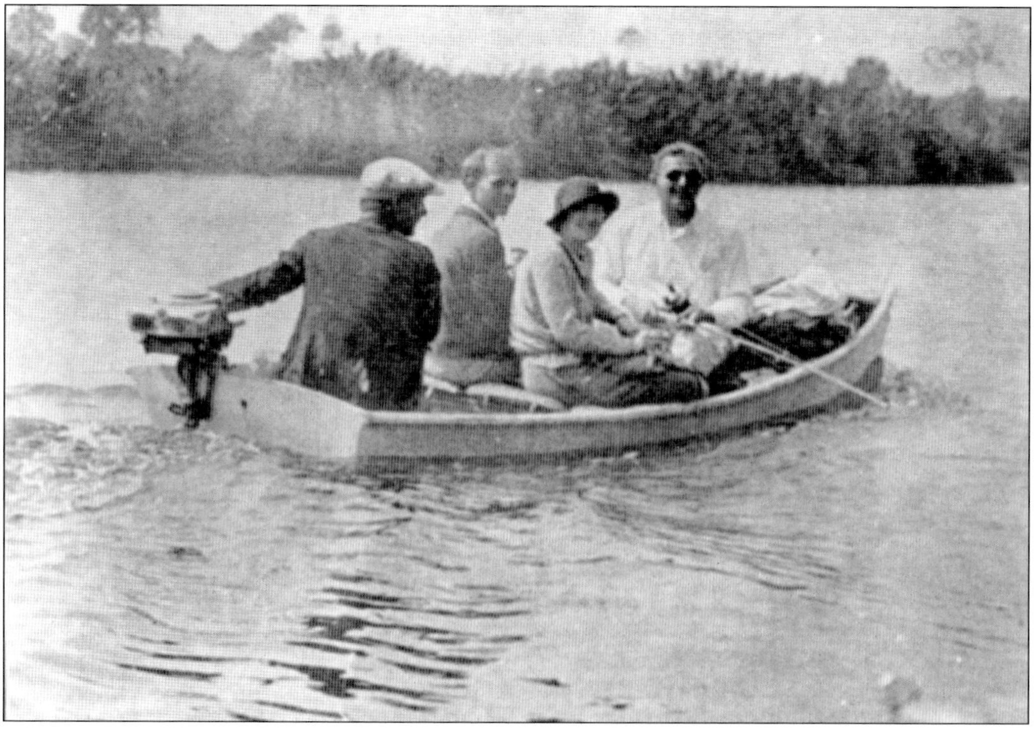

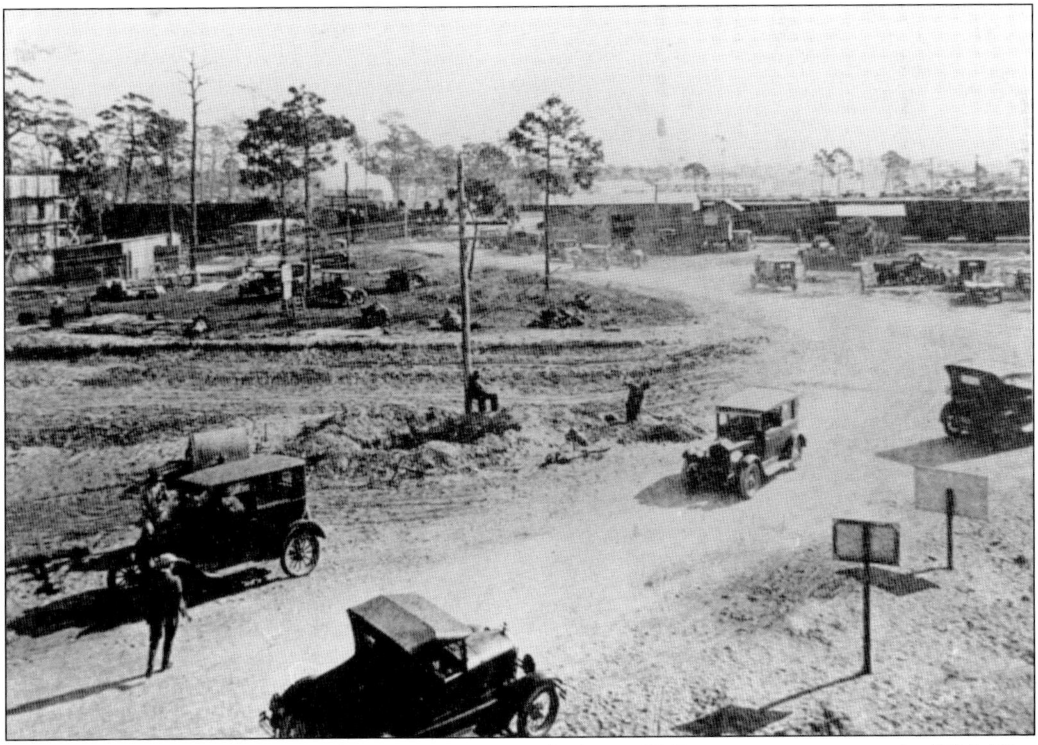

This photograph, taken from the San Marco Hotel, shows BLE construction in early 1926. The old Palmer railroad depot, at the top right-hand side, is near St. Augustine Avenue and Nokomis Avenue. The new BLE train depot, relocated east, opened in 1927 at its current location now on the east side of the Intracoastal Waterway. (NP0872.)

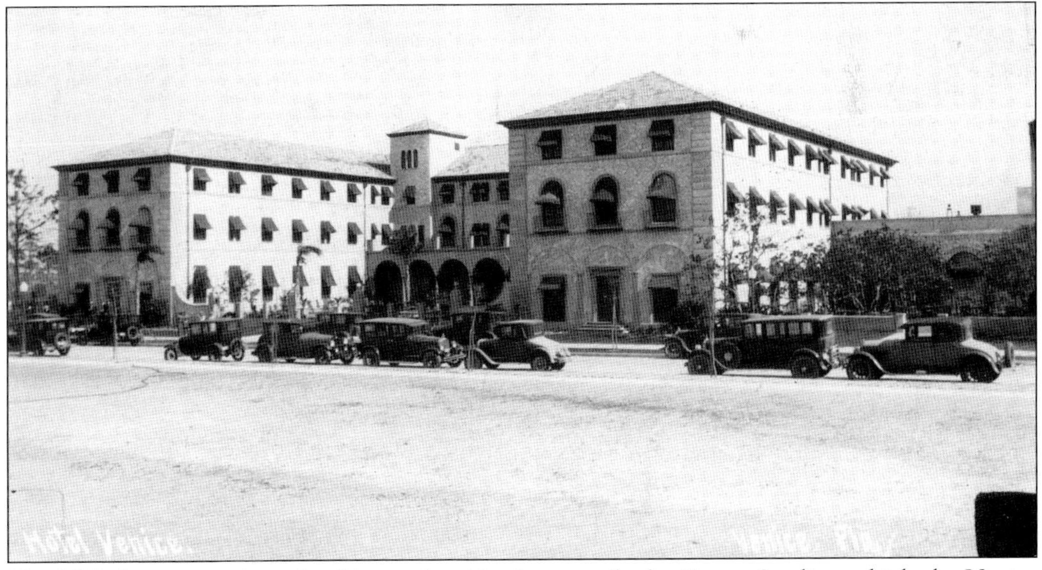

The BLE documented much of its work with photographs by Koons Studios, which the Venice Historical Resources, Museum & Archives, has in its collection. Pictured here is Hotel Venice on the northeast corner of what is now Tampa Avenue West and Nassau Street. After serving as a KMI facility, it is now an assisted living center. (NP0021A.)

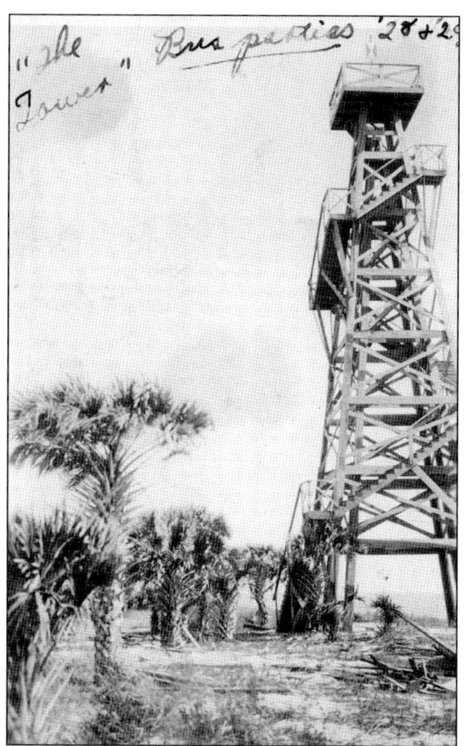

Three triangulation points are necessary for surveying. This BLE wooden tower was most likely located on the island, but it is not known where. Perhaps another triangulation point was the top of the Beach House built by Dr. Albee. Based on what is handwritten on the back of the photograph, teenagers "partied on" this tower. (PH26.0194, CD024, 10 of 37.)

The BLE described most of its Venice hotels as luxury hotels, with the latest accoutrements, including fully staffed restaurants and cooking facilities, as shown in this picture from Hotel Venice. More affordable hotels and rooming houses were also available for Brotherhood members. After the BLE left in early 1929, a number of its employees stayed on and made their homes here. (NP1242.)

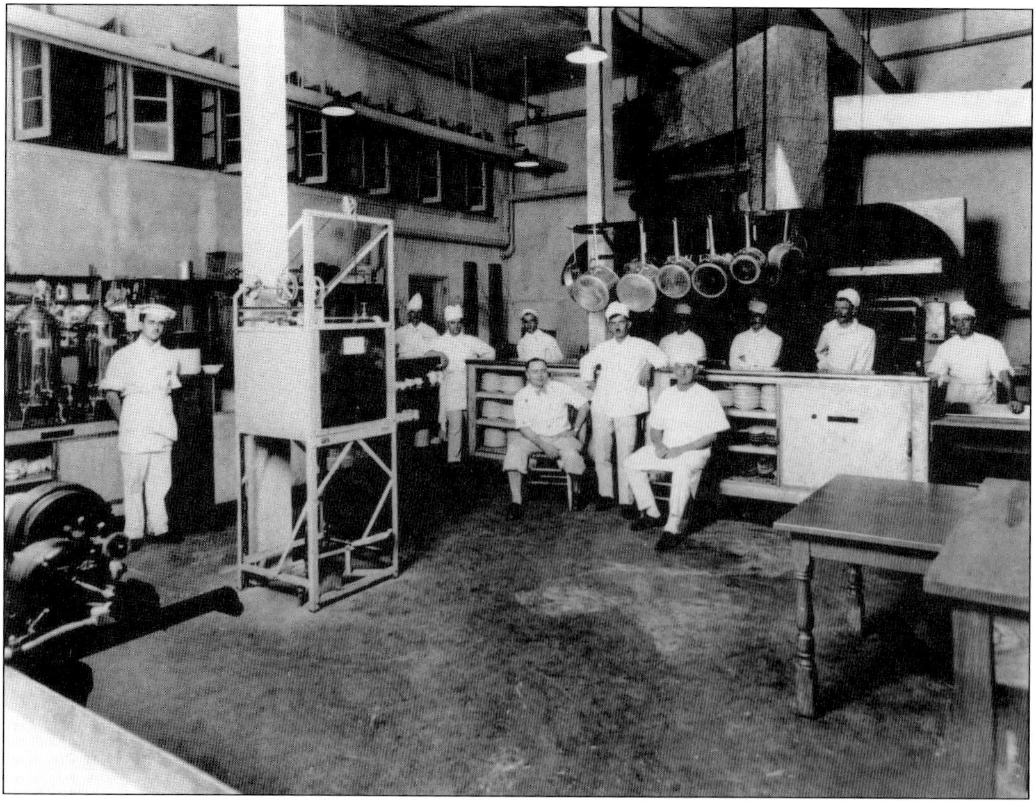

Several BLE buildings no longer exist. Its Venice-Nokomis Bank was a showpiece of the downtown area, as demonstrated by its professional lighting in this 1968 photograph. The bank was located at the corner of West Venice Avenue and Nassau Street. It was demolished in December 1975. (PH09.01.3.)

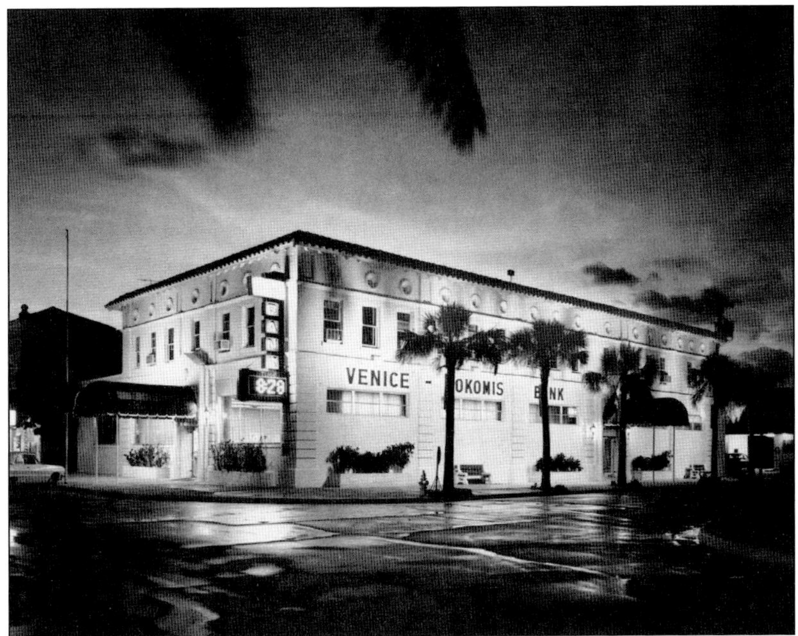

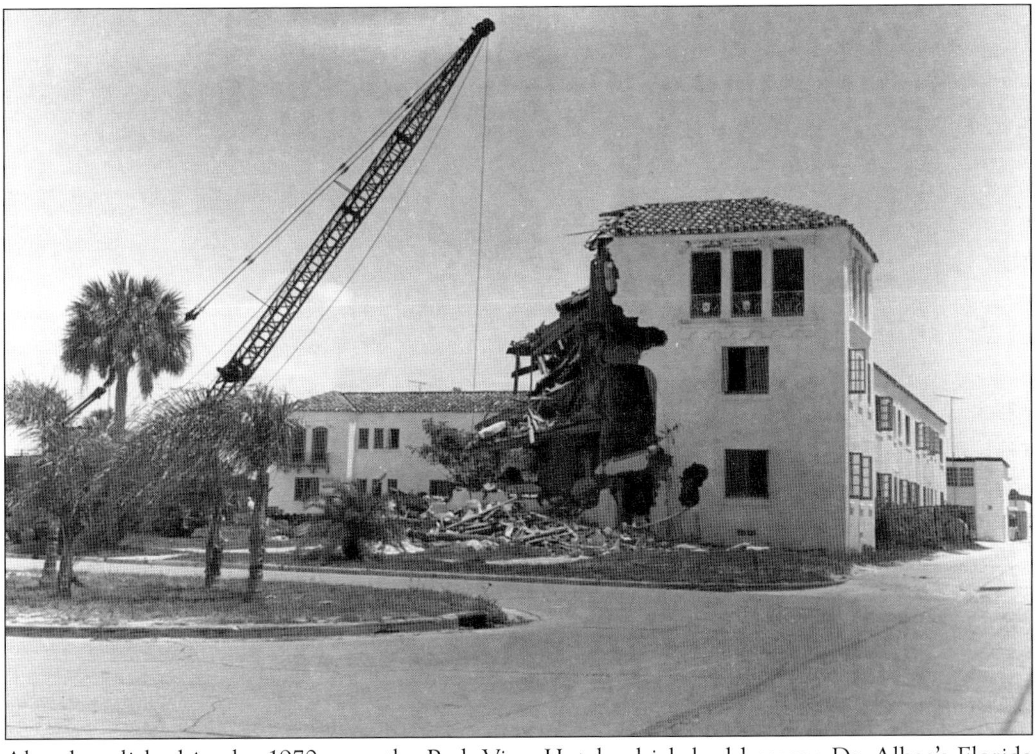

Also demolished in the 1970s was the Park View Hotel, which had become Dr. Albee's Florida Medical Center and then the Venice Army Air Corps hospital during World War II. It had a few more tries as a hotel, but eventually the building was torn down to be replaced by the Venice Post Office, located at the corner of North Harbor Drive and Tampa Avenue. (PH26.06.22.)

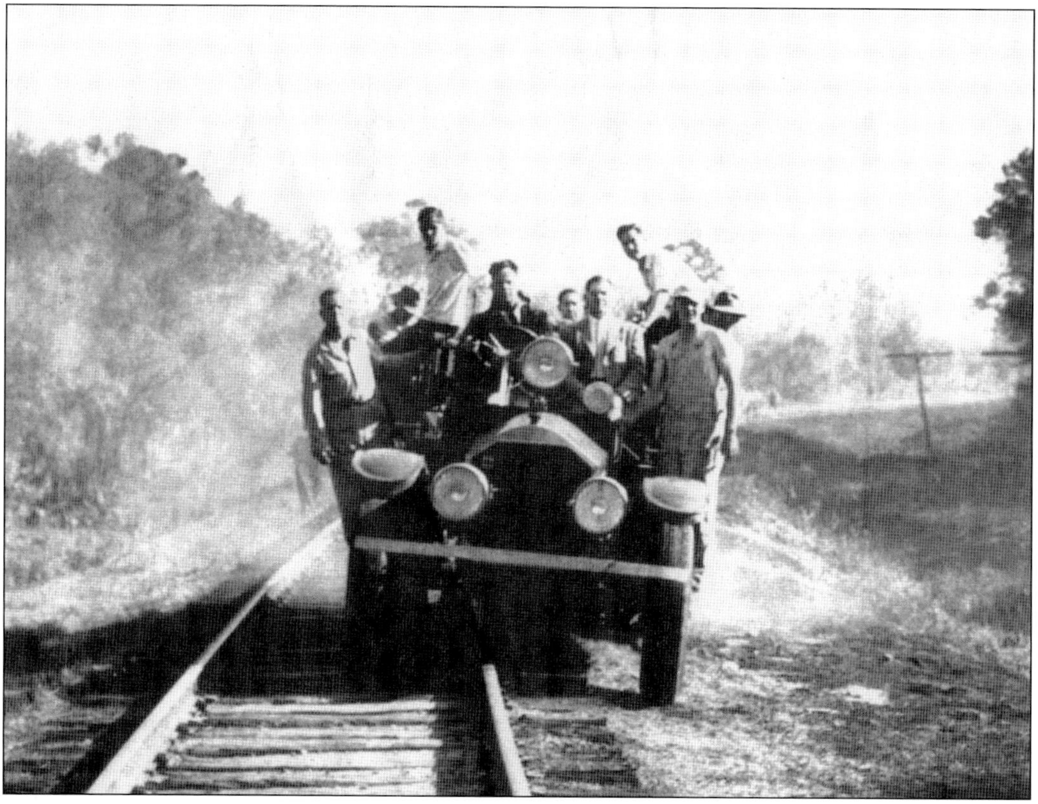

This probably is not how the BLE envisioned using Old Betsy, Venice's 1926 fire truck. Here it is seen straddling one of the railroad tracks in 1927. Old Betsy still graces the annual nighttime Christmas parade and other events. It is lovingly cared for by Earl Midlam and other volunteers. (PH26.0571.)

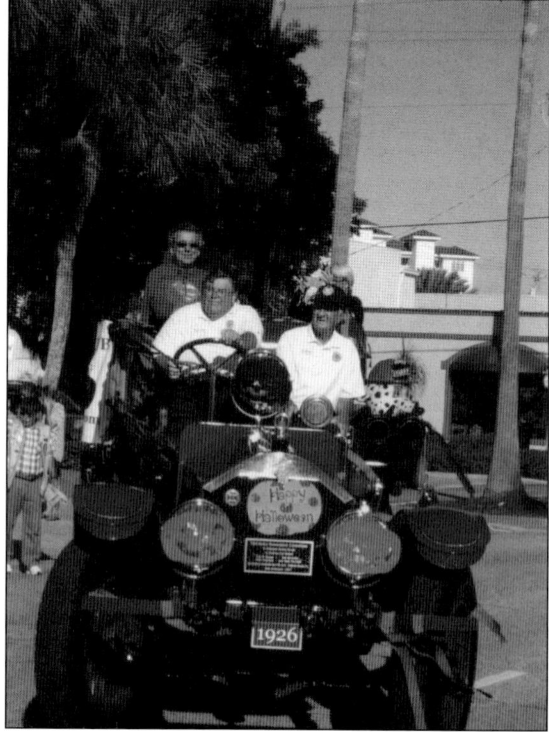

This could be any one of the many Venice parades in which Old Betsy has participated, but this image, with Earl Midlam driving and a crew behind him, is wryly recollective of the previous image. The 1926 fire engine has its own museum display building, funded by individual donations, Venice Heritage Inc., and city resources. (PH26.0565, image 5 of 10.)

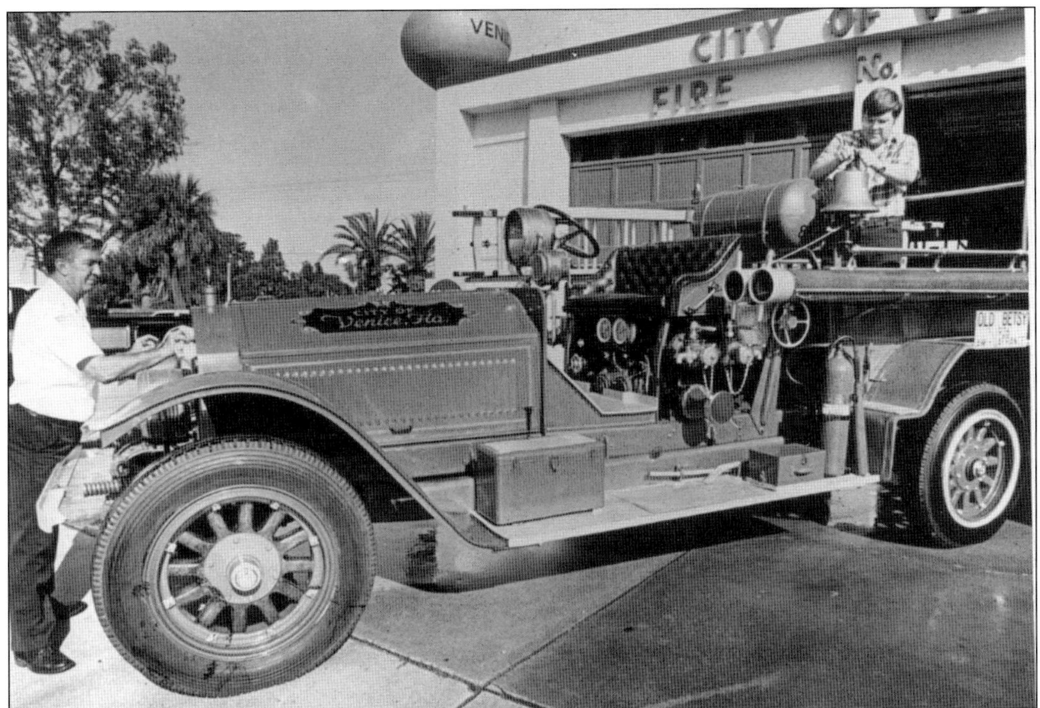

Earl Midlam, seen here on the right in the 1970s with Gaylord George (left), is a Venice native known for his enthusiasm and outreach capabilities. He is the loving caretaker and mechanic for Old Betsy and a founder of the Old Timers, which annually celebrates its Venice heritage. Membership was limited to those whose families had been here for 50 years or more. (NP0352.)

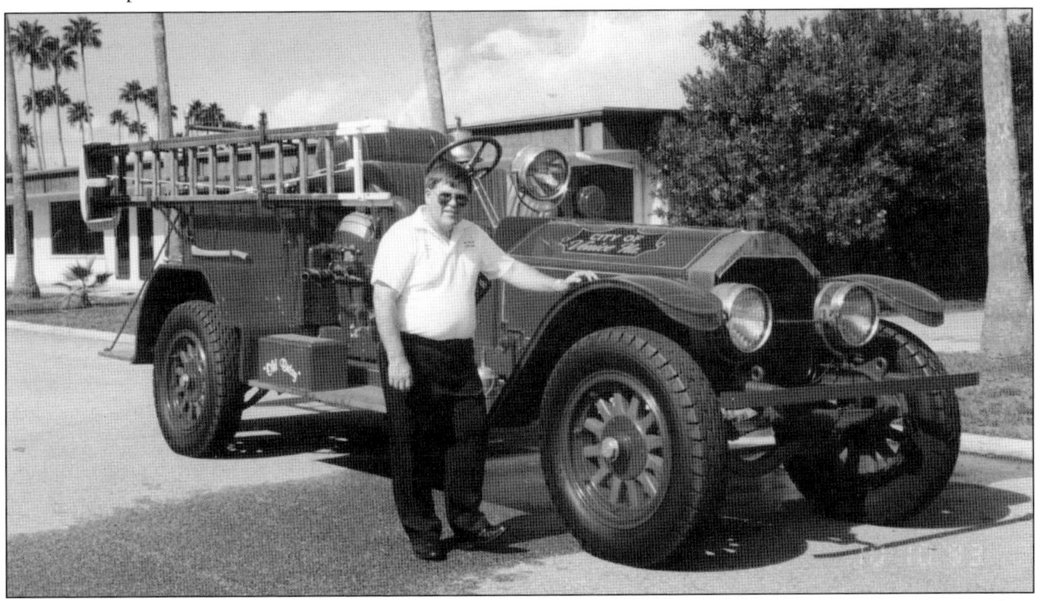

Earl is a former Venice fireman, city council member, and vice mayor and has had many other roles and interests. With items gathered from family members, friends, and the Old Timers, he is a prolific donor to Venice Historical Resources with one-of-a-kind photographs, articles, and objects. (PH26.0569, image 6 of 8.)

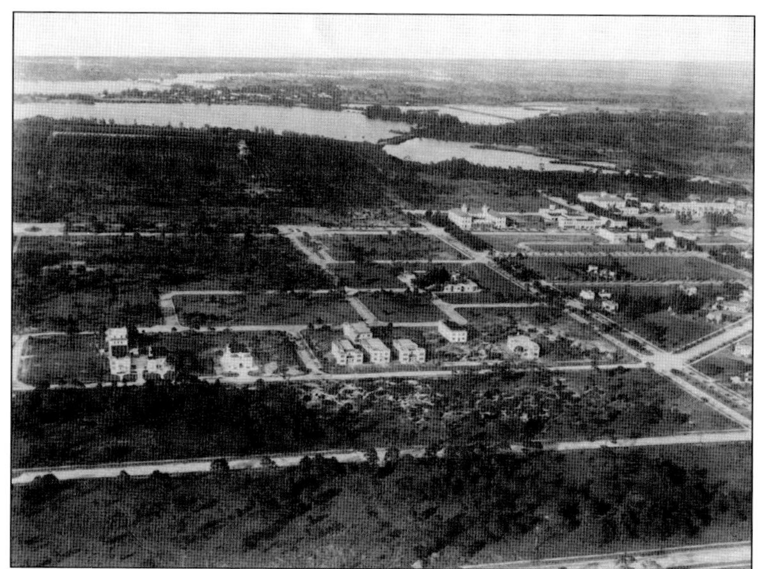

The BLE was forced to pull out of its Venice project due to the failing structure of Florida development. Its Venice property then reverted to the previous owners. Albee resold much of his portion to the Palmer family, who sold it to the Caspersen family, whose initiatives drove much of Venice's later development. (LIB 975.961 KOR, CD119, 16 of 27.)

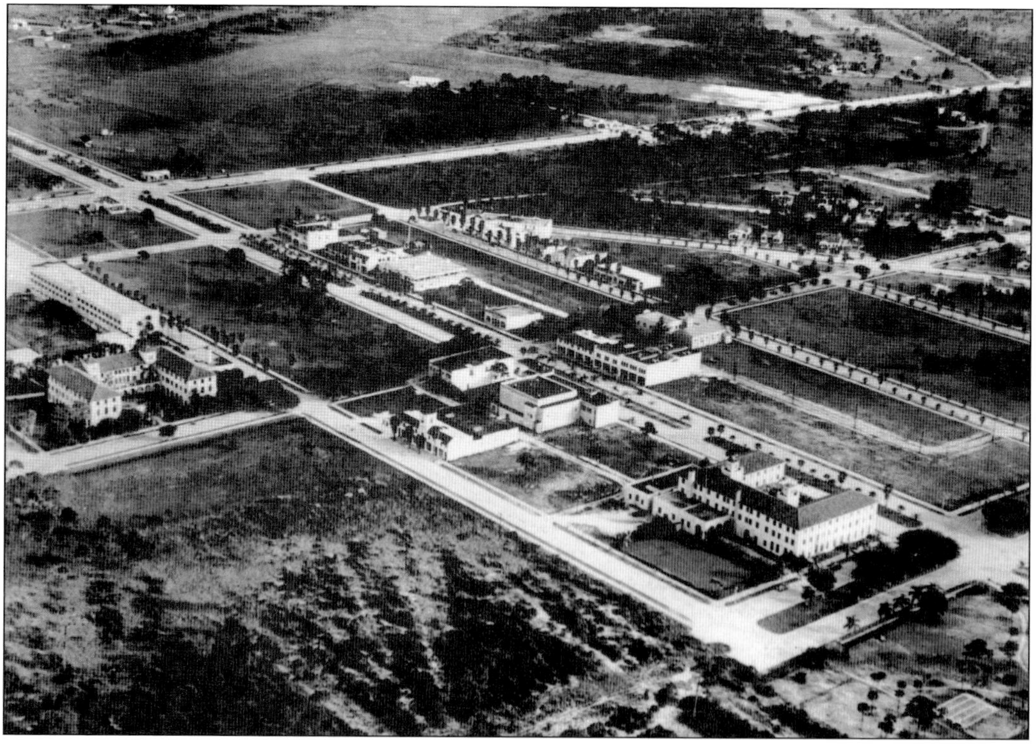

This 1940s aerial of downtown, taken from the north looking southeast, shows extensive vacant space. Venice Avenue is just a straight road east, to the left. There is no bridge, because the Intracoastal Waterway did not exist until the 1960s. Albee Airfield is at the very top, with the Tamiami Trail just below it. (SCHC, PH26.0464, image 9 of 15.)

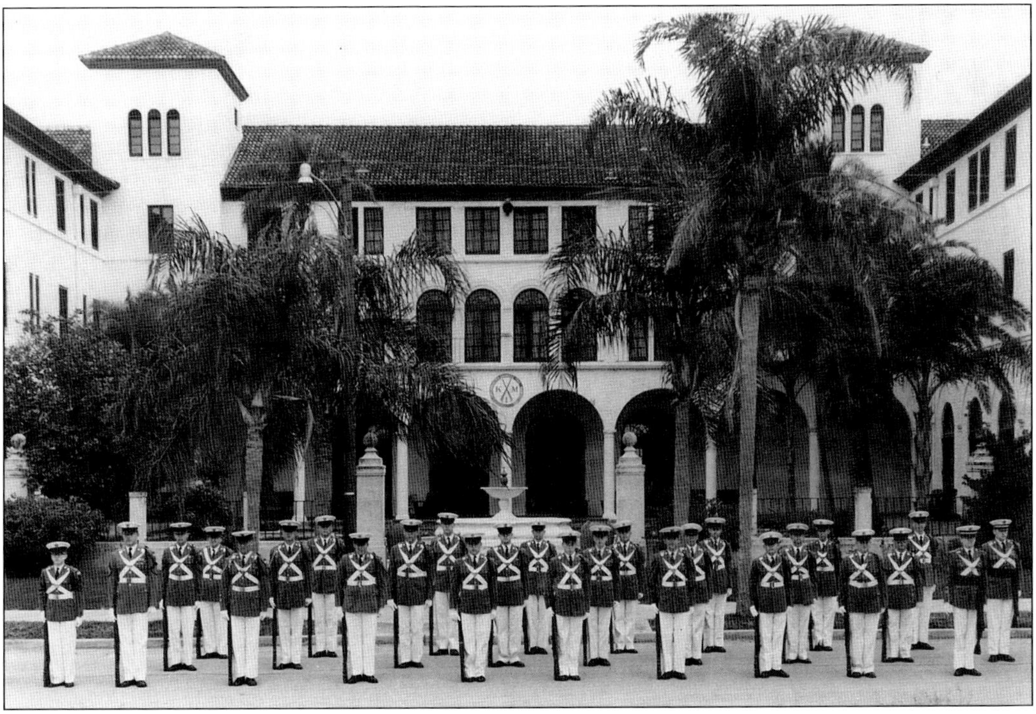

When the Kentucky Military Institute was looking for new winter headquarters in 1930, the abandoned BLE buildings looked like a god-sent gift. Buildings were already erected; they were fireproof, storm-proof, and hurricane-proof. There was a railroad depot, and Venice was a secluded location for a group of often rambunctious cadets, pictured here in front of the old Venice Hotel. (LAT 6J.)

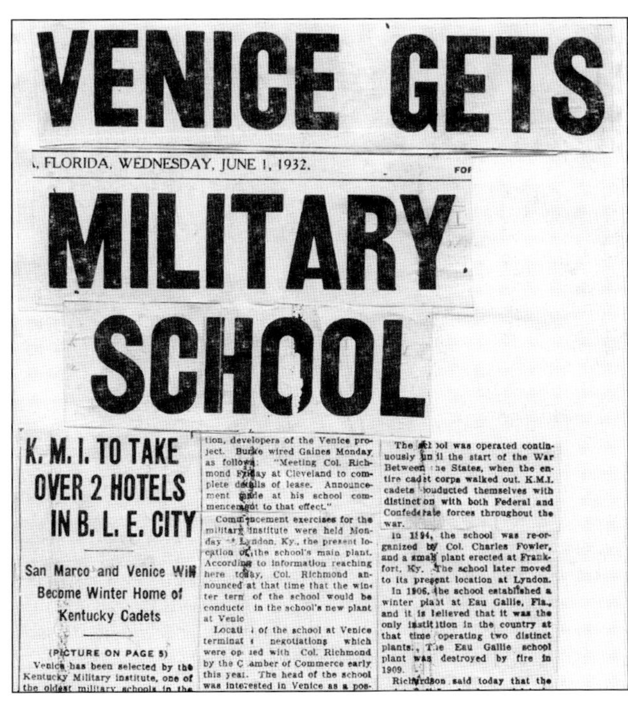

VENICE GETS

, FLORIDA, WEDNESDAY, JUNE 1, 1932.

MILITARY SCHOOL

K. M. I. TO TAKE OVER 2 HOTELS IN B. L. E. CITY

San Marco and Venice Will Become Winter Home of Kentucky Cadets

(PICTURE ON PAGE 5)

Venice has been selected by the Kentucky Military institute, one of the oldest military schools in the

tion, developers of the Venice project. Burke wired Gaines Monday as follows: "Meeting Col. Richmond Friday at Cleveland to complete details of lease. Announcement made at his school commencement to that effect."

Commencement exercises for the military institute were held Monday at Lyndon, Ky., the present location of the school's main plant. According to information reaching here today, Col. Richmond announced at that time that the winter term of the school would be conducted in the school's new plant at Venice.

Location of the school at Venice terminates negotiations which were opened with Col. Richmond by the Chamber of Commerce early this year. The head of the school was interested in Venice as a pos-

The school was operated continuously until the start of the War Between the States, when the entire cadet corps walked out. K.M.I. cadets conducted themselves with distinction with both Federal and Confederate forces throughout the war.

In 1894, the school was reorganized by Col. Charles Fowler, and a small plant erected at Frankfort, Ky. The school later moved to its present location at Lyndon.

In 1906, the school established a winter plant at Eau Gallie, Fla., and it is believed that it was the only institution in the country at that time operating two distinct plants. The Eau Gallie school plant was destroyed by fire in 1909.

Richardson said today that the

From 1932 to 1972, the KMI (from Lyndon, Kentucky) had winter quarters here. Venice was a location attractive to parents on holiday, there were marching sites available, and it was close to the beach for swimming and sailing lessons. Thanks to numerous donations by KMI men, the collection of KMI's materials at the Venice Museum & Archives is outstanding. (LAT 6J.)

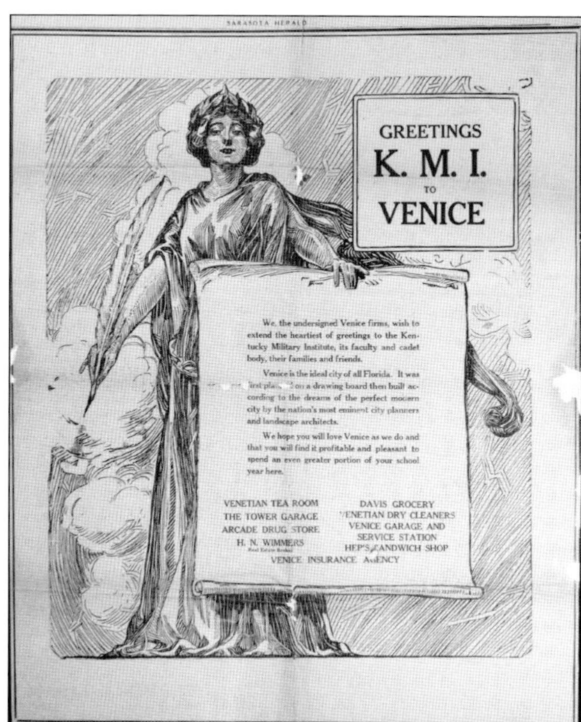

SARASOTA HERALD

GREETINGS
K. M. I.
TO
VENICE

We, the undersigned Venice firms, wish to extend the heartiest of greetings to the Kentucky Military Institute, its faculty and cadet body, their families and friends.

Venice is the ideal city of all Florida. It was first pla[illegible] on a drawing board then built according to the dreams of the perfect modern city by the nation's most eminent city planners and landscape architects.

We hope you will love Venice as we do and that you will find it profitable and pleasant to spend an even greater portion of your school year here.

VENETIAN TEA ROOM
THE TOWER GARAGE
ARCADE DRUG STORE
H. N. WIMMERS
Real Estate Broker

DAVIS GROCERY
VENETIAN DRY CLEANERS
VENICE GARAGE AND SERVICE STATION
HEP'S SANDWICH SHOP

VENICE INSURANCE AGENCY

The resident population of Venice was eager to welcome KMI, as this 1933 newspaper advertisement in the *Sarasota Herald Tribune* demonstrates. Nine local businesses paid for the welcome promotional, including Bud Wimmers, a real estate broker who remained in Venice after the BLE left. The Venetian Tea Room at the Triangle Inn, built by the BLE, also welcomed KMI. (MS46, 2015.00.29.)

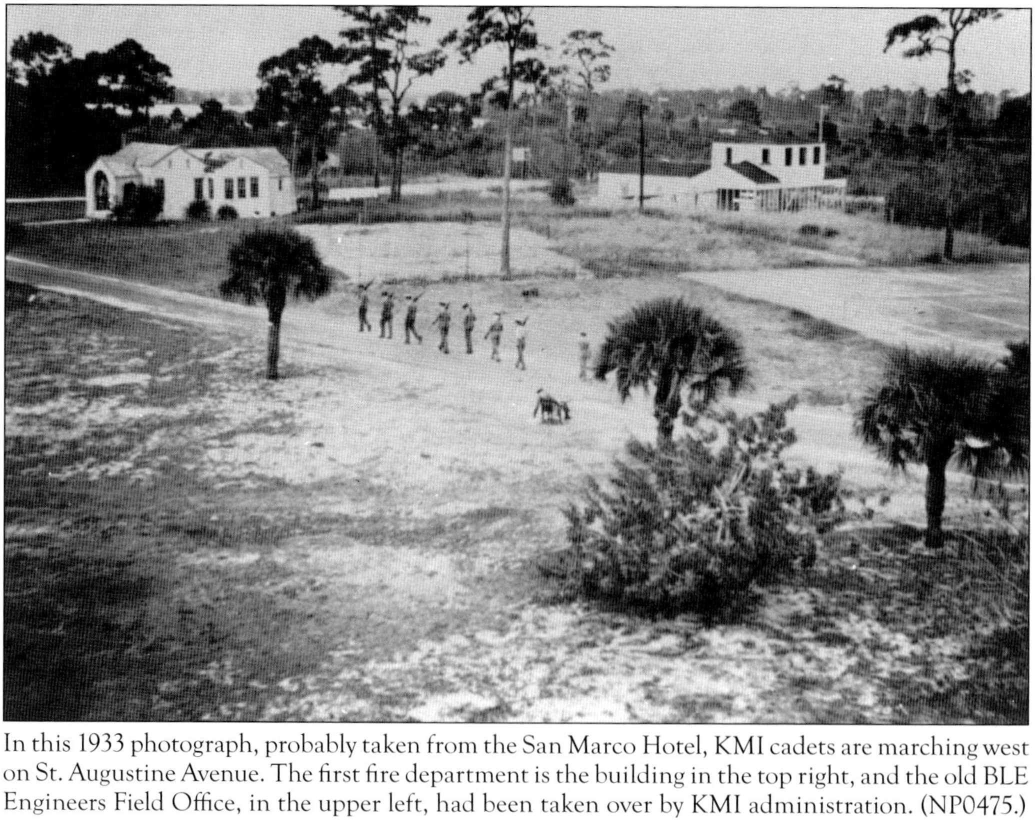

In this 1933 photograph, probably taken from the San Marco Hotel, KMI cadets are marching west on St. Augustine Avenue. The first fire department is the building in the top right, and the old BLE Engineers Field Office, in the upper left, had been taken over by KMI administration. (NP0475.)

A few local boys, like James Cousins, seen here in 1933, were educated at KMI. James's father, Mitt Cousins, was KMI's grounds superintendent and a construction contractor. In the 1940s, he was also the mayor of Venice. Mitt's wife, Carmen, not pictured here, operated the Triangle Inn rooming house, now the Venice Museum & Archives. James's little sister Julia Cousins-Laning is also pictured. (NP0416.)

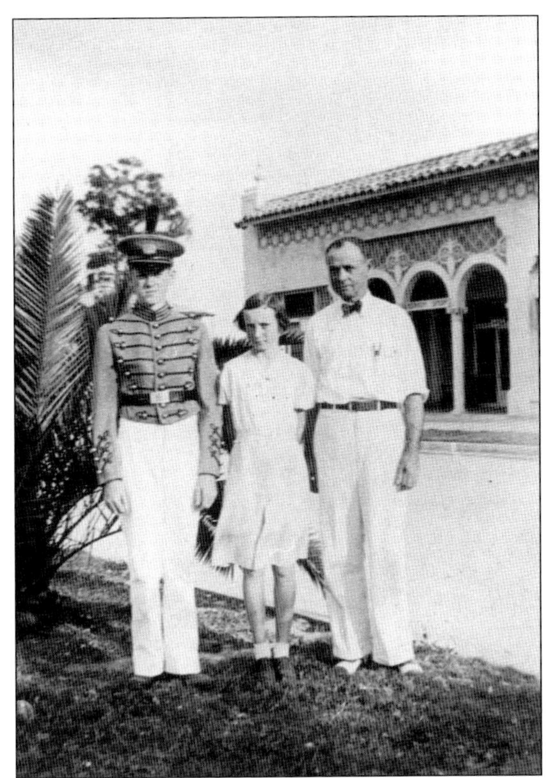

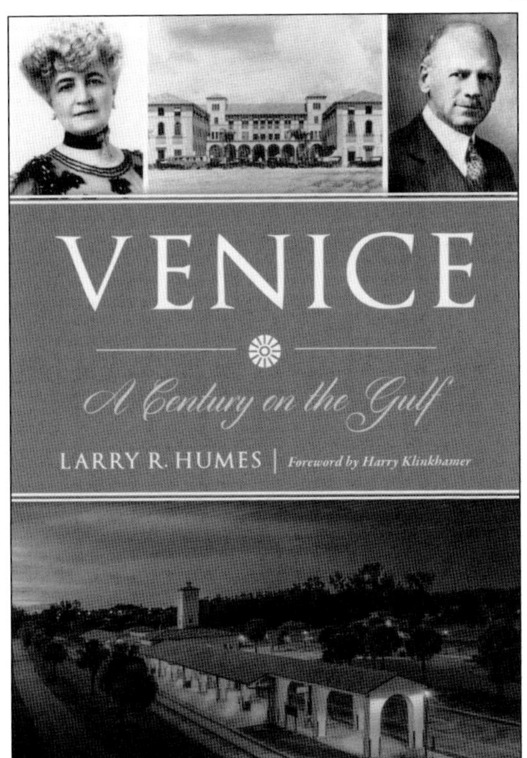

This History Press book, *Venice: A Century on the Gulf*, is by local historian and *Venice Gondolier* newspaper reporter Larry R. Humes, a former KMI cadet. Harry Klinkhamer, director of the Venice Historical Resources, Venice Museum & Archives, wrote the foreword and assisted in the gathering of materials. It provides many, many more details about KMI, the BLE, and other Venice topics. (LIB 975.)

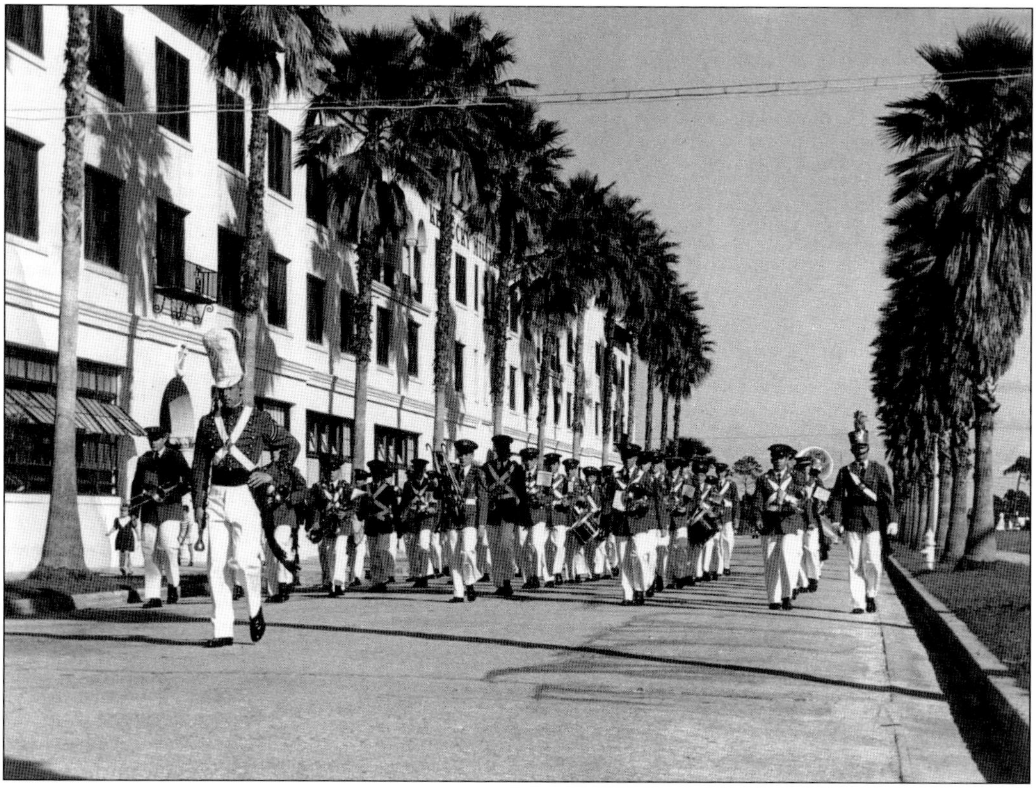

Even the marching band uniforms were striking, as shown here in 1965 in front of the old San Marco Hotel. In 2018, the exhibit of KMI memorabilia was expanded for viewing on the first floor of the hotel, alongside restaurants and shopping. The second floor became condominiums. (PH06.1.2, Box 1.)

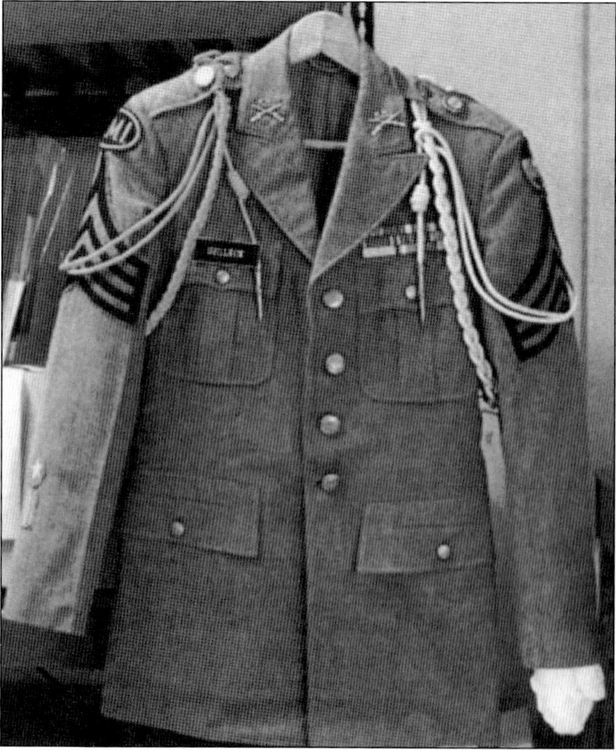

The KMI uniform was stunning. (No wonder local girls found the cadets attractive.) This 1966 dress jacket, worn by Richard H. Selleck II, has gold braid and brass buttons and sports stripes, ROTC emblems for officers, plus a name tag on the right pocket. (1999.28.01 image 4 of 4.)

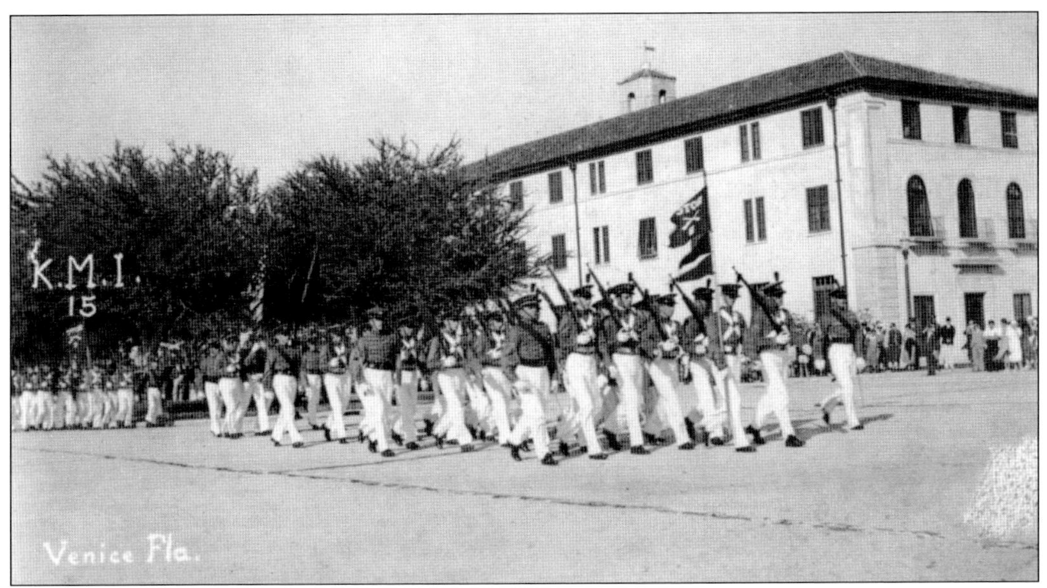

Marching in formation in full uniform in a photograph taken on February 25, 1934, by Sunshine Press, the cadets were the delight of local girls and a torment to local boys but a boon to the local economy. Some of the cadets later married local girls and stayed in town; others came back in retirement, all with fond memories. (2013.41.20, CD024 image 5 of 37, 2008.21.024.)

With local girls gathered at the Seaboard Air Line Railroad depot to say goodbye, the boys of the Kentucky Military Institute leave their winter headquarters in Venice on the train for Lyndon, Kentucky, departing until the next winter quarter. (PH06.14.15, image 3 of 3.)

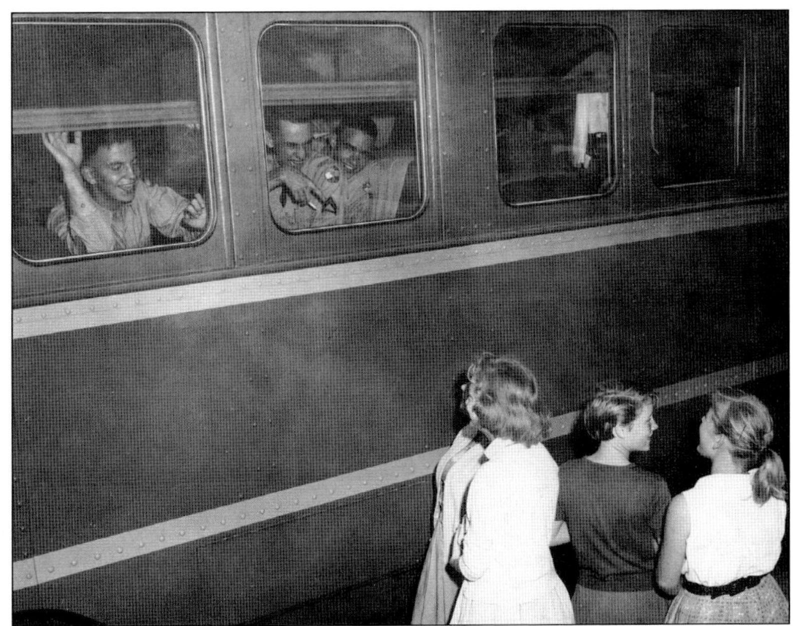

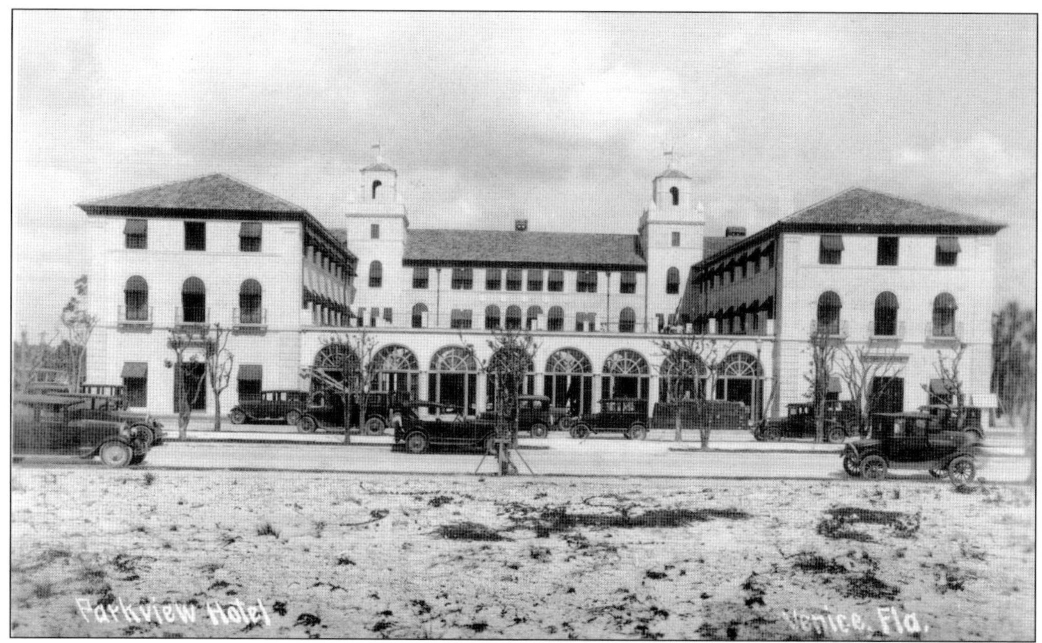

After the BLE left and while KMI was in Venice, Dr. Albee purchased the BLE's Park View Hotel to establish the area's first hospital, the Florida Medical Center. He also established the first airfield in Venice in 1932 to fly his patients to the hospital. (NP0021B.)

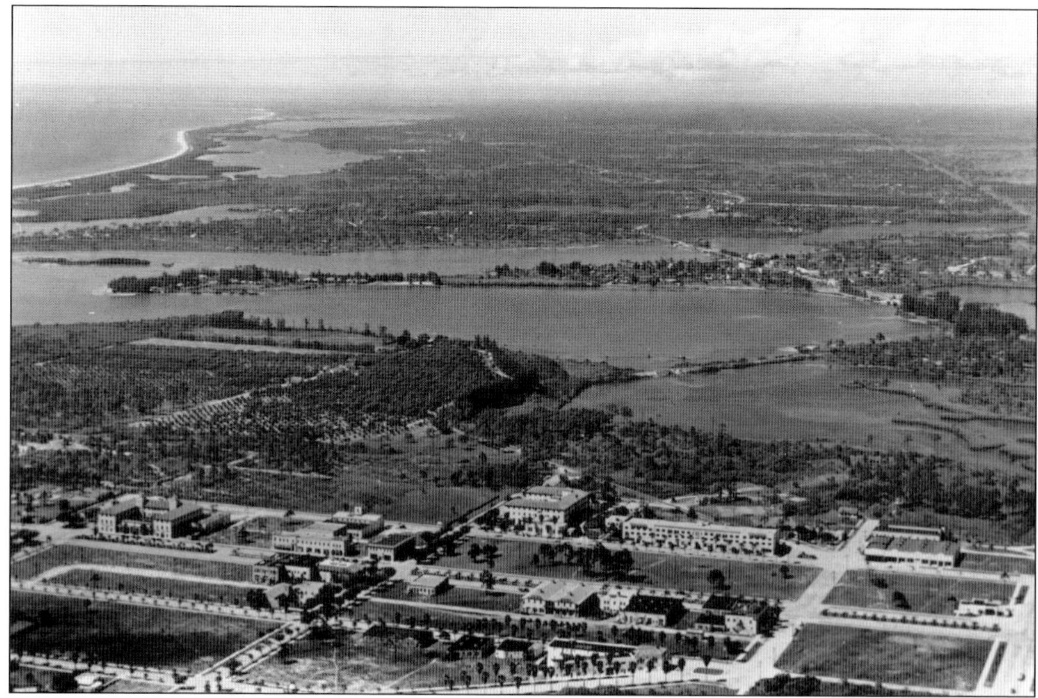

Even in 1943, Venice was still mostly unbuilt. Shown in this aerial by Vaughan Pitman, looking northwest, are the apartments on Armada Road South and other homes, mostly built by the BLE. The causeway for the nine-foot Hard Road, abandoned in 1927, still comes into the citrus grove at the center from Eagle Point Resort. (Eric Duda, 2021.17.07.)

This and the following image were shot at almost the same location 40 years apart. This aerial from 1943 shows very little development, with Venice still a quiet place with few churches, no condominiums, and few homes. Treasure Island, now known as Casey Key, plus Nokomis and Laurel are primarily cattle ranches and citrus groves. (PH26.0465, SCHR, image 8 of 9.)

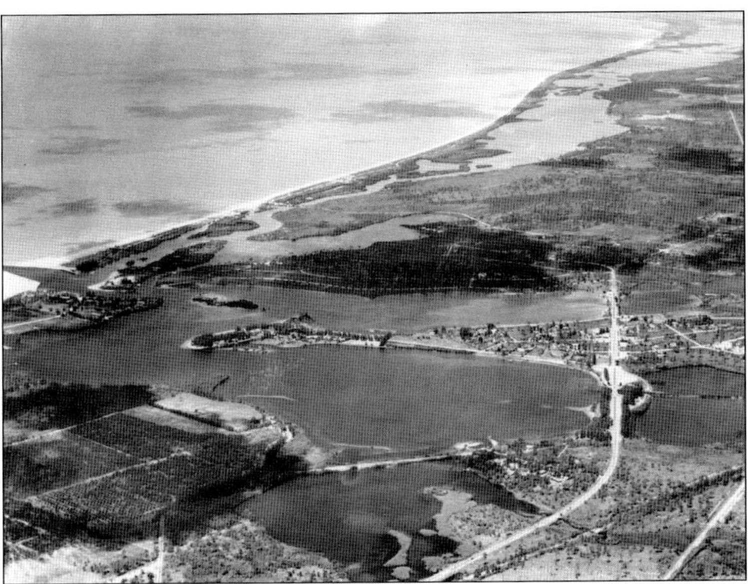

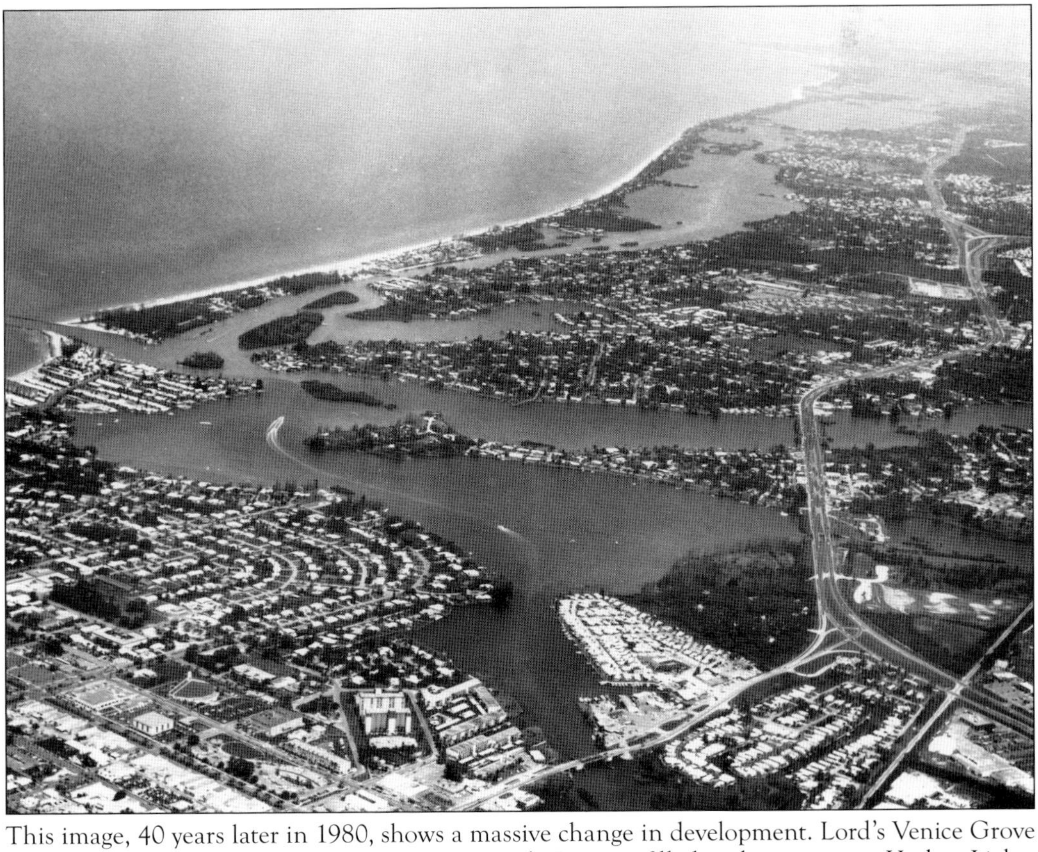

This image, 40 years later in 1980, shows a massive change in development. Lord's Venice Grove is now almost built out as Bayshore Estates. Eagle Point is filled with vegetation. Harbor Lights Mobile Home Park was expanded, built on dredged material from the Intracoastal. The causeway is gone, with a two-lane Hatchett Creek Drawbridge over the Intracoastal coming in from the north. (PH26.0464.)

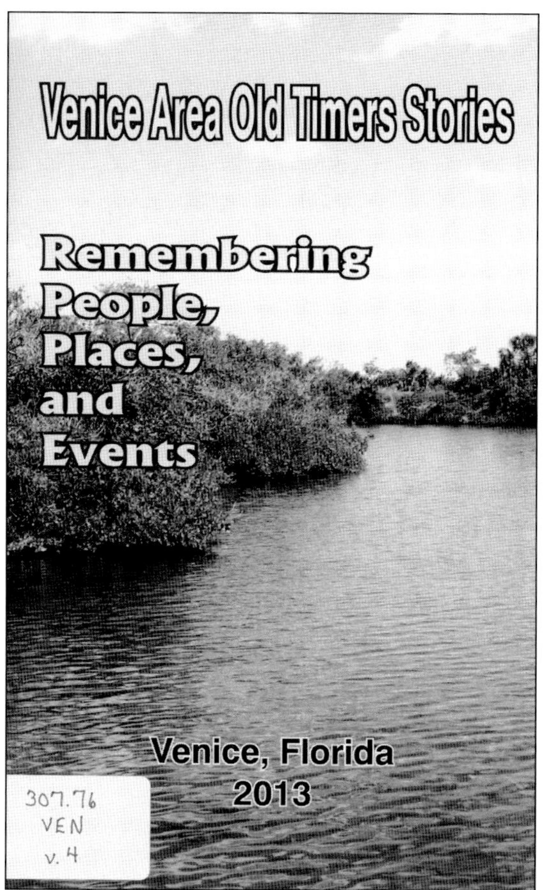

Each promoter of the area, whether listed in this book or not, left a legacy of accomplishments. At the Venice Area Old Timers picnic, stories were collected and published. All of the settlers, innovators, and promoters in Venice brought new residents to the area. (LIB 307.76 VEN.)

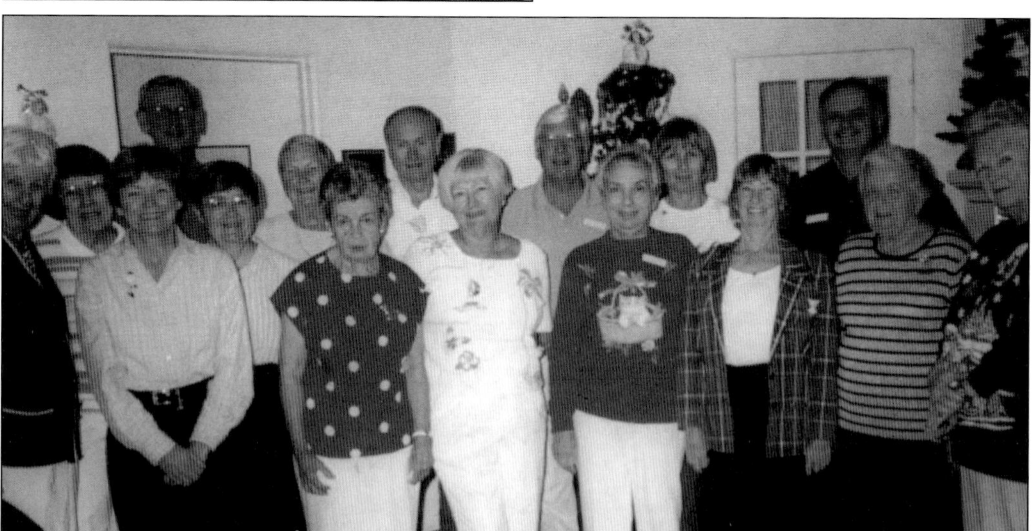

Many volunteer opportunities exist for newcomers, part-time residents, and old timers, as this 2003 image shows. A second book, *Venice, Nokomis, and Laurel*, will talk about the city, shell mounds, the settlers' families, and local residents who made, and continue to make, an impact following in the footsteps of the original promoters. (2008.21.100, image 25 of 48.)

Five

SEEKERS AND SAVERS

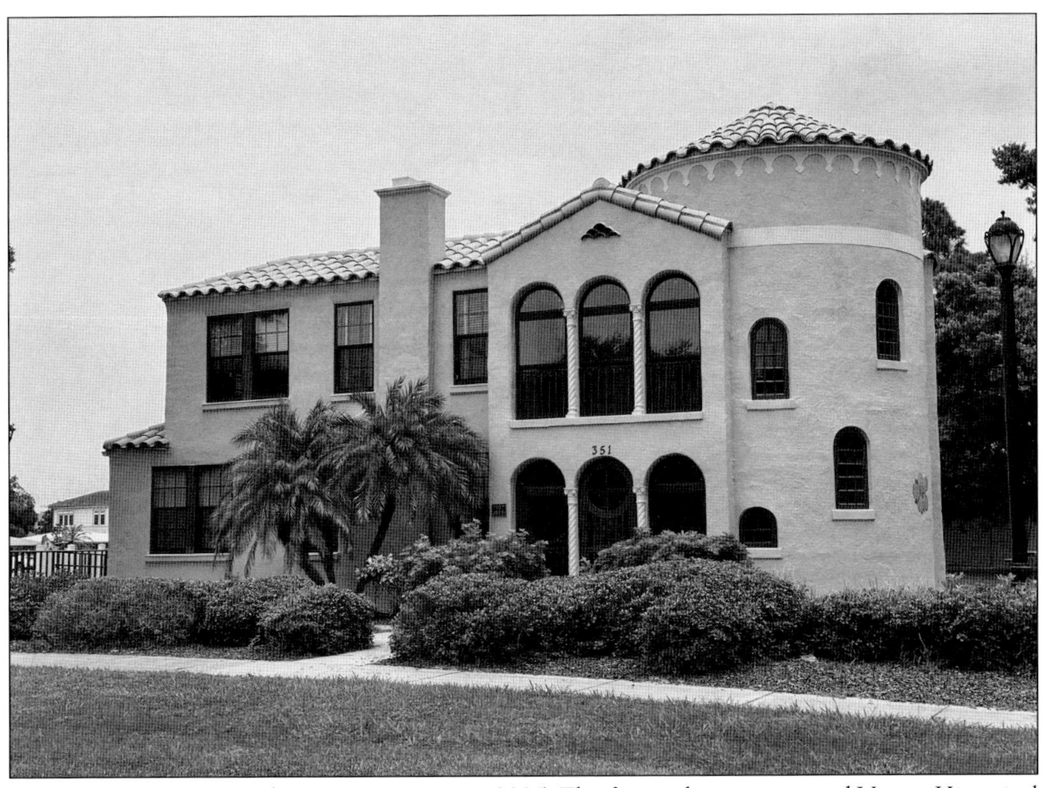

There are three historical groups in Venice in 2025. The first is the city-operated Venice Historical Resources, also known as the Venice Museum & Archives. It is based at the Triangle Inn and also at the CLARC building. It offers a museum, programming, tours, and resource help, plus an online database. Its collections include donations of maps, photographs, and memorabilia. (RR.)

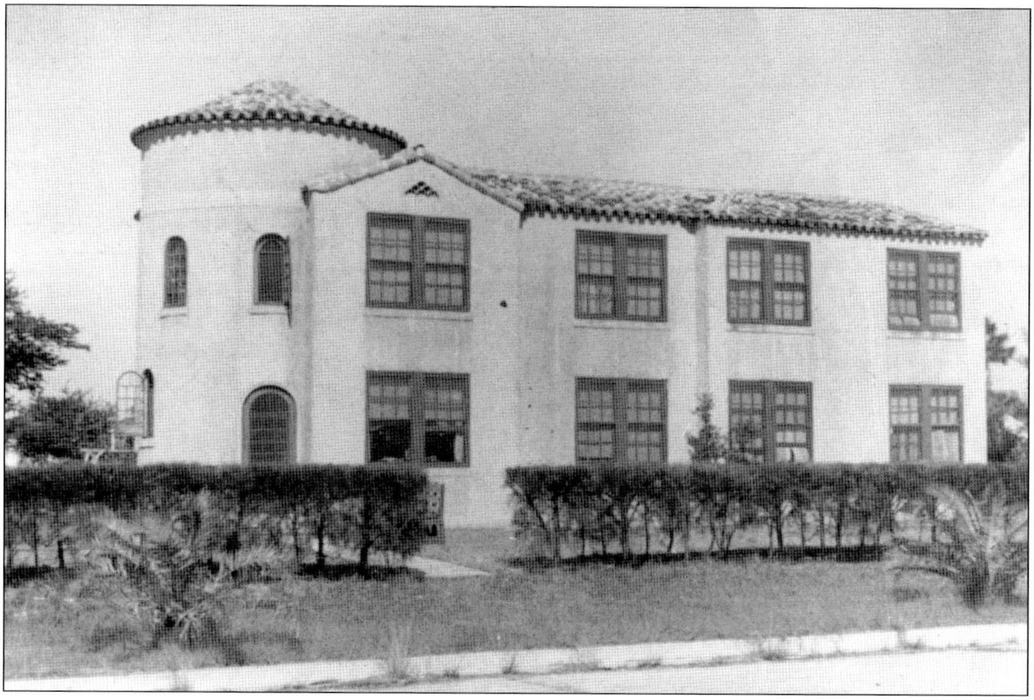

The Triangle Inn, built in 1927 and shown here in the 1930s, was originally a rooming house for BLE staff, visiting KMI parents, and World War II Army Air Corps base military families. But by 1991, it was tired and out of date and scheduled to be torn down. Thankfully, it was donated by the owners and moved by the city to 351 South Nassau Street on "Venice's Cultural Campus." (VHR and SCHR, NP0974 LAT 15A.)

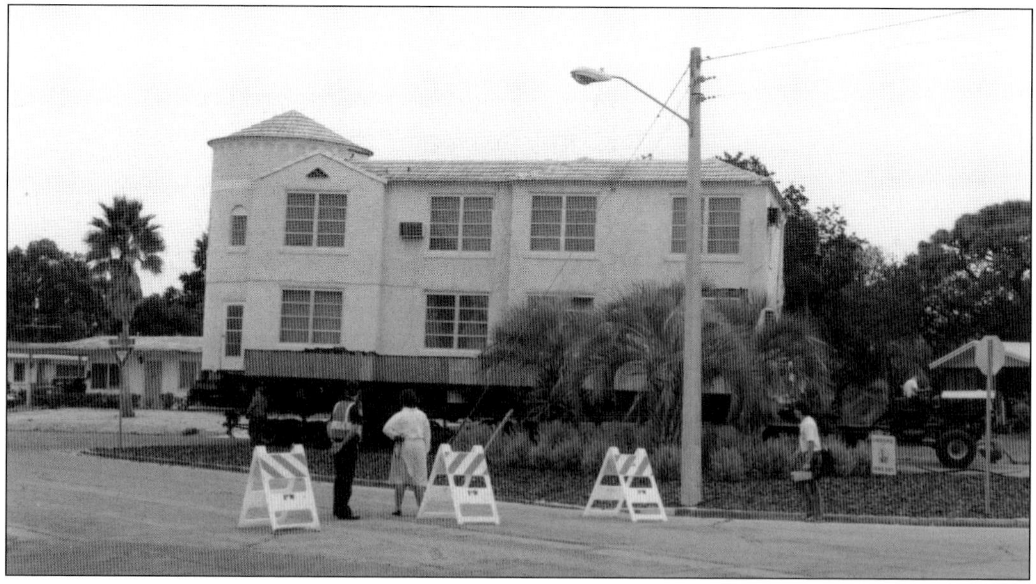

Dorothy Korwek, a Venice city councilwoman at the time, volunteered to coordinate the Triangle Inn's move, pictured here, to Venice's Cultural Campus. Later, as director of historical resources, she oversaw the renovation of the old inn into a proper museum with both permanent and changing exhibits. (MS244 File 2.)

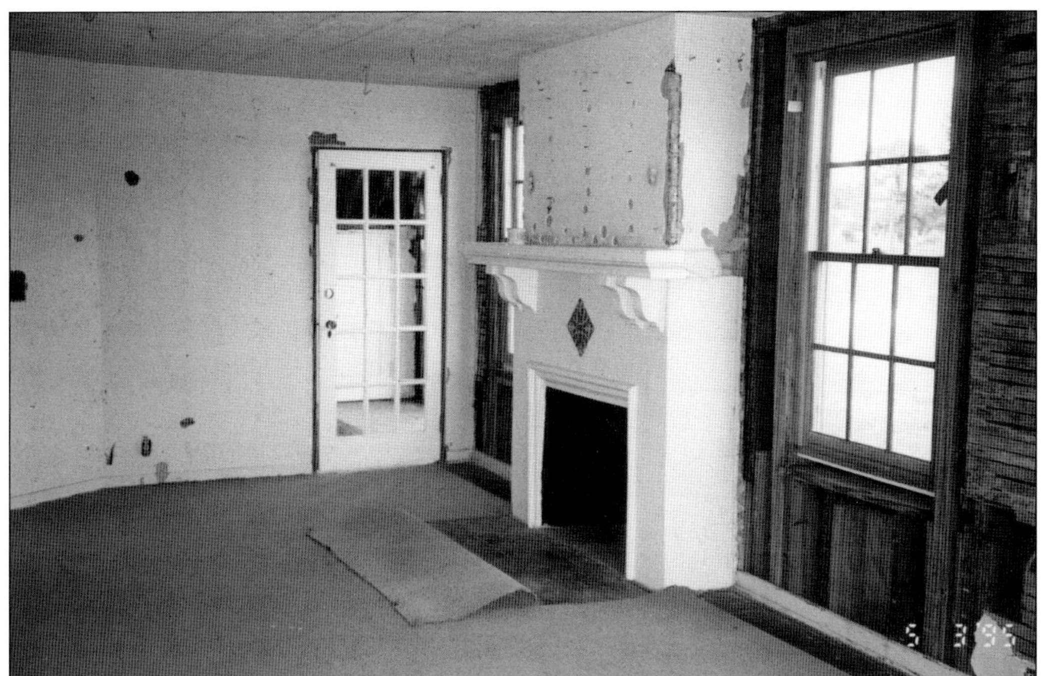

Much work was required to make the building usable as a museum and offices. Walls were removed in order to make the space workable for exhibits, archival storage, and staff and volunteer offices. Out-of-date windows and deteriorated ceilings were replaced or repaired. It was placed in the US National Register of Historic Places on February 23, 1996. (MS235 Box 6 File 2.)

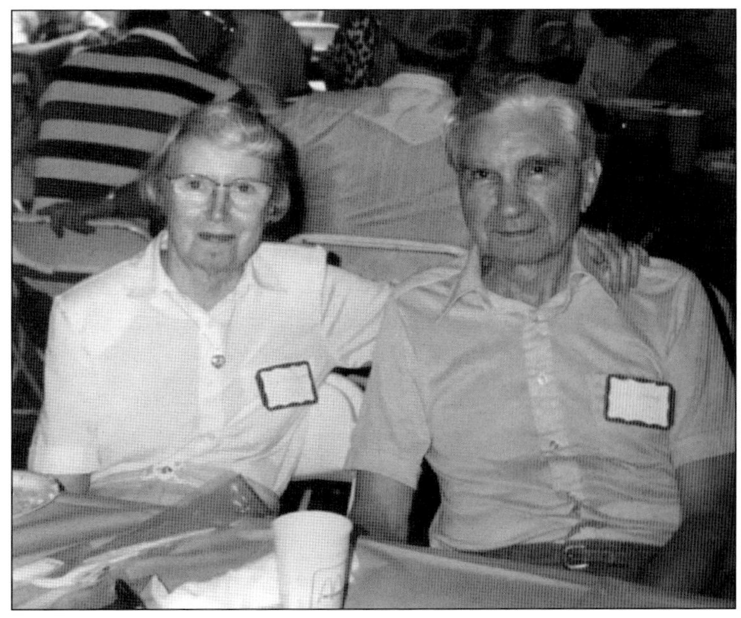

Originally, the collection of photographs, postcards, documents, objects, clothing, and more was housed on the second floor. But donations grew, and the weight of the collection eventually became too much for the old building. Julia Cousins-Laning and her husband, Dale, donated $1 million in 2011 to rehouse the collection. (PH26.0631.)

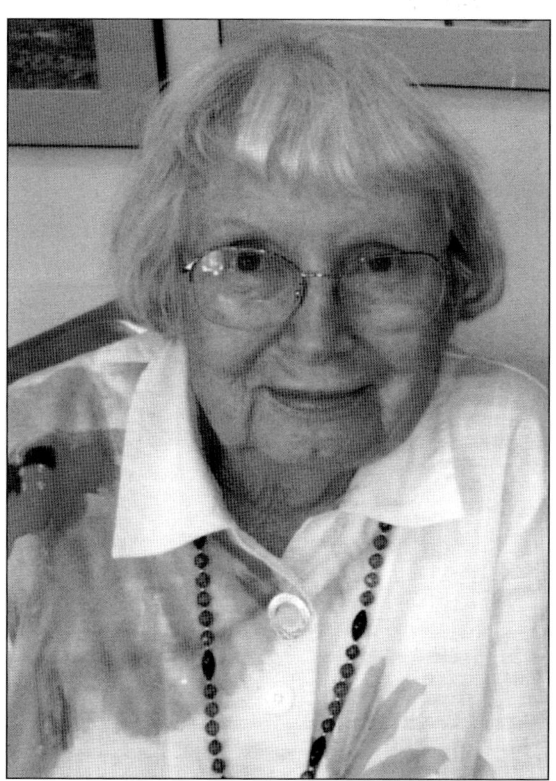

With a degree in art from Florida Southern University and at the urging of Dr. Fred and Louella Albee, Julia Cousins moved to New York and then returned to Venice in 1970. Dale died at the age of 93 in 2008. Julia funded the permanent exhibit on Dr. Albee as well as many other initiatives. (PH26.0632, RR.)

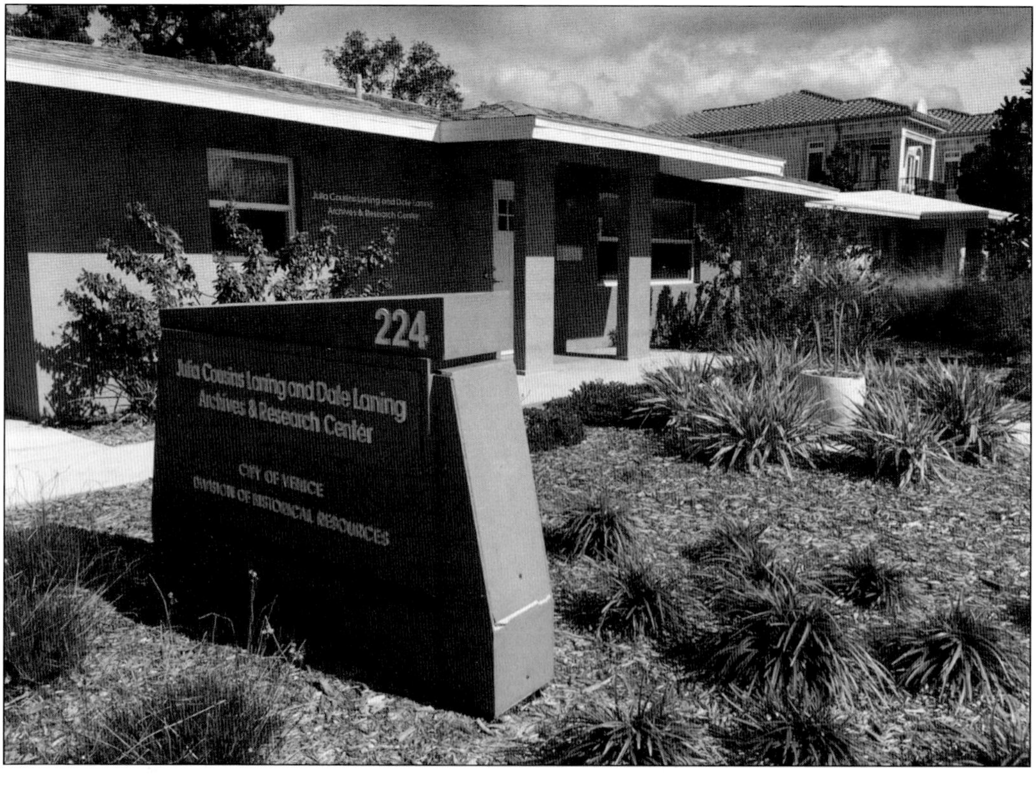

Most of the images in this book were made available by the Venice Historical Resources and can be found online or by contacting the CLARC building of VHR at 224 Milan Avenue. Like Julia Cousins, the "staff" are actually volunteers, who often act as researchers in answering queries from the public. With the collections manager, they also process donations into the collection. (RR.)

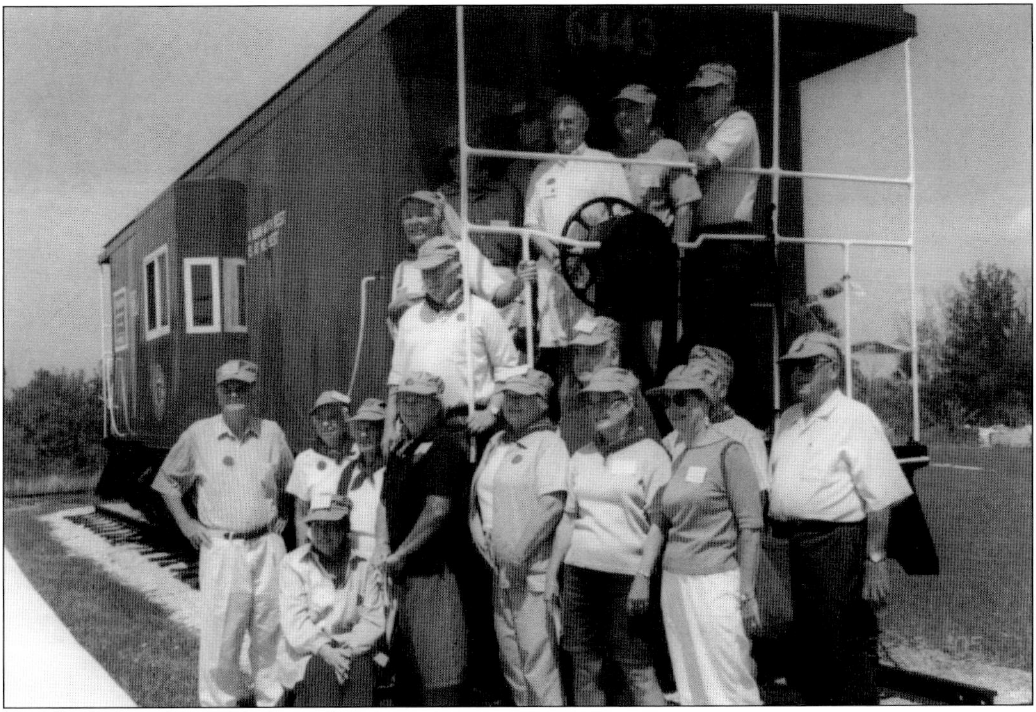

The second history organization is the Venice Area Historical Society (VAHS). It offers historical programming and train depot tours. It looks after the Sarasota County–owned railroad depot as well as operating a train caboose museum (shown here in 2005 in a photograph by Gary Youngberg) and a former Ringling Bros. and Barnum & Bailey Circus car museum at the depot. (PH26.0518.)

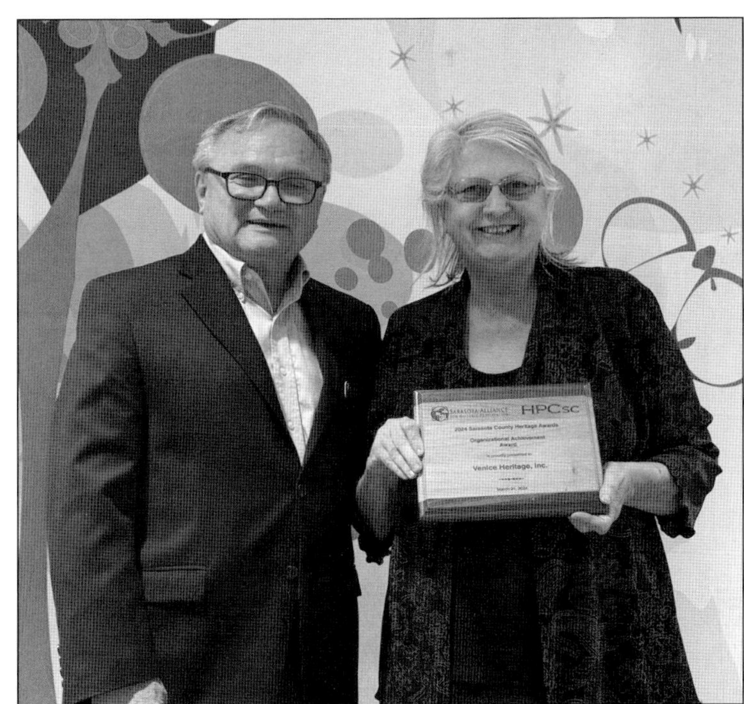

The third history organization is named Venice Heritage Inc. Originally a friends group for the Triangle Inn, then the Lord-Higel House, it does extensive fundraising for projects, publishing books, and providing educational programming open to the public. Here, Jean Trammel collects an award in 2024 from the Sarasota Alliance for Historic Preservation for the Venice Heritage Foundation. (SAHP.)

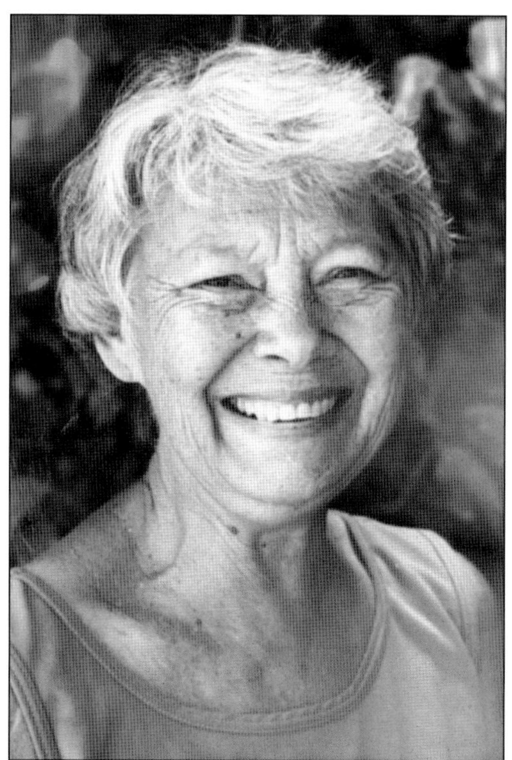

Venice Historical Resources was founded by Betty Hauser Arnall. Her family had moved here in 1926, and she realized that the area was unique. In 1984, Betty, as a volunteer in the Friends of the Venice Public Library group, took action to save and collect the history of Venice, Nokomis, Laurel, and Osprey. (PH26.0445.)

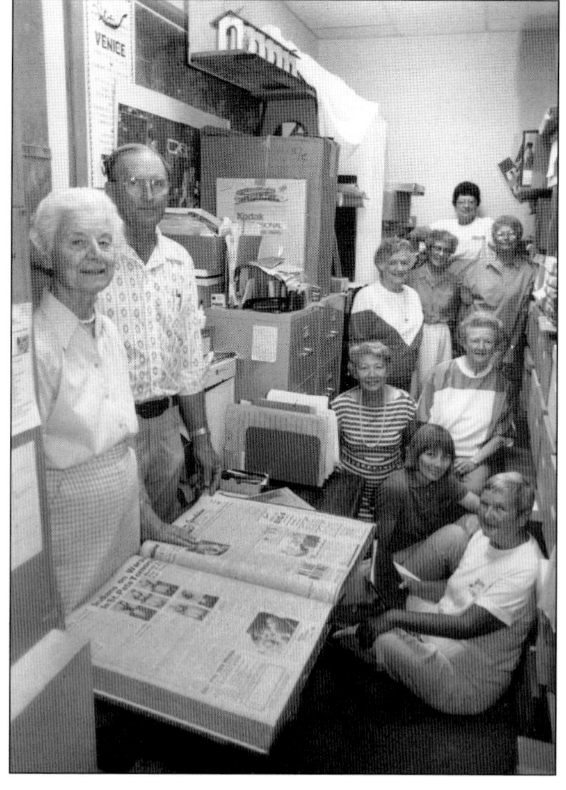

The first Venice library offered this small closet for processing, sorting, and storage. In this 1990 photograph are history volunteers; from left to right are (standing, foreground) Vera Schierenberg and Glenn Stephens; (seated, foreground) Barbara Dein and Pat Hobbs; (kneeling) Betty Arnall and Milie Nugent; (standing) Peg Fintel, Louise Ingram, Virginia Shufflebarger, and Dottie Jechorek. (NP1290.)

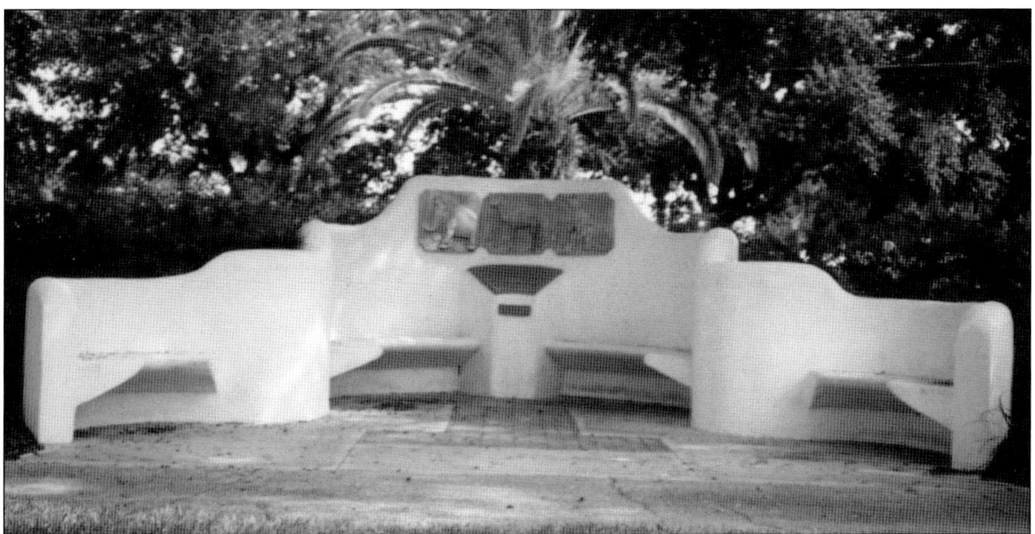

Donations of photographs and memorabilia kept pouring in, and in 1986, Arnall proposed that the city council, with the Venice Historical Commission, establish and administer historic preservation with a city historian and a museum. Betty Arnall became the first director of Venice Historical Resources. By 1987, the Architectural Review Board was established, and planning for an updated Heritage Park along Venice Avenue began. (PH26.0369, image 1 of 10.)

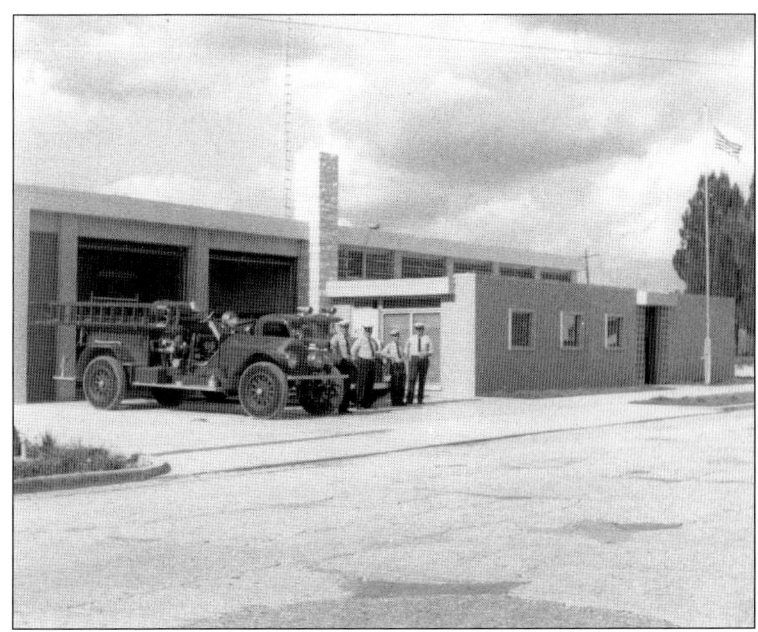

Betty Arnall promptly traveled to Cleveland, Ohio, and gathered pertinent BLE records. There are many stories of her persistence and initiatives in the area history that grew the files of VHR, such as collecting a negative of the fire station with Old Betsy at one of the annual Old Timers' picnics and processing it into this photograph. (NP1232.)

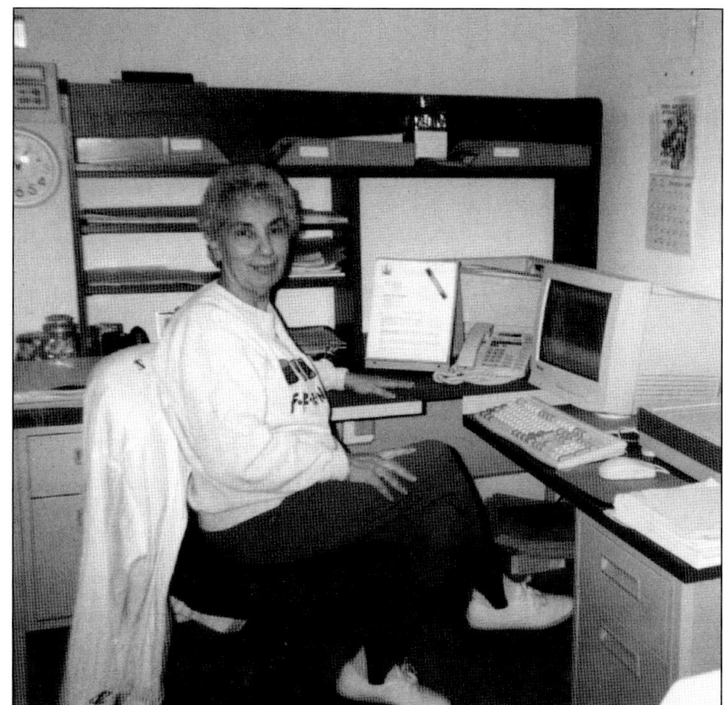

Mary Charles has been a volunteer working with the historical collection for over 50 years. As a clerk in the mayor's office and then as an early collections volunteer at both the Triangle Inn and the CLARC building, she is a font of information on people, places, and events in Venice. (RG201 Box 8.)

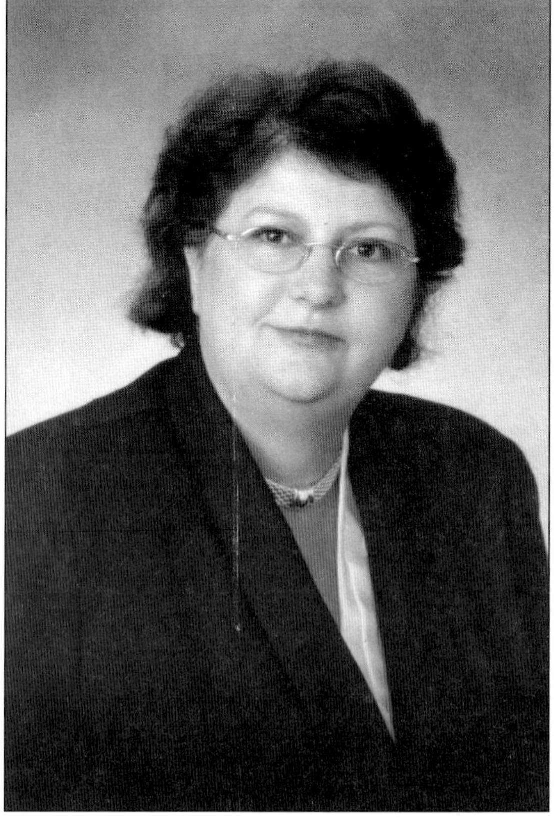

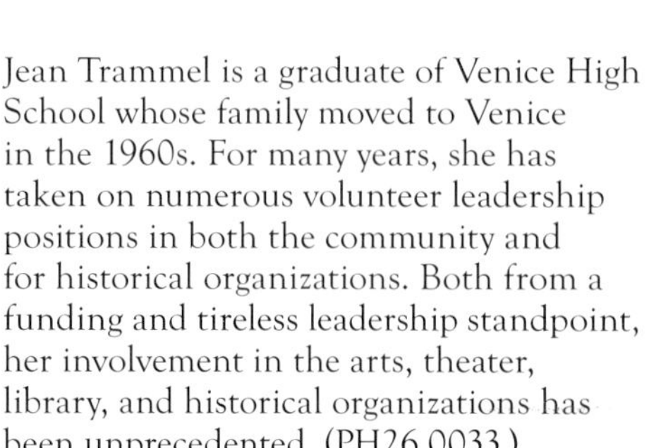

Jean Trammel is a graduate of Venice High School whose family moved to Venice in the 1960s. For many years, she has taken on numerous volunteer leadership positions in both the community and for historical organizations. Both from a funding and tireless leadership standpoint, her involvement in the arts, theater, library, and historical organizations has been unprecedented. (PH26.0033.)

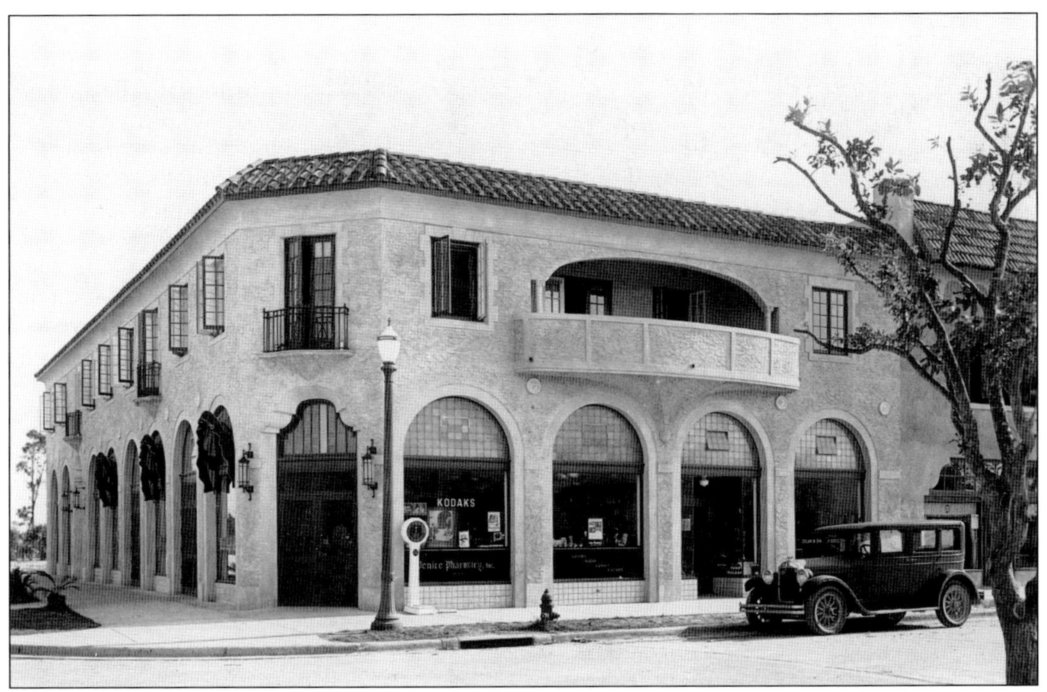

Trammel authored the National Register of Historic Places application for the BLE's Johnson-Schoolcraft building on Miami Avenue, pictured here by Jay Brown. The application was notably so complete and well-researched that it was approved on the first submission. That building is now owned by her family's organization, the Venice Company. (NP0063.)

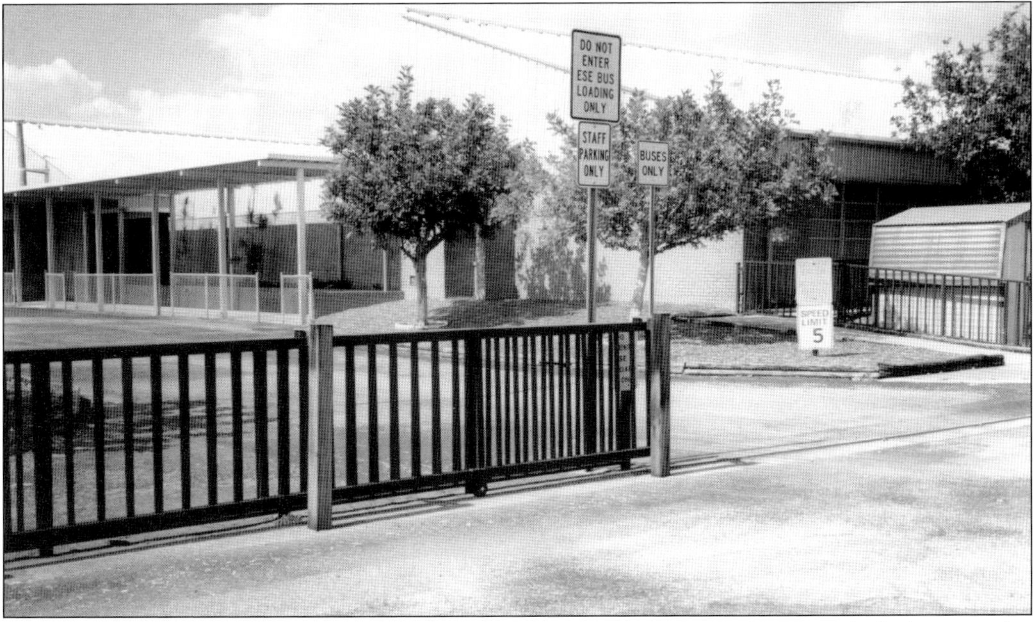

Dorothy Korwek has been a photographer for over 40 years. Her many "current day" photographs, for example this 2004 image of Venice Elementary School, Venice street scenes, buildings, and events, tell an interesting story of "what we looked like before" and help answer research questions such as "where was 'this' located?" or "why is 'that' the way it is?" (NP0737.)

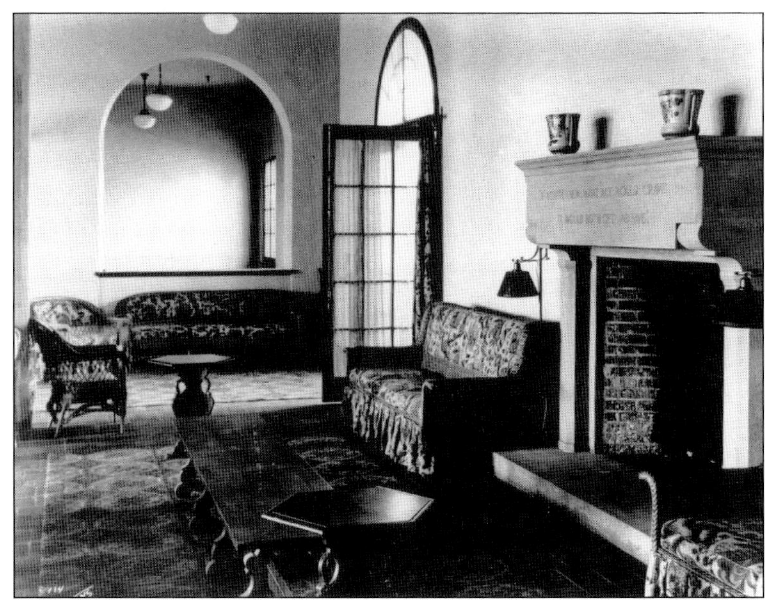

Several photographers must also be recognized. From 1925 to 1929, Grover Cleveland Koons and his studio were hired by the BLE to film the day-to-day work of building out Venice. The most prolific photographer of the time, Koons produced several hundred photographs for the BLE, many of which the Venice Archives holds. (NP1237.)

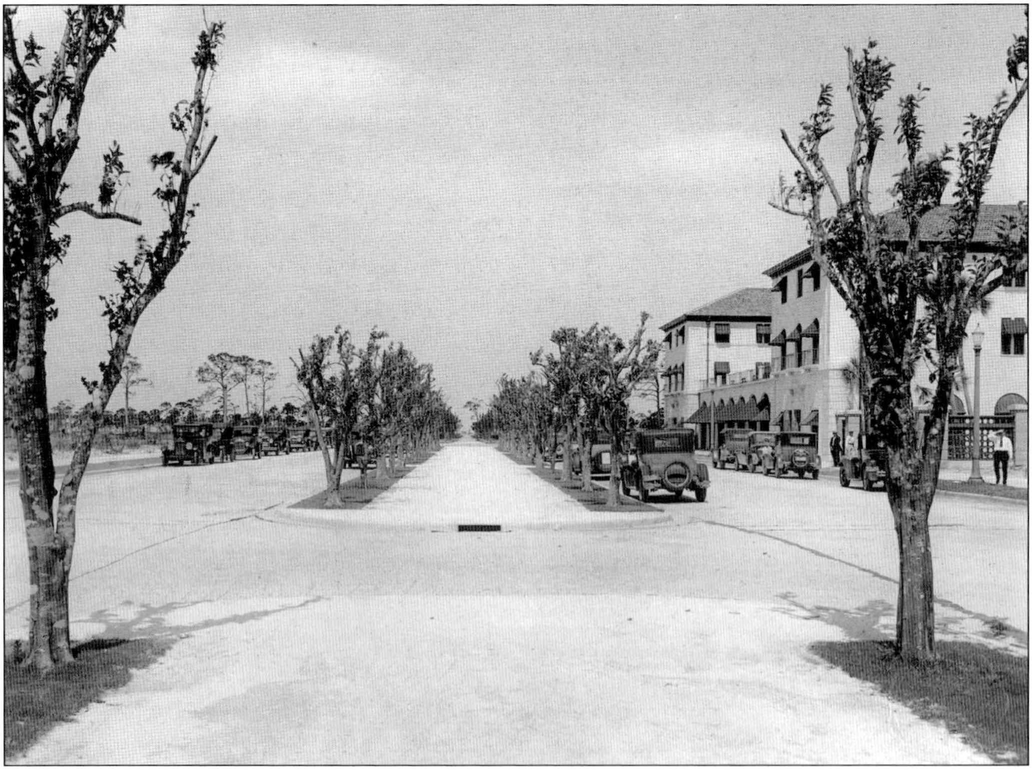

Jay Brown was a 1920s photographer whose images are still extremely popular. Both his and Koons's photographs can often be seen displayed in homes and offices across the area. Their documentation of early Venice gives a sense of the people and the place. (NP0006.)

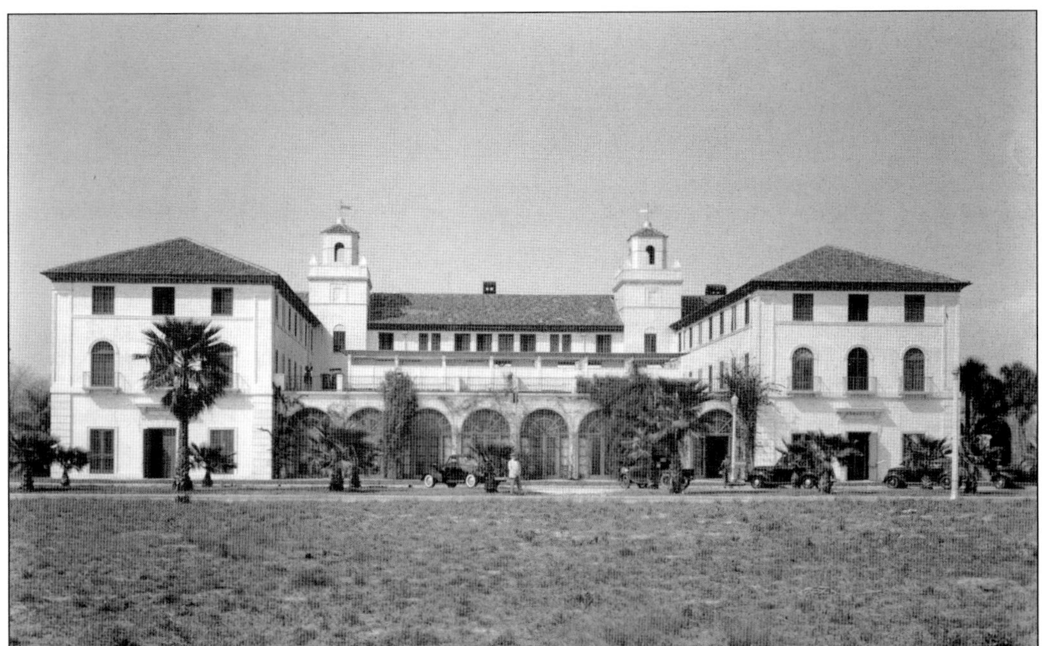

In the 1930s and 1940s, the Burgert Bros. Studio often photographed the Venice area, such as Dr. Albee's Florida Medical Center in 1940. Working for various companies as well as their own, their distinctive and interesting photographs are very popular. (PH26.0620.)

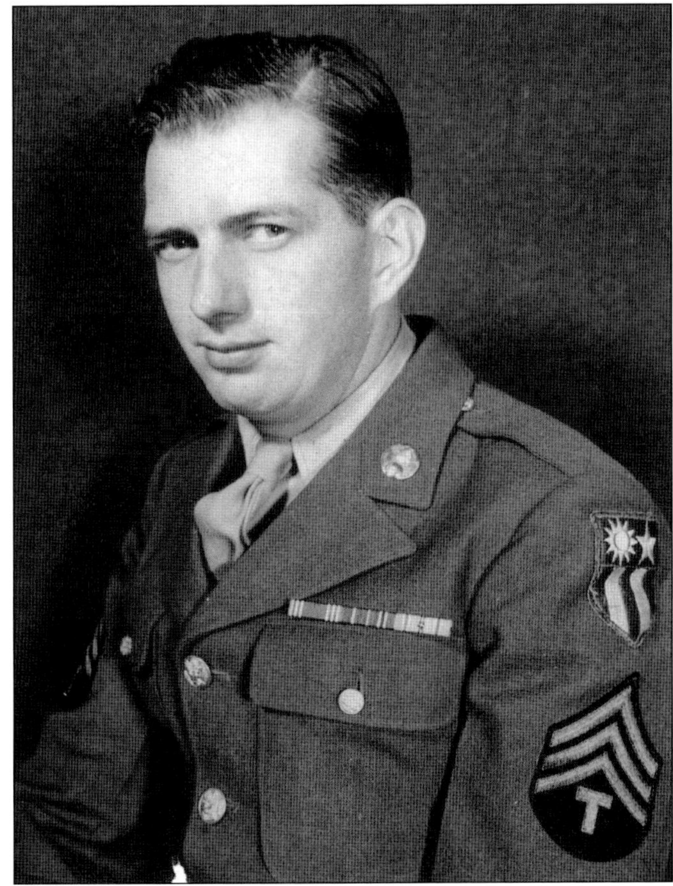

From the 1950s through the 1970s, Woody Thayer was a photographer for a number of local newspapers. While numerous images exist of his family, local people, tourists, events, and places, almost none exist of him. Thayer was a radio announcer, was married with two boys, and took the opportunity to insert members of his family into many of his photographs. (PH26.08.07.61.)

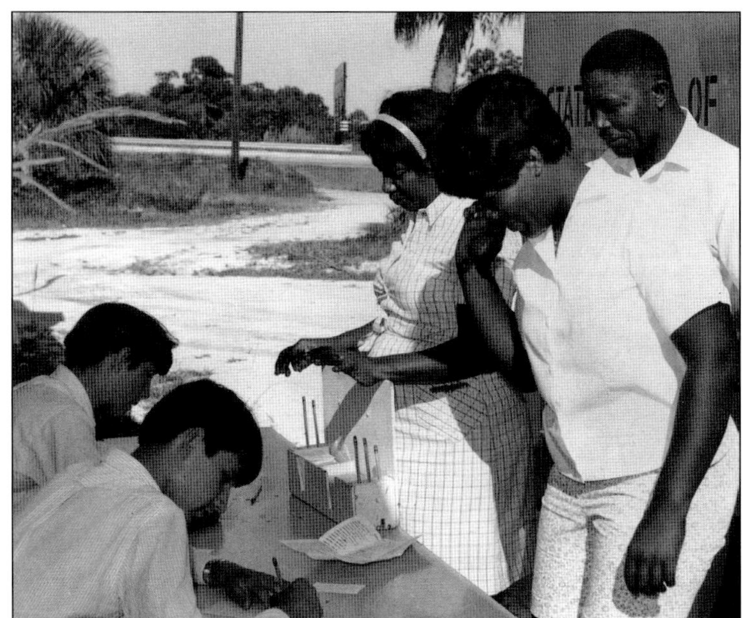

Thayer's images of everyday people, places, and events are nostalgic and insightful to view. As an example of his using his family members as subjects for his art, seen here from left to right in 1962, Bill Royal and Woody Thayer Jr. are signing up Juanita and Annie Mitchell and Jack Bryant for free tuberculosis chest x-rays. (M5.215.1.)

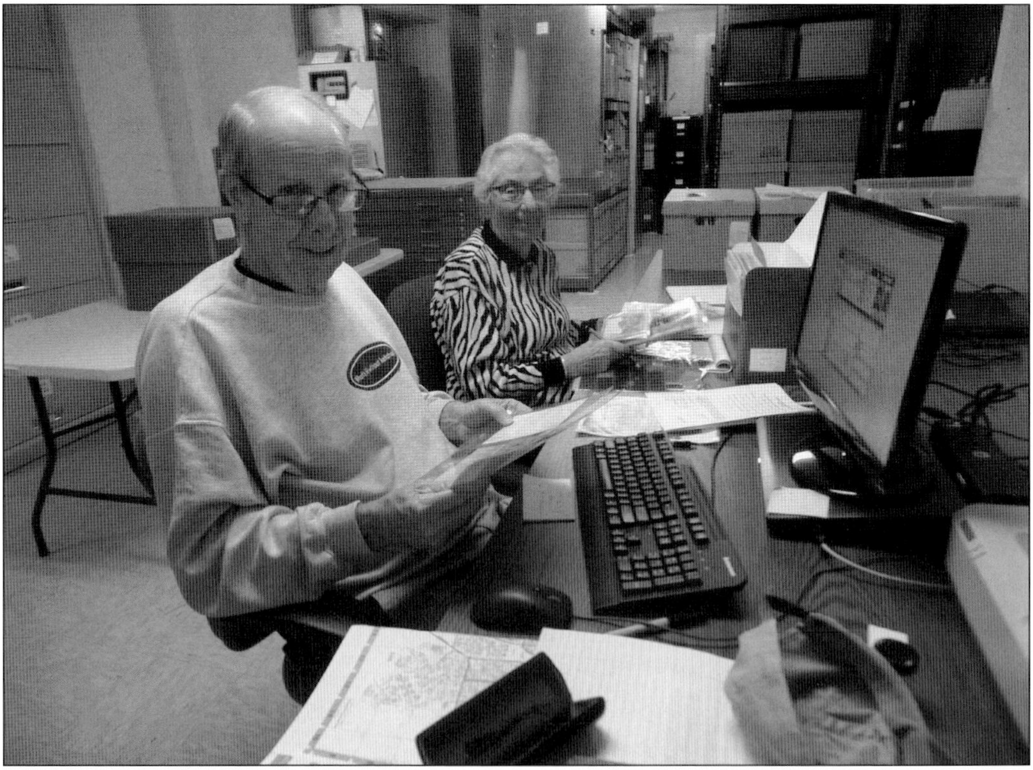

Over the years, many have donated originals or permitted scans to be done of numerous photographs, aerials, and documents about families, events, buildings, and historical activities. Here, volunteers are processing donations that have been received. Unfortunately, some donations come without documentation, so in spite of best efforts and desires, it is not possible to give attributions to all the materials. (RR.)

Six

Churches, Hospitals, and Airports

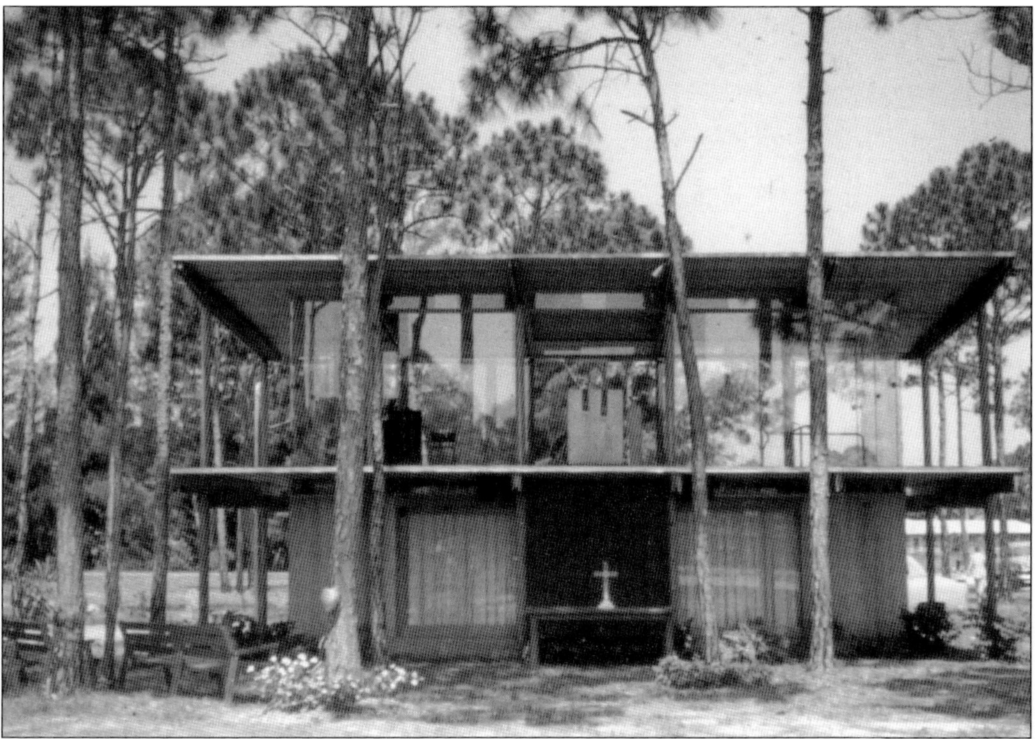

The Venice-Nokomis Presbyterian Drive-In Church was unique when it was built in March 1954 on Firenze Avenue. It was set in a pine grove that had formerly been part of the Venice Army Air Corps Base (VAAC). Over 30 parishioners funded the two-story glass-walled structure, modeled after the then-popular drive-in movie format. With speakers mounted on poles, the congregants sat in cars listening to services. (PH26.0406, 1 of 12, compiled by Gary Youngberg.)

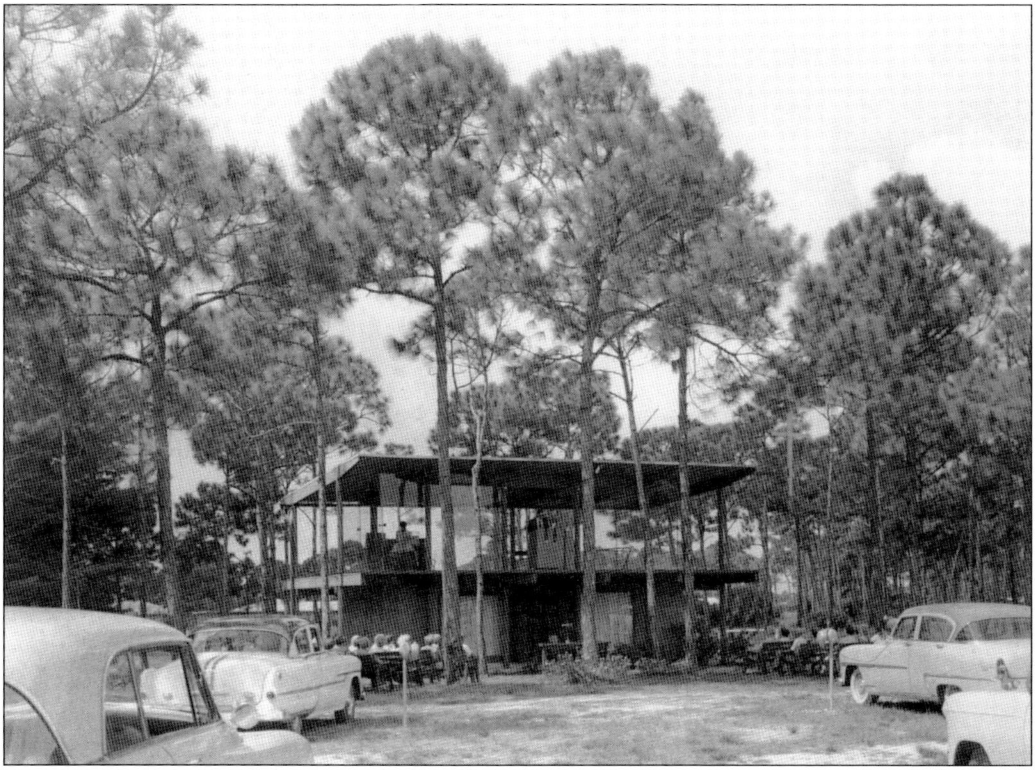

Ushers would set up the speakers, returning later with collection plates. The top floor accommodated the pastor, choir, and organ. Sunday school was on the ground floor. After services, families gathered for picnics. *Life* magazine featured the church in its April 18, 1955, issue. By 1957, membership was growing rapidly, so an arched-domed fellowship hall was built. (PH26.0406, image 3 of 3.)

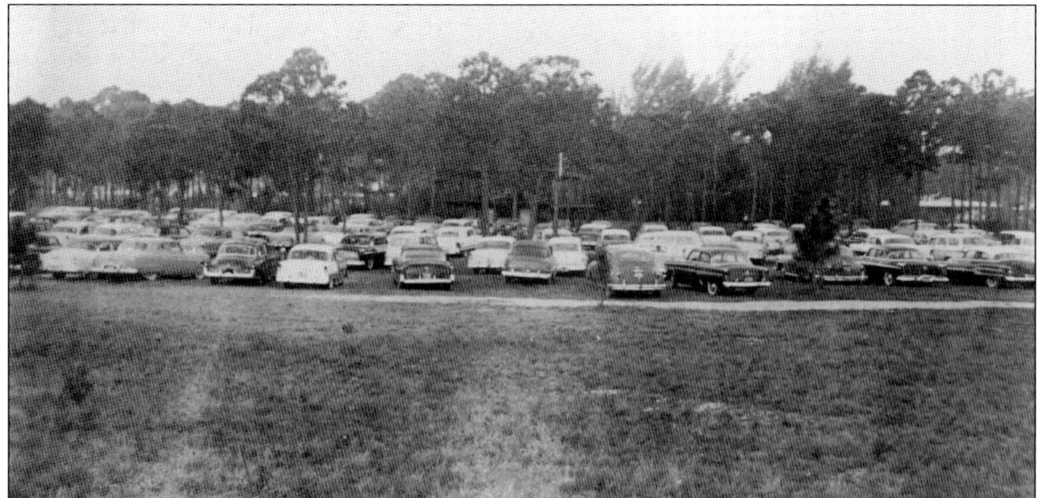

In September 1960, the glass walls blew out as Hurricane Donna pushed up the center of the state after coming ashore at Naples. Winds were still 120 miles an hour when it hit Arcadia, 50 miles to the east. Parishioners replaced the glass, but in 1962, Hurricane Alma came ashore in Miami, moving up the East Coast over 200 miles away, and caused damage to the church. (NP0143.)

Insurance companies then refused to insure the building, and the Drive-In Church was dismantled to become a beach house on Thornton Key, west of Englewood. The fellowship hall, pictured here by Lionel Murphy Jr., was remodeled with air-conditioning and opened as the Venice Presbyterian Church in August 1965. (PH01.03.21, image 2 of 2.)

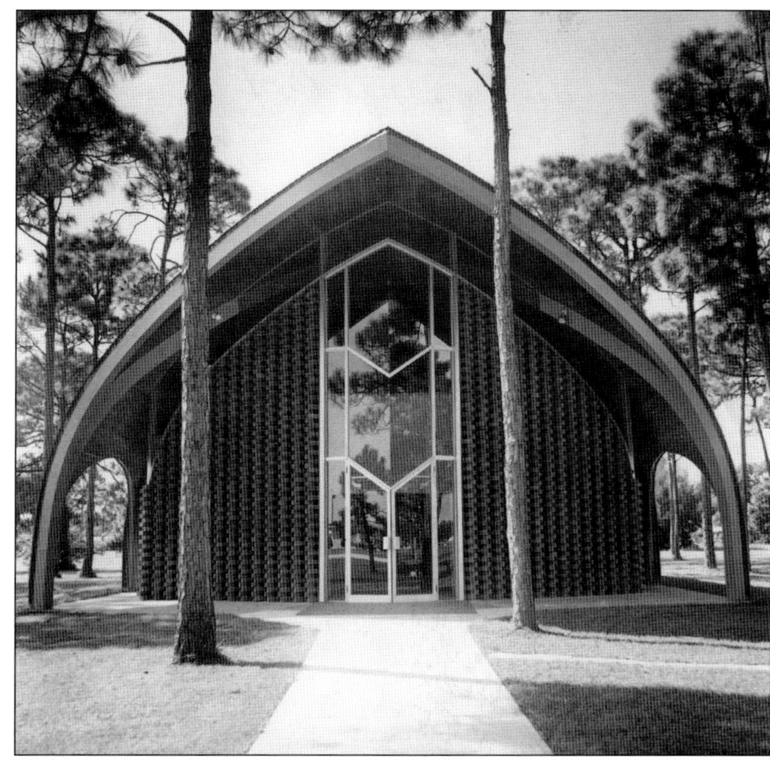

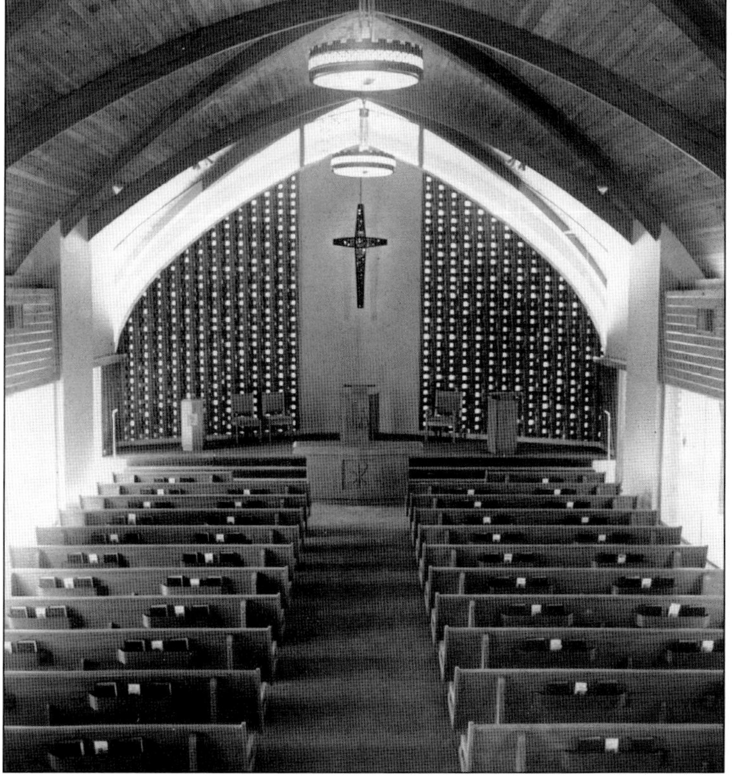

Both the Drive-In Church and the parish hall, which became the second church, were designed by Victor Lundy of the Sarasota School of Architecture. They were stunning. After two more renovations, the second building still serves the Venice Presbyterian Church congregation. (PH01.03.21.06.)

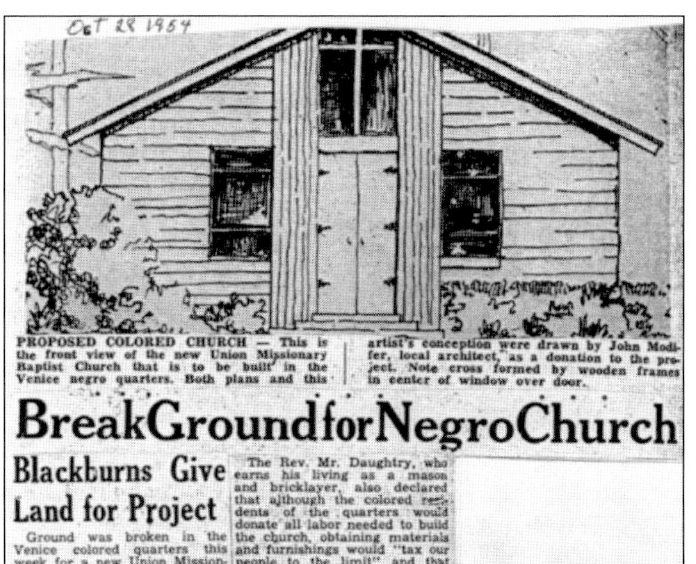

Oct 28 1954

PROPOSED COLORED CHURCH — This is the front view of the new Union Missionary Baptist Church that is to be built in the Venice negro quarters. Both plans and this artist's conception were drawn by John Modifer, local architect, as a donation to the project. Note cross formed by wooden frames in center of window over door.

Break Ground for Negro Church

Blackburns Give Land for Project

Ground was broken in the Venice colored quarters this week for a new Union Mission-

The Rev. Mr. Daughtry, who earns his living as a mason and bricklayer, also declared that although the colored residents of the quarters would donate all labor needed to build the church, obtaining materials and furnishings would "tax our people to the limit" and that

The Union Missionary Baptist Church was formed in 1954. It moved into a new home on Warfield Road between Hatchett Creek and US 41 on a 100-foot-by-100-foot lot was donated by Albert and Dorothy Blackburn of Laurel. Baptist services had formerly been held in a 1925 BLE building, once a dormitory for 400-plus BLE laborers, that had burned down in 1953. (LAT 81.)

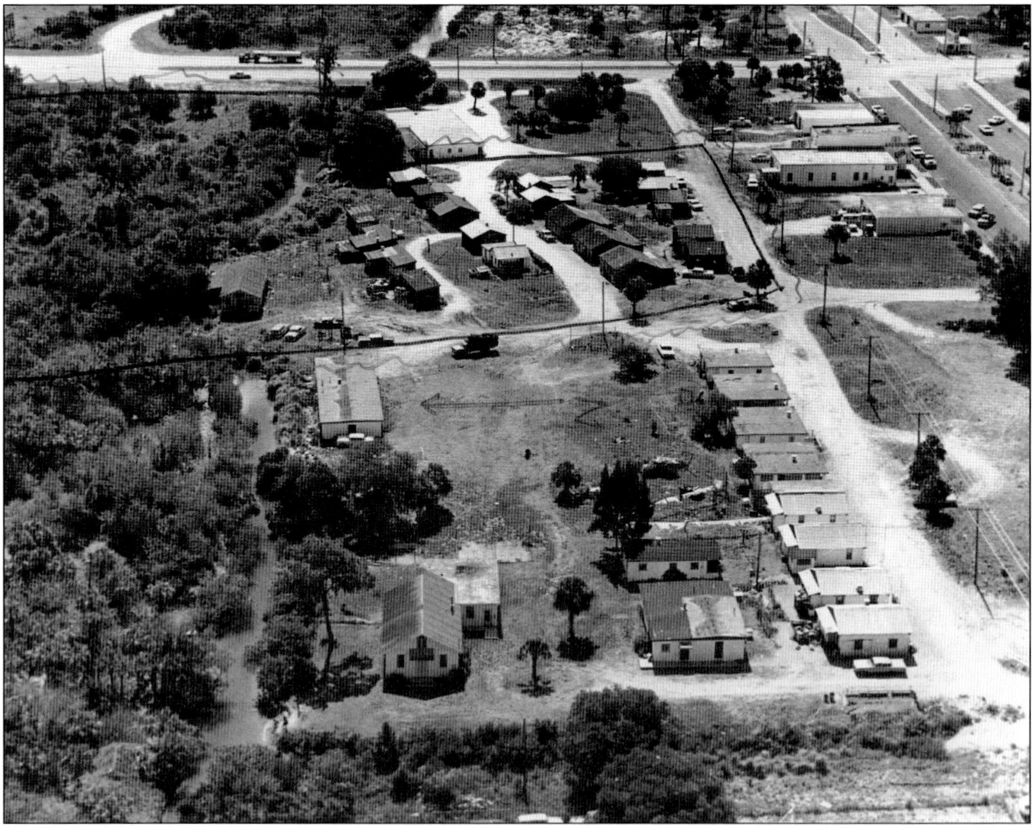

In 1947, the Venice City Council ruled that this quarter was the only area where "Negro residents" could live. This 1970s aerial by Woody Thayer, looking east, shows about 30 homes plus several buildings erected by the Blackburn family (who then owned the property), including the church in the bottom left corner. The first pastor was Rev. Joseph Daughtry, who served 12 years, until 1967. (NP1095.)

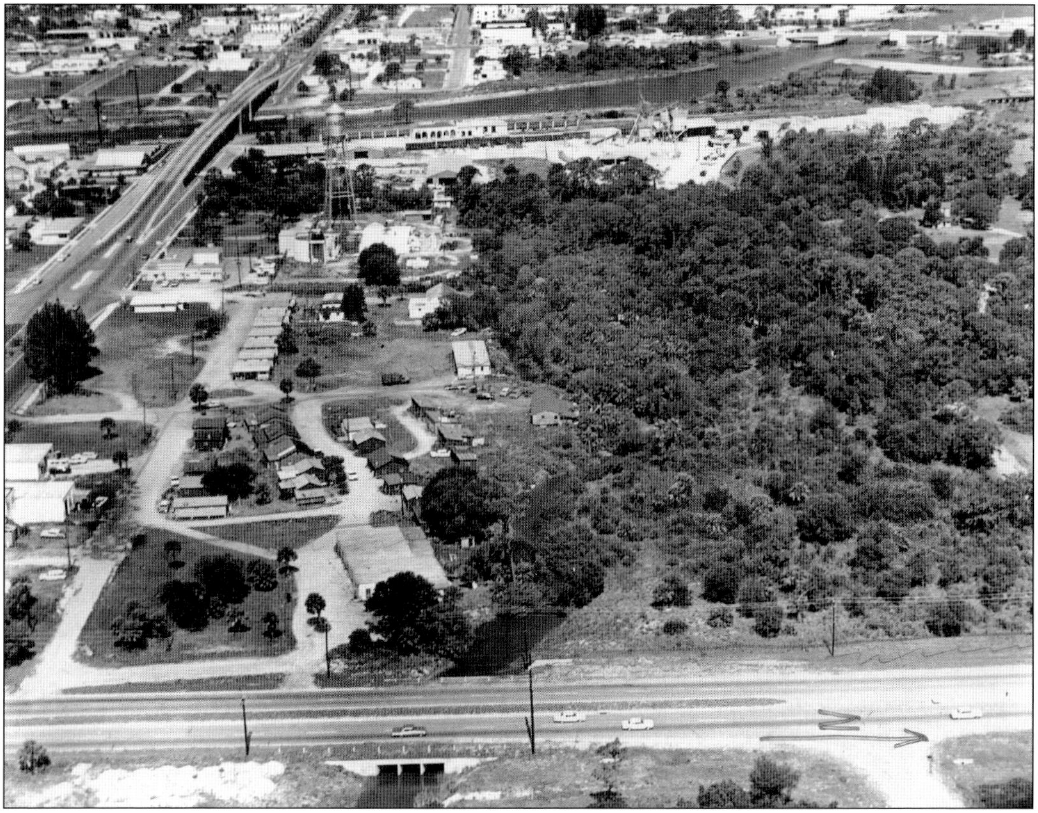

In another 1970s aerial, but looking west through the Blackburn Quarter, US 41 is at the bottom, and East Venice Avenue is at the far left. The Intracoastal Waterway has been built, and the rambling flowage of Hatchett Creek was tamed by ICW dredging, including the eastern section coming out under US 41. (NP1090.)

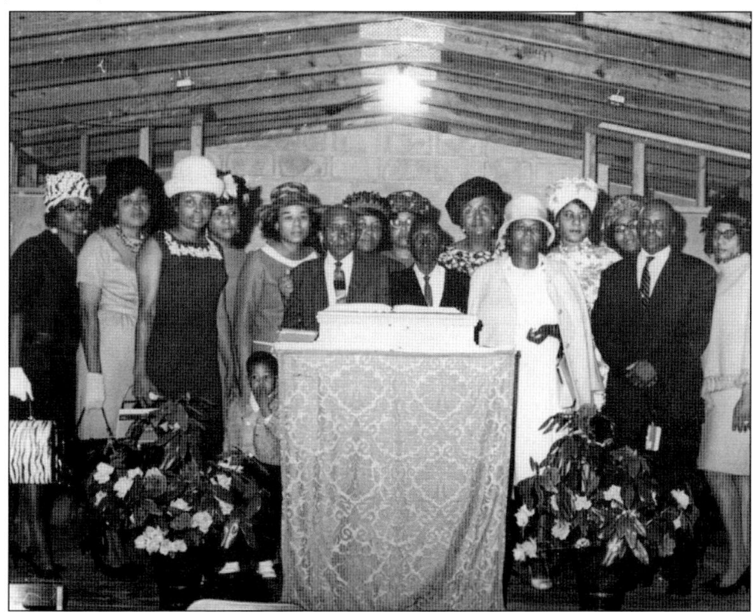

In 1974, the Black community was devastated when the city tore down their homes to build the water treatment plant and a fire station. The residents were moved to Grove Terrace Public Housing until the late 1970s, when that building was demolished. Rev. J.C. Sims, pictured here with some of his congregation, served 38 years, from 1967 to 2005. (PH06.05.22.01.)

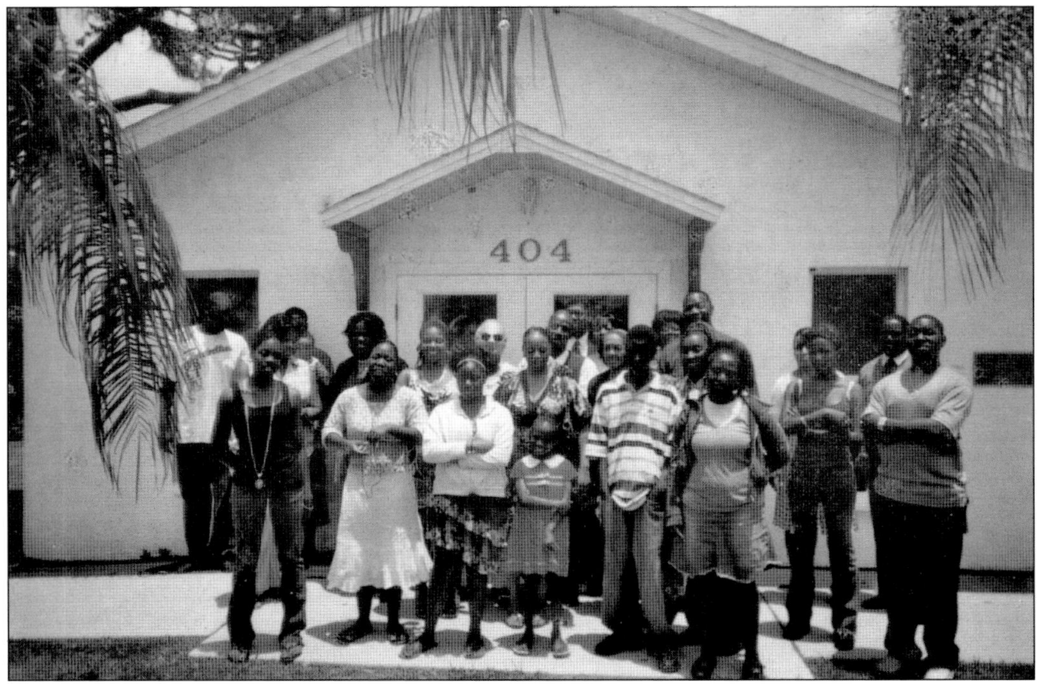

Unfortunately, on June 22, 2003, the little church was flooded with 500 gallons of raw sewage that poured from the Venice Sewage Treatment Plant next door. Nine months of inaction resulted in extensive mold buildup and raw sewage damage. The church was completely gutted, and all-new furnishings were purchased. Pictured here are some people who worked to reopen the church. (Rev. James Juan Mitchell of the Union Missionary Baptist Church.)

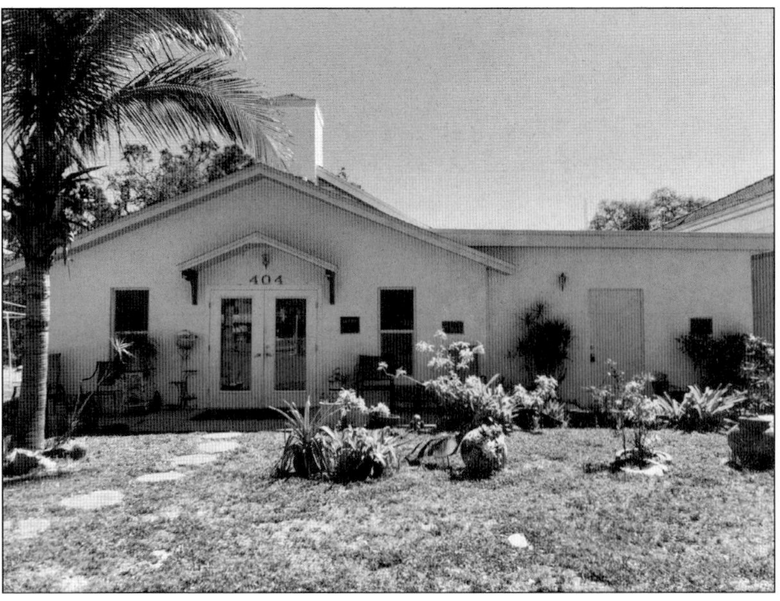

Only the church remains in the old neighborhood. It has been designated a Venice historical site. The current pastor, Rev. James Juan Mitchell, has served since 2005. In April 2025, the Union Missionary Baptist Church celebrated 70 years of fellowship. As Reverend Mitchell said, "This is not a Black church, this is God's church. Whosoever will, let him come." (MMK.)

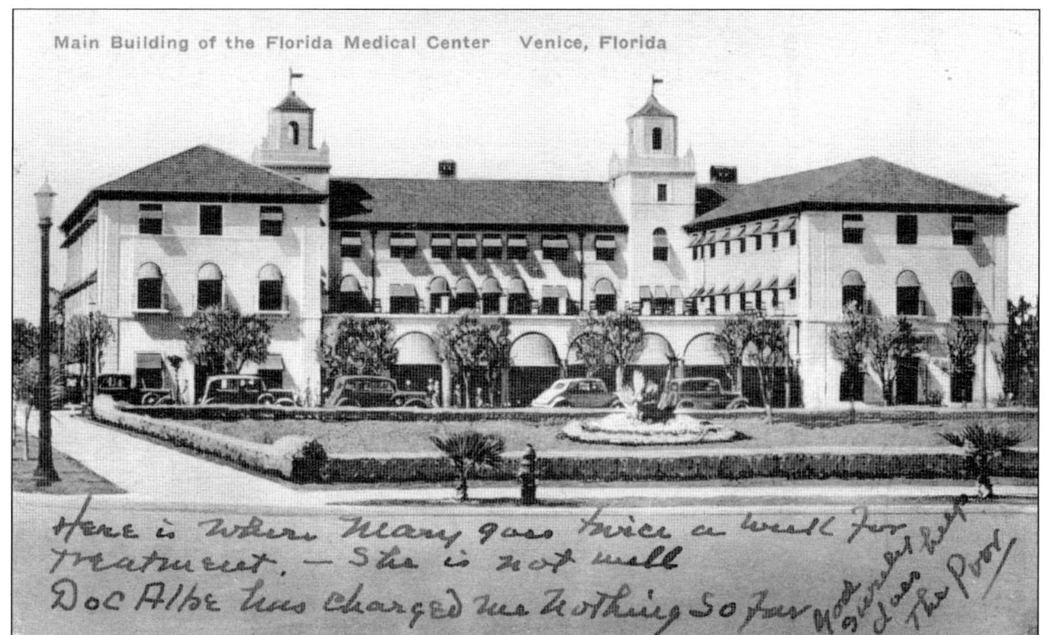

Dr. Fred Albee did not neglect his physician instincts and character. In 1932, the first hospital in Venice was his Florida Medical Center in the unused Park View Hotel, which was constructed by the BLE in 1926. Orthopedic patients were flown in to Albee Field for treatment, and local families requiring treatment were welcomed. (Postcard MS.215.1.4.)

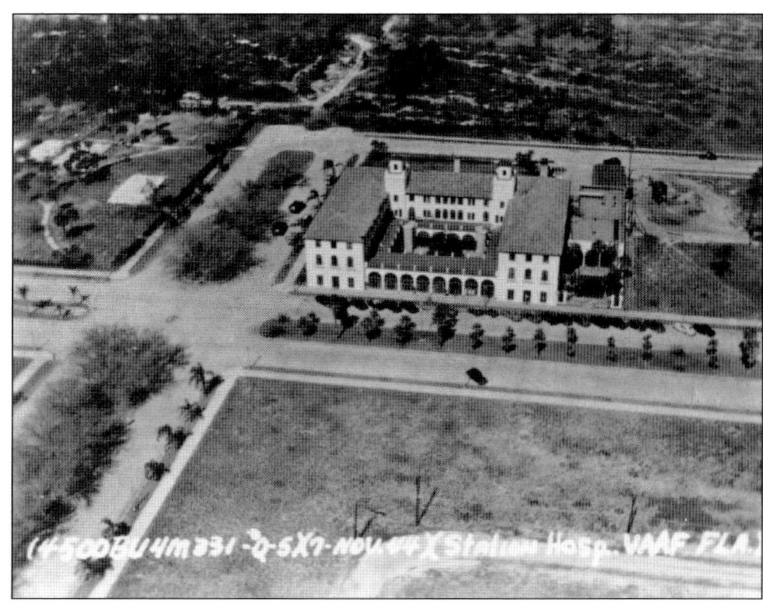

In 1942, the Army Air Corps took over Albee's Florida Medical Center. Servicemen, their pregnant wives and families, and support personnel, who were often local Venice area residents, were treated here. Nurses were housed in the Granada Apartments, across from Palmetto Court Park (current-day John Nolen Park). The first "service baby" was born in September 1943. (NP1166.)

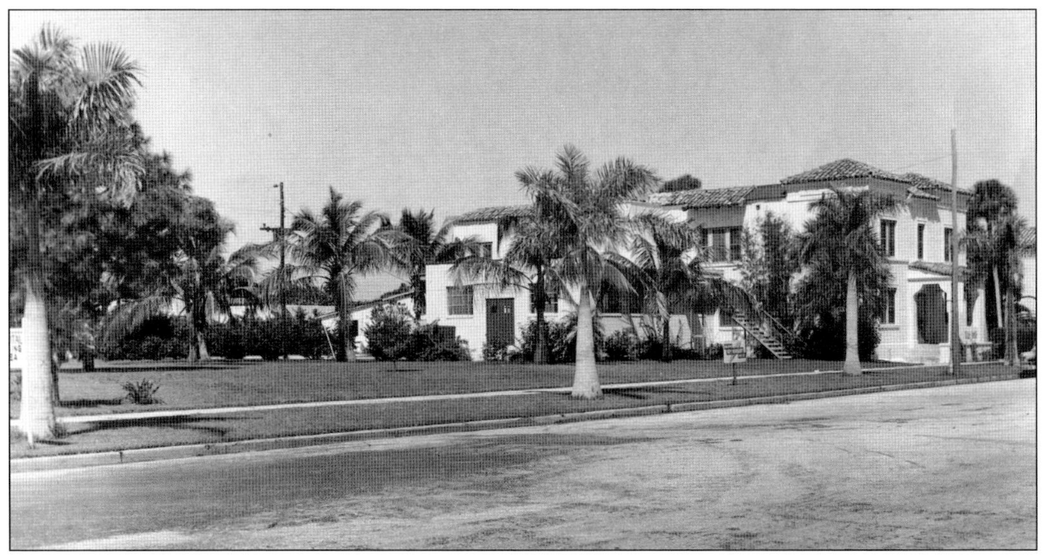

After 1945, the military hospital became a local hospital again. Later, the Worthington Apartments, on The Rialto, were remodeled to accommodate hospital patients. A new building, originally named South Sarasota County Memorial Hospital, was built in 1951 with only 14 beds, no operating room, and no elevator. (NP0233.)

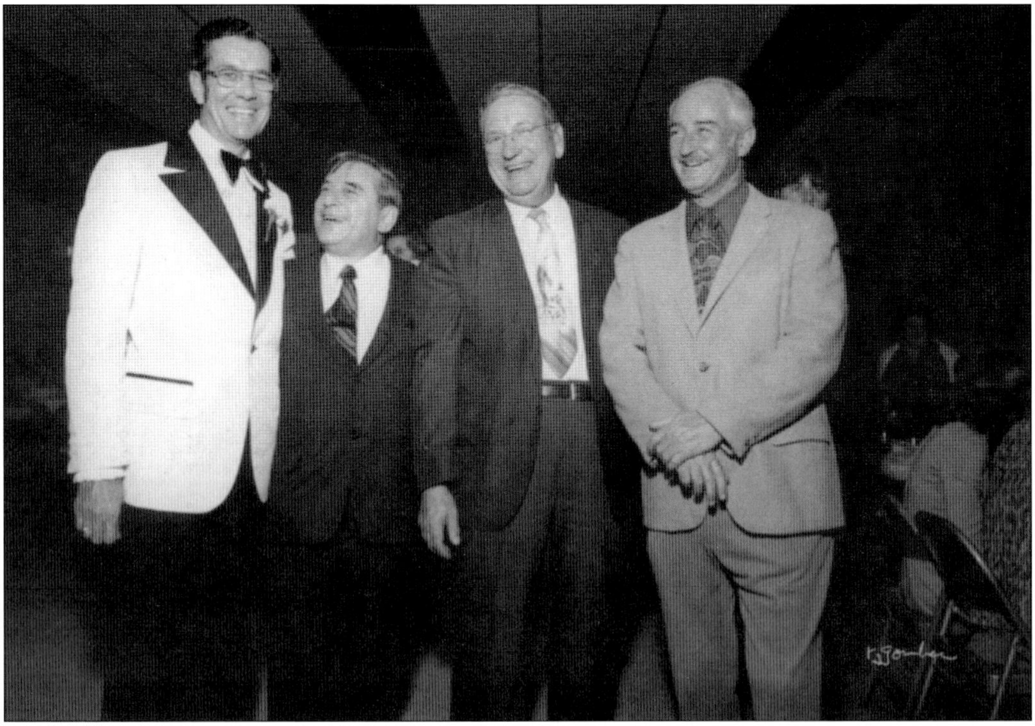

In early 1952, fundraising built an operating room in the renamed Venice Memorial Hospital. A second fundraising drive added an elevator. The Founders Way Walkway in the 200 block of West Venice Avenue commemorates hospital volunteers and the four doctors who founded Venice Hospital in 1951: from left to right, Talmadge Thompson, MD; Samuel Kaplan, MD; James Blades, MD; and Douglas Murphy, MD. (PH26.0535.)

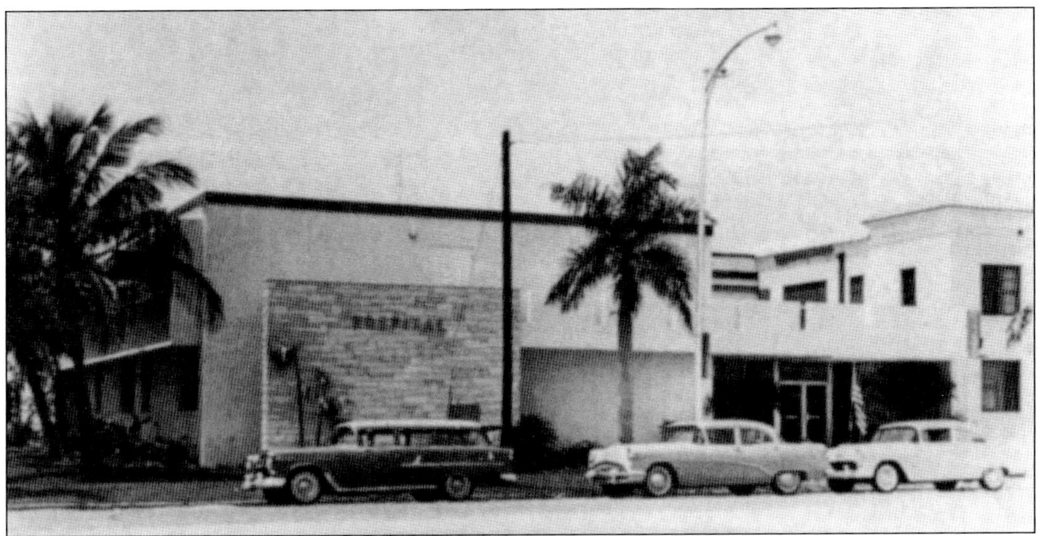

Since 1951, the distinctive limestone wall on the front entrance has been the one constant throughout repeated expansion of services and name changes. On the right side are the 1927 Worthington Apartments. The hospital was renamed Bon Secours Venice Hospital in 1995, Venice Regional Medical Center in 2004, Venice Regional Bayfront Health in 2014, and finally, in 2021, Shore Point Health Venice. (PH26.0577.)

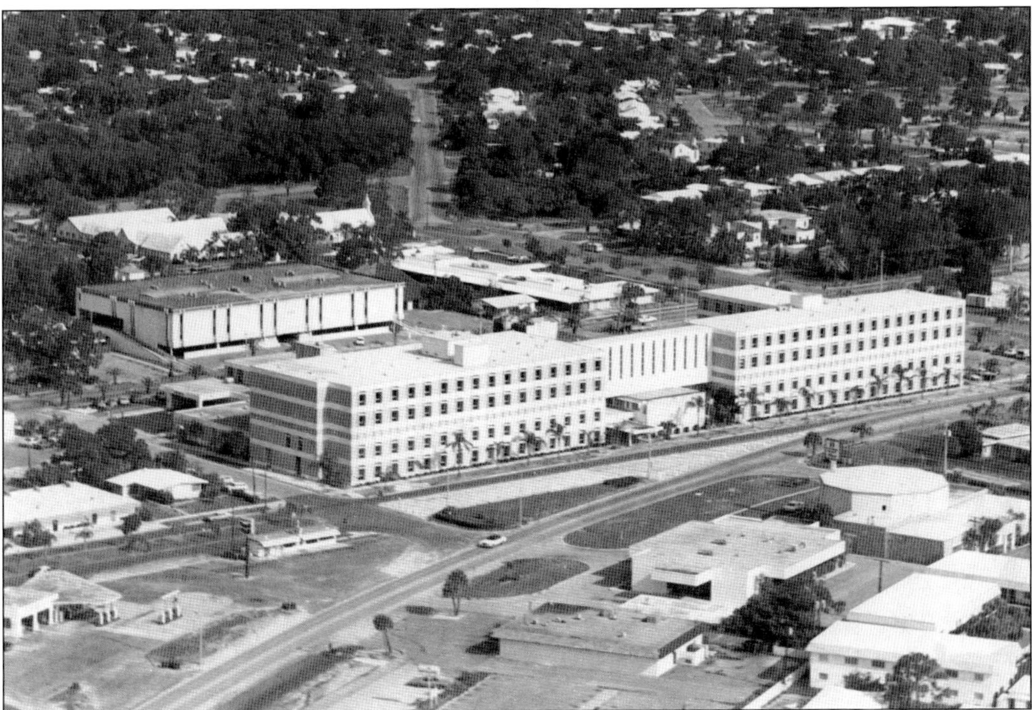

While expanded services and construction occurred repeatedly for 50-plus years, for local residents, it was always "Venice Hospital." Plans to build a new hospital building in southern Sarasota County never came to fruition, and hospital services at the building ended in September 2022. Emergency and hospitalizations were taken over by the new Sarasota Memorial–Venice Campus at Pinebrook and Laurel Roads. (PH01.04.22.)

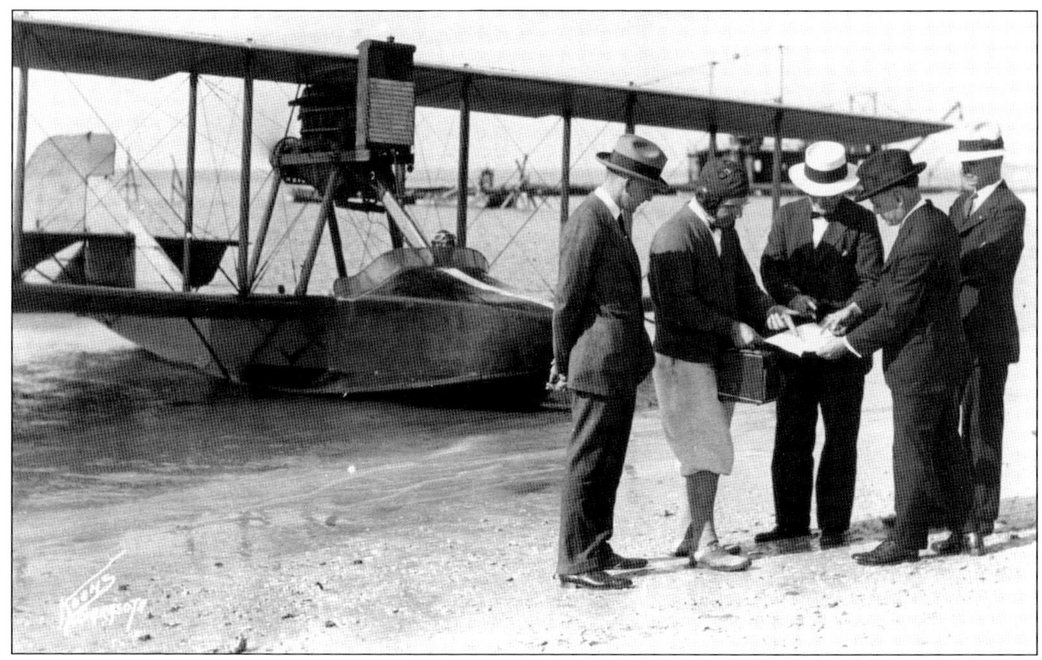

There have been three official airports in Venice: the 1930s Albee Field, the 1941 Venice Army Air Corps Field, and the 1947 Venice Municipal Airport. But, around 1917, Dr. Fred Albee utilized seaplanes, which could land on the water in Roberts Bay, for aerial shots of the Venice-Nokomis area. Pictured in this image by Koons Studios is pilot Asa Cassidy (secon from left) with Dr. Albee (third from left) and three other unidentified men. (NP0313.)

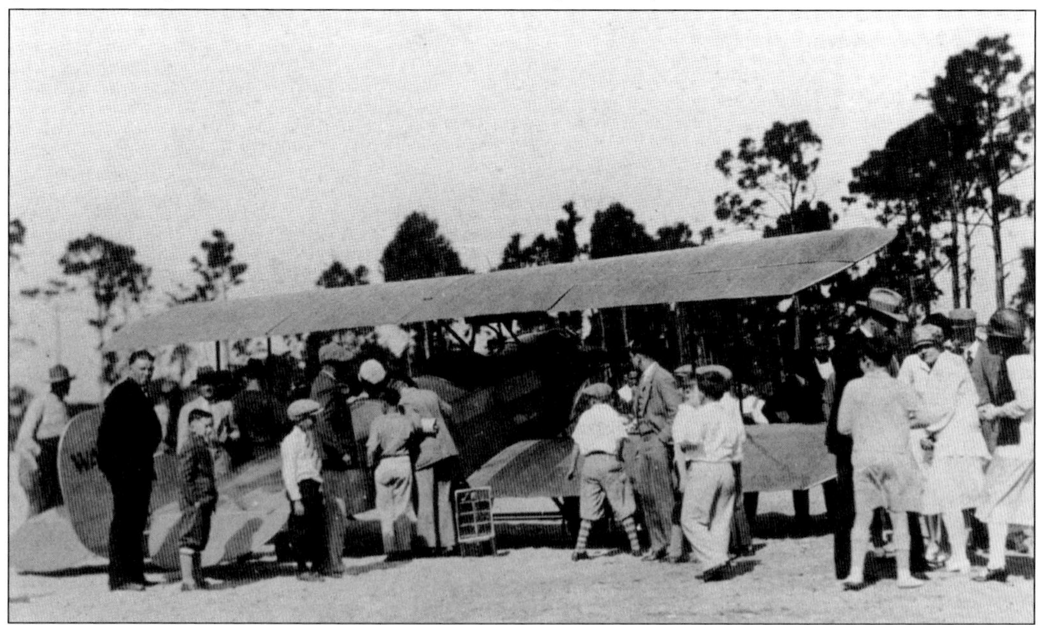

The BLE never built an airport in Venice, but the first recorded on-land arrival into Venice was on January 13, 1927, by George Haldeman, who landed on Nassau Street. He delivered strawberries to the Hotel Venice, and, as this photograph records, gathered a crowd. Emergency landings occasionally occurred, but no municipal airport existed until the 1930s. (NP0372.)

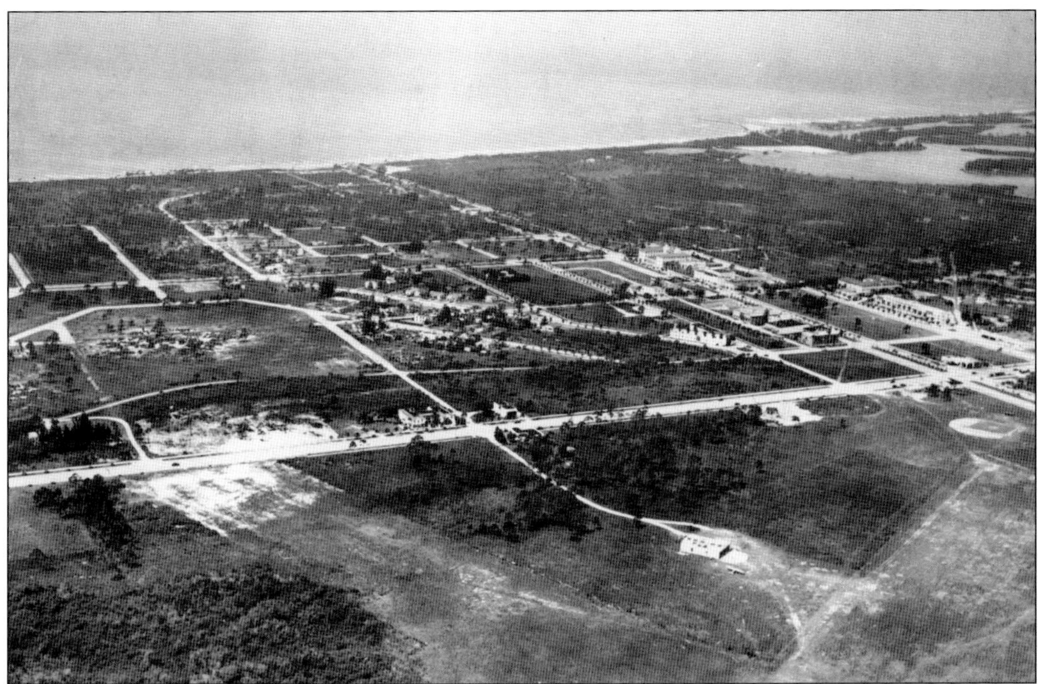

Authorized in 1933, the Works Progress Administration (WPA) built two air strips on property owned by Dr. Albee north of the Venice Golf and Country Club (now a shopping area). It was not until 1939 that it was dedicated as the Fred Albee Municipal Airport, also referred to as the "Downtown Municipal Airport." A hangar and repair shop were also constructed. (PH26.0627, image 2 of 2.)

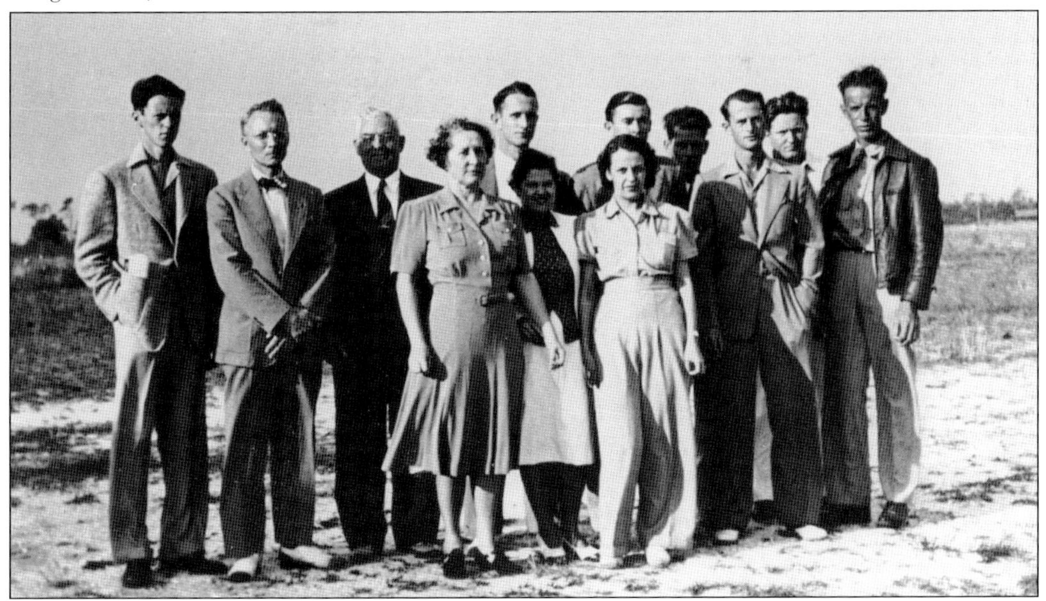

The Venice Flying Club was formed in 1939. From left to right are (first row) Helga Roess Siede, Ann Dorso Moreman, Mae Wrede, Tom Wrede Jr., and Claude Archer; (second row) James Cousins, George H. Hauser, James E. Darby, Albert W. Moreman, George Surls, Finn Caspersen, and Jack Wilkinson. (NP0383.)

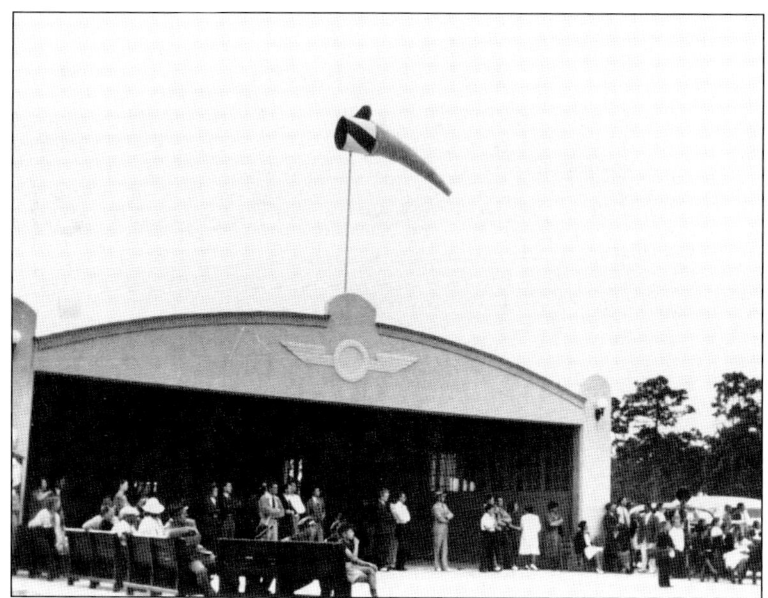

This group of flying enthusiasts, including Betty Hauser Arnall and Steve Albee (nephew of Fred Albee), and their instructor attended classes in the airport hangar. Instructor J.J. "Doc" Chiddix taught courses in air navigation, meteorology, maps, and map reading. Four of the 13 members were women, which is an interesting statistic for the 1930s. (NP0394.)

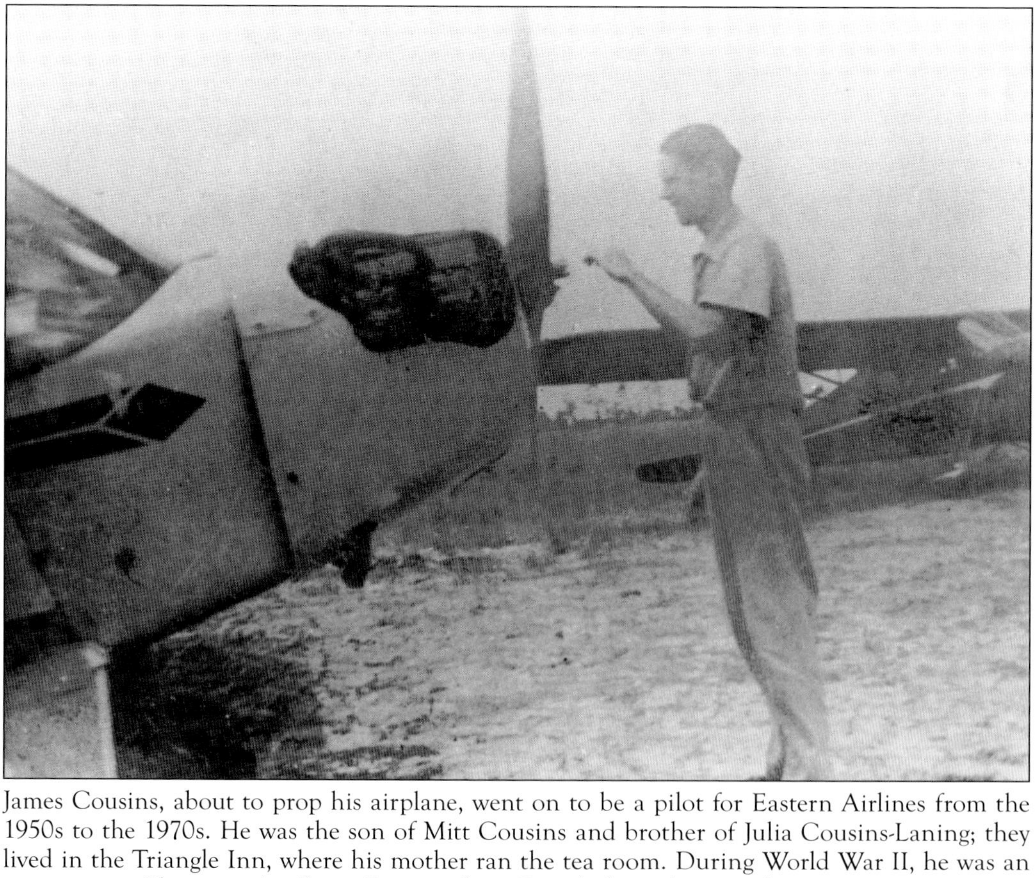

James Cousins, about to prop his airplane, went on to be a pilot for Eastern Airlines from the 1950s to the 1970s. He was the son of Mitt Cousins and brother of Julia Cousins-Laning; they lived in the Triangle Inn, where his mother ran the tea room. During World War II, he was an instructor at Clewiston Air Corps Base teaching British flyers. (NP1053.)

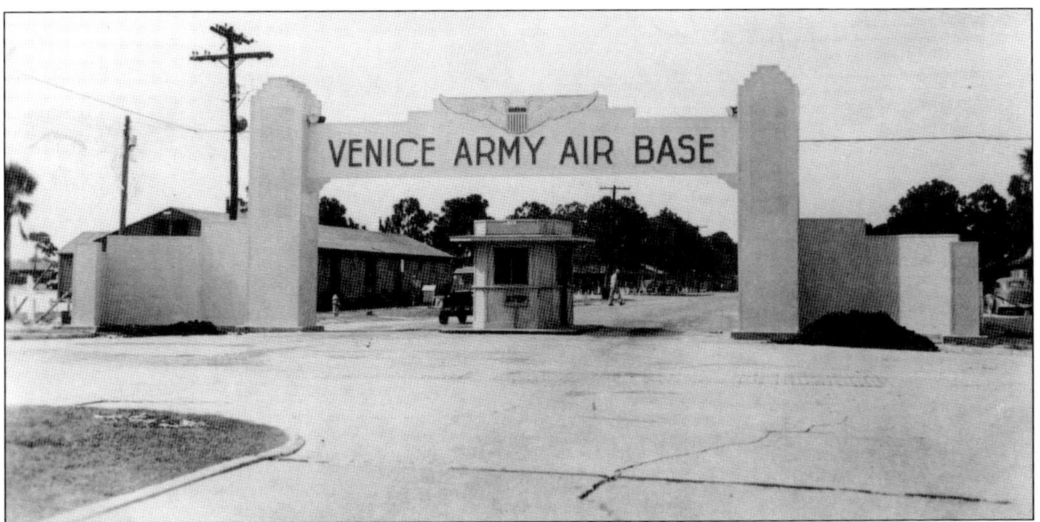

The US Air Force was not formed until September 1947, thus the base was named the Venice Army Air Corps base. With the outbreak of World War II, Finn Caspersen, whose family owned 3,000 acres, sent a telegram to the War Department about land it could lease/use, and soon, a 1,699-acre Army Air Corps base replaced the initial idea for a shooting range. (NP0075.)

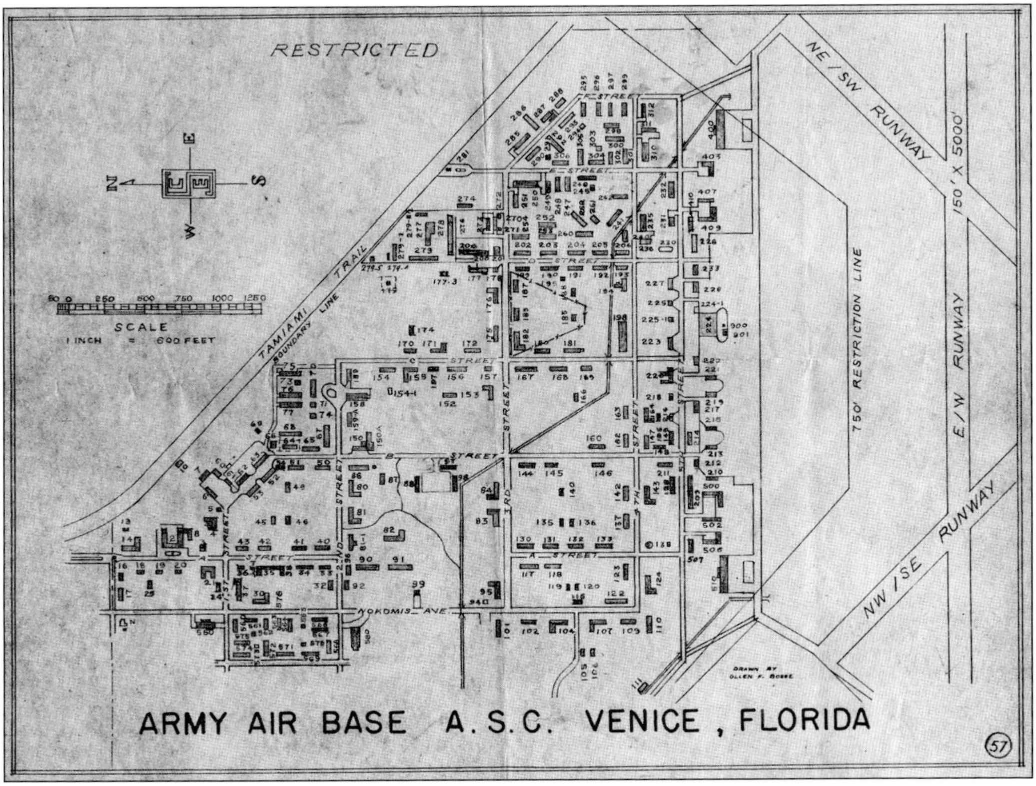

RESTRICTED

ARMY AIR BASE A. S. C. VENICE, FLORIDA

57

The base entrance was at the east corner of The Rialto and US 41. It extended down San Marco Drive to the Gulf and south to Lemon Bay. Extensive planning and construction were necessary to accommodate approximately 5,000 military members and staff on-site. It opened in June 1942. (0S61.01.)

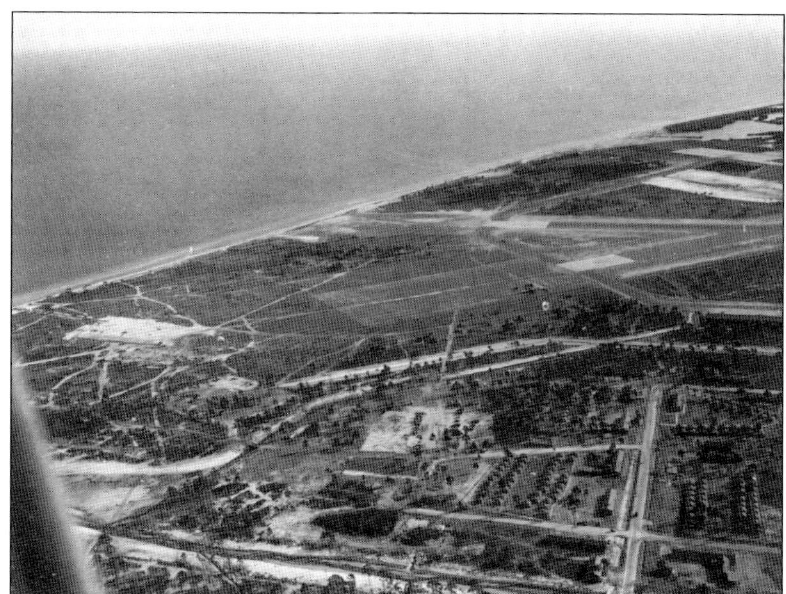

This 1943 aerial by Vaughan Pitman, looking north, has a clear view of most of the air base. On the bottom right are the tents and huts used by military personnel. Buzzard (now called Red) Lake, plus what is now Caspersen Beach, is on the top and left with the airplane runways in between. (Eric Duda, 2021.17.127.)

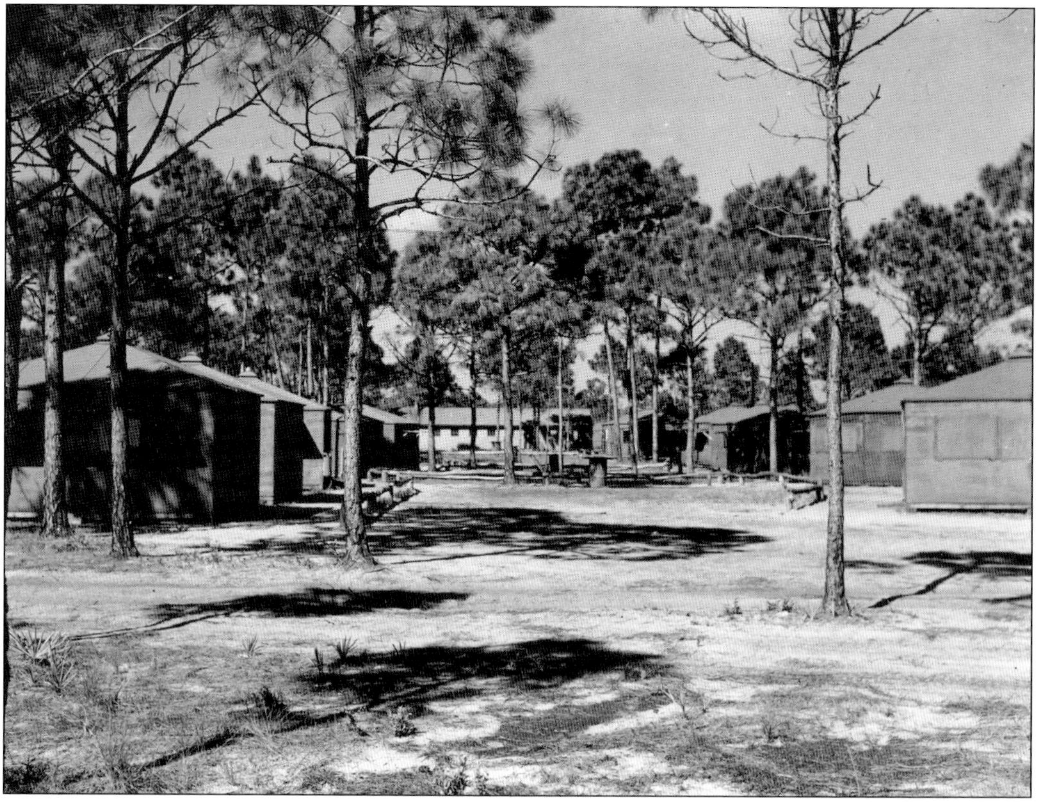

Living on the base was rough, even in 1943, as photographed by Vaughan Pitman. There was no air-conditioning, and tar paper huts or tents served as accommodation. Single men lived on base, and married men lived in town or sometimes as far away as Sarasota. Local residents also took civilian jobs at the base. (Eric Duda, 2021.17.037.)

Vaughan Pitman, a draftee from New Hampshire, was a photographer who underwent training in the autumn of 1943. He served in the Army Air Forces from 1943 to 1945 in Normandy, northern France, the Rhineland, and Central Europe. The website vaughanpitman.com, with many of his photographs, is extremely interesting to review. (Eric Duda, 2021.17.111.)

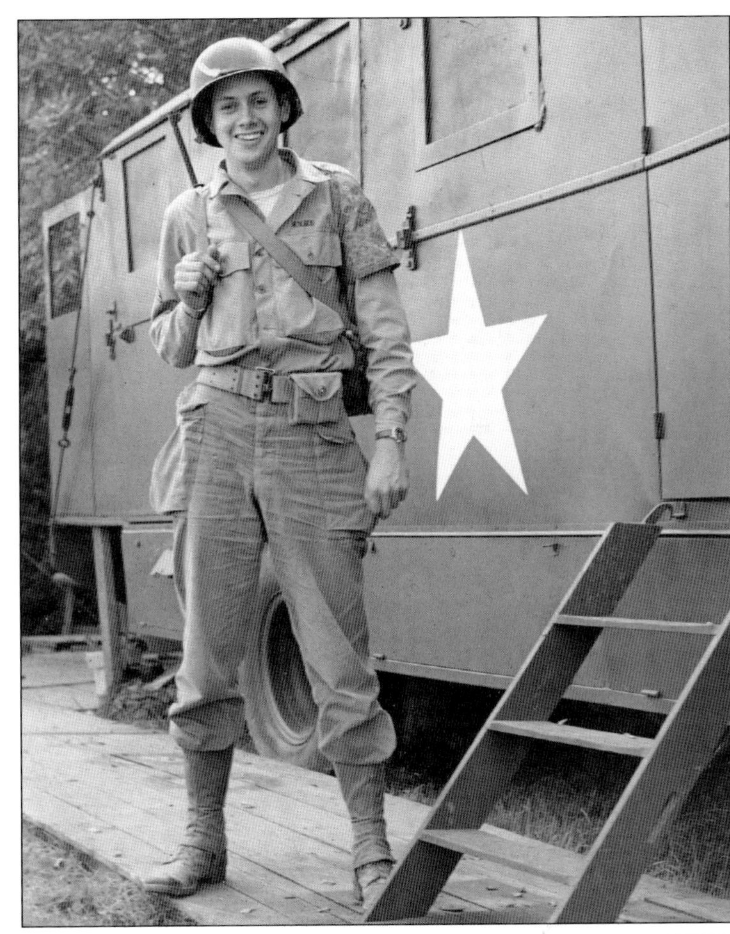

Pictured in 1943 by Pitman are Curtiss P-40 fighter trainee planes. At the far right sits an old C-78, a four-seater plywood transport utility craft affectionately nicknamed the "Venice Queen." All these planes are lined up outside the maintenance hangar. (Eric Duda, NP0564.)

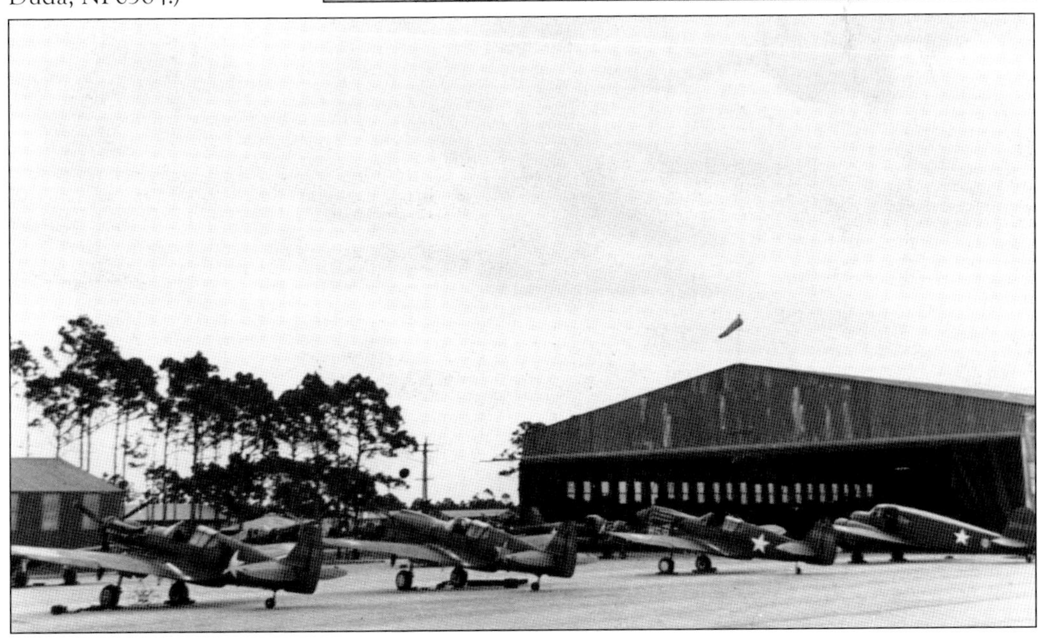

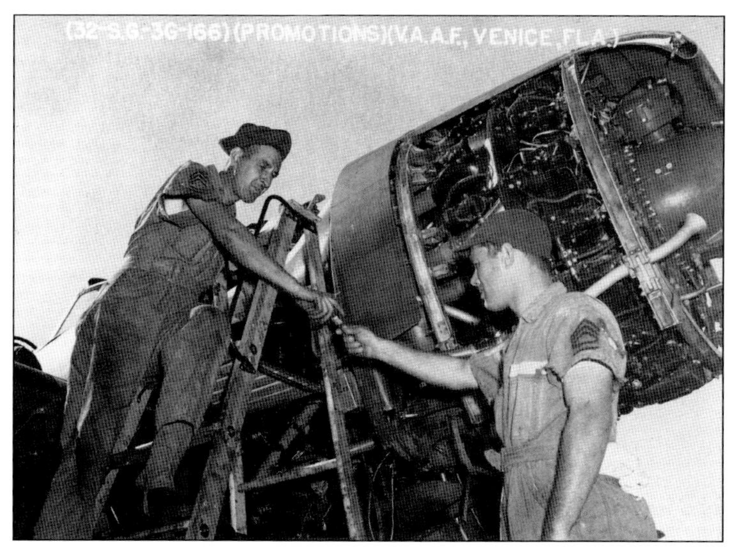

The base provided training for over 22,000 maintenance crews and pilots for P-40 Warhawks, P-38 Lightnings, P-39 Airacobras, P-47 Thunderbolts, and P-51 Mustangs, with engine factory representatives from Rolls-Royce and Pratt & Whitney as instructors. Two hundred German war prisoners also arrived in 1945 to work as electricians, plumbers, in the mess hall, and on local farms. (Eric Duda, 2021.17.056.)

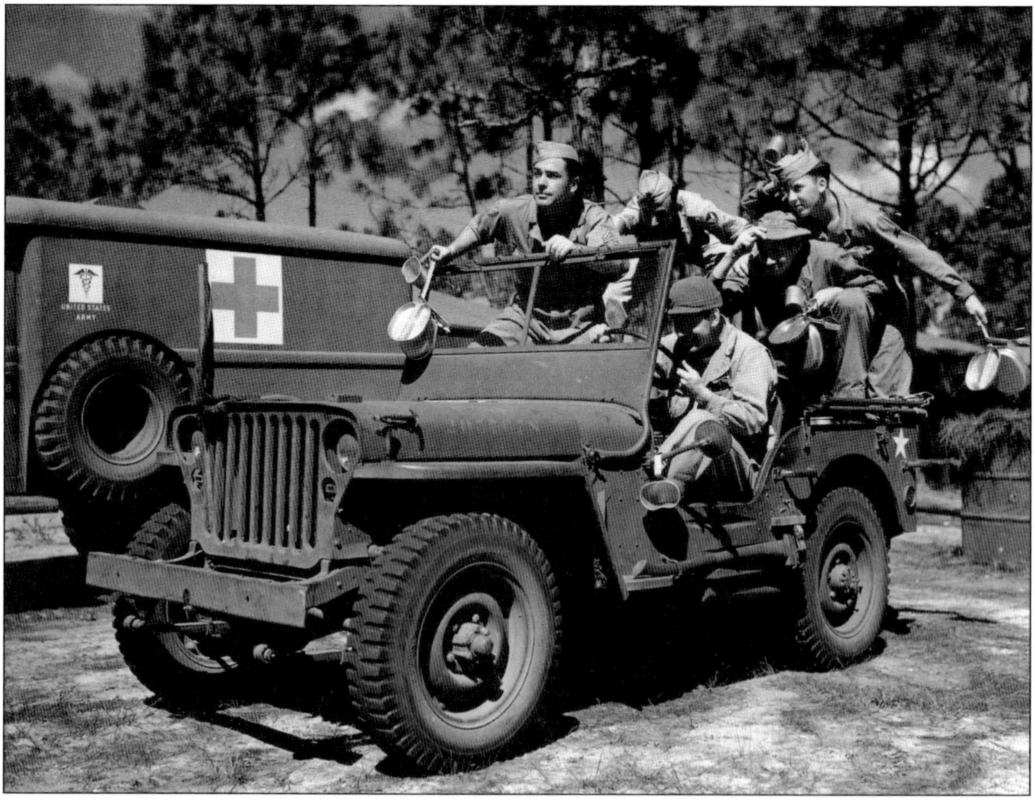

Army personnel with downtime coached Little League teams, held Christmas parties, and with community organizations, hosted dances and concerts and conducted bond drives. Base staff included military trainees, engine maintenance, doctors, nurses, food service staff, teachers, lawyers, military police, chaplains, entertainers, K-9 dog units, and engineers. (Eric Duda, 2021.17.019.)

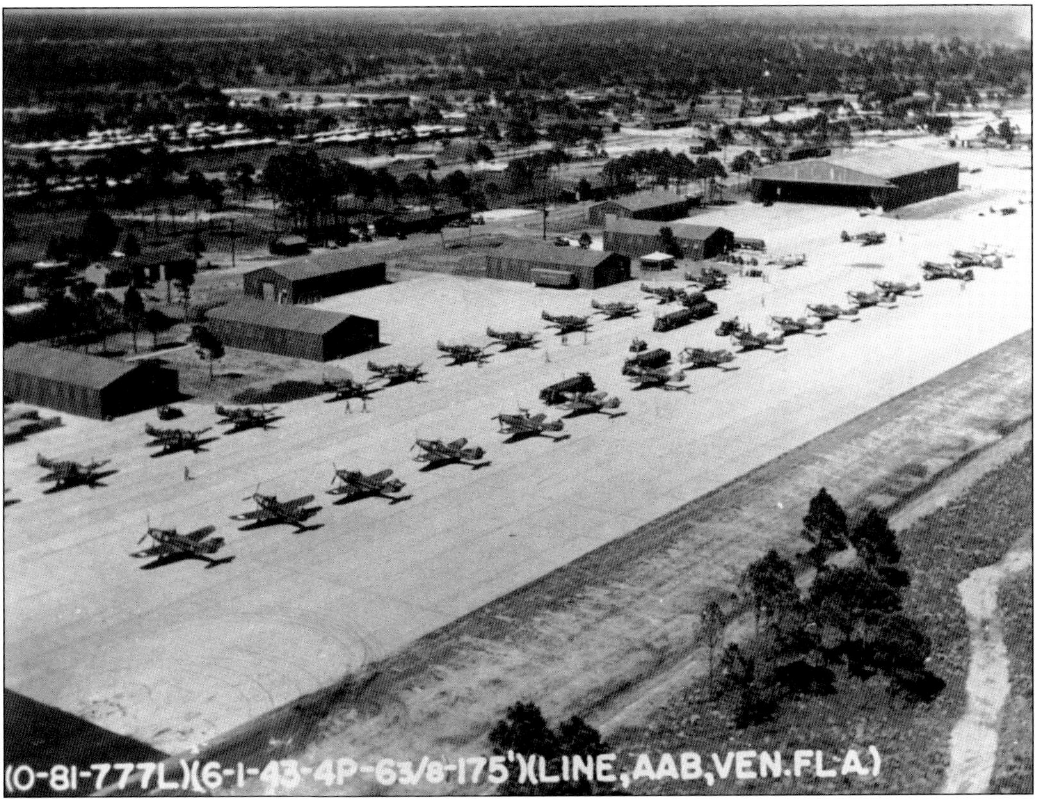

(0-81-777L)(6-1-43-4P-63/8-175')(LINE, AAB, VEN. FLA.)

The military had taken over much of the city, with thousands of military and support personnel (including POWs), and was driving the economy. There were also over 300 civilian employees working as firefighters, clerks, or truck drivers. A number of residents can recount their families moving to Venice seeking employment with the airport's training center. (Eric Duda, NP1340.)

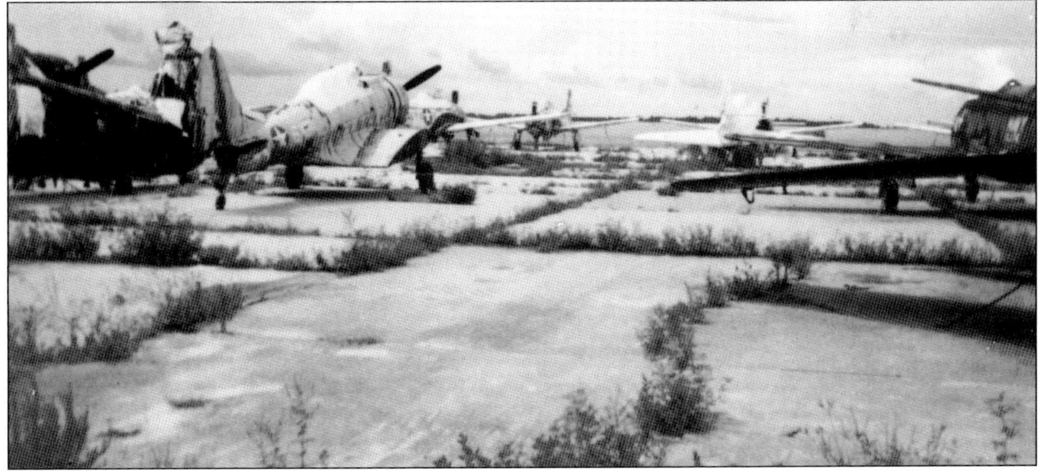

The war ended on September 2, 1945, and the base closed in December that same year. Donations to the Venice Historical Archives over the years have included photographs, documents, and letters written by trainees while stationed at the VAAC base. Even today, occasionally after heavy storms, armaments or plane parts are found in the water or washed up onto Venice-area beaches. (PH26.0447, image 3 of 4.)

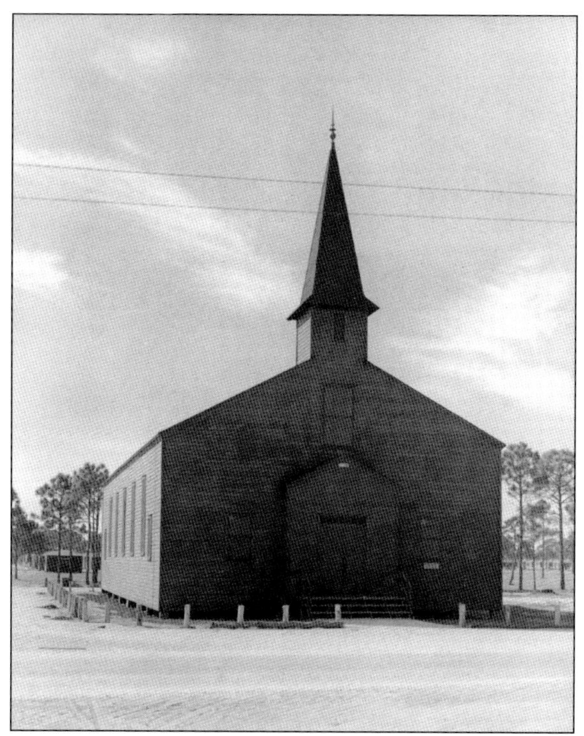

After the base closed, some of its buildings were repurposed as housing for Golden Beach or were moved to other locations. The base church was moved to become Epiphany Mission Church. For a short time, a warehouse became the Little Theatre. Later renamed the Venice Theatre, it moved into the old Orange Blossom Garage/KMI gymnasium at Nokomis Avenue North and Tampa Avenue West. (NP0495.)

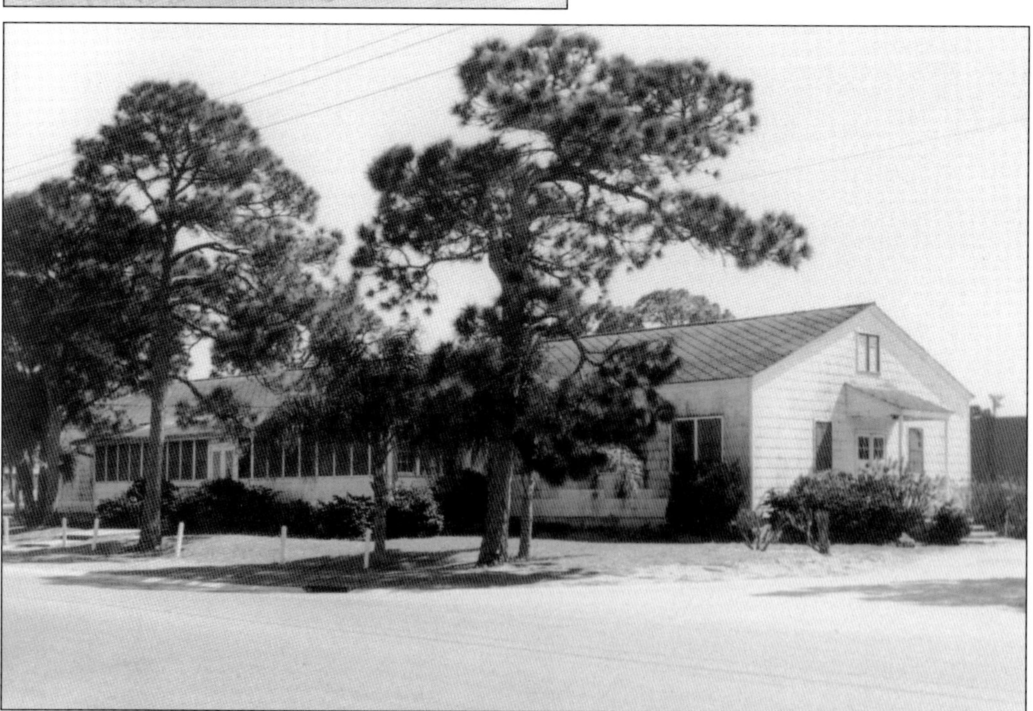

In 1947, a base mess hall was moved to Harbor Drive and Venice Avenue to become the city hall. When a new city hall was erected in the 1960s, the mess hall was again moved and became the chamber of commerce building. In 2025, only the Student Officers' Club remains in its original location as the clubhouse at the Venice Municipal Mobile Home Park. (NP1371.)

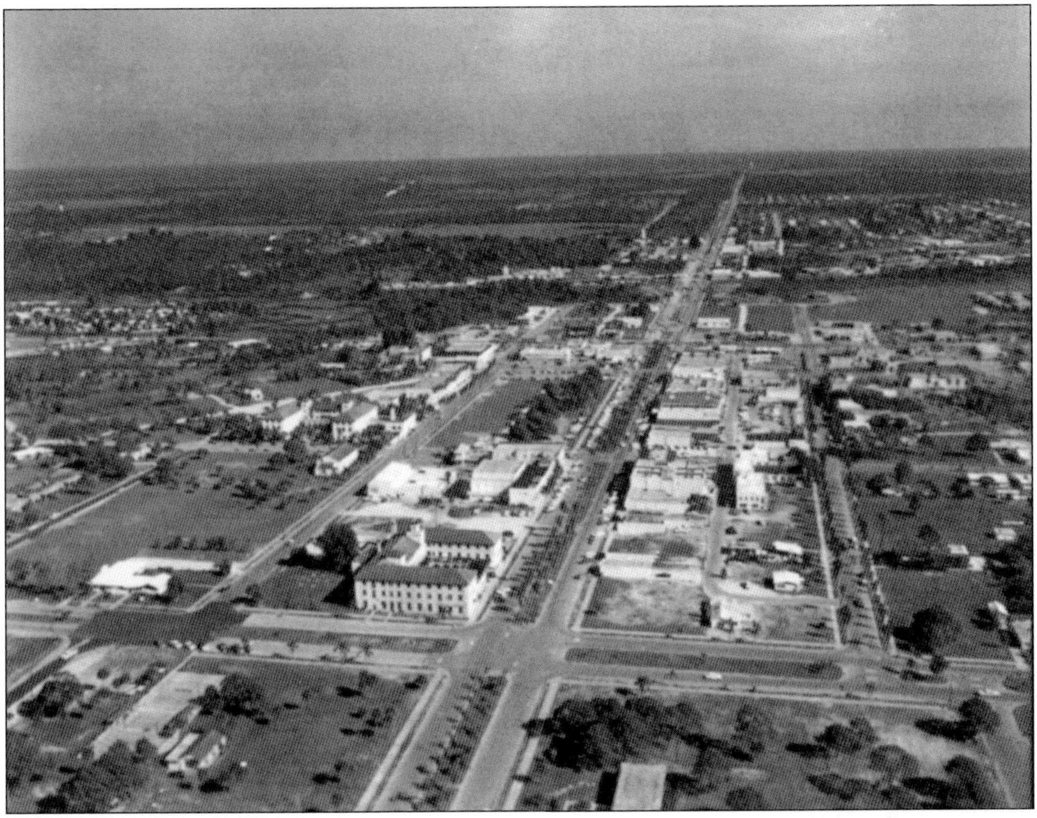

In this 1950s aerial, the Orange Blossom Garage (now Venice Theatre) and the former base chapel (now Epiphany Church's parking lot) can be seen along Tampa Avenue. Dr. Albee's Florida Medical Center (now the post office) and the former mess hall (now city hall) are on Venice Avenue. (PH26.0466, 6 of 13.)

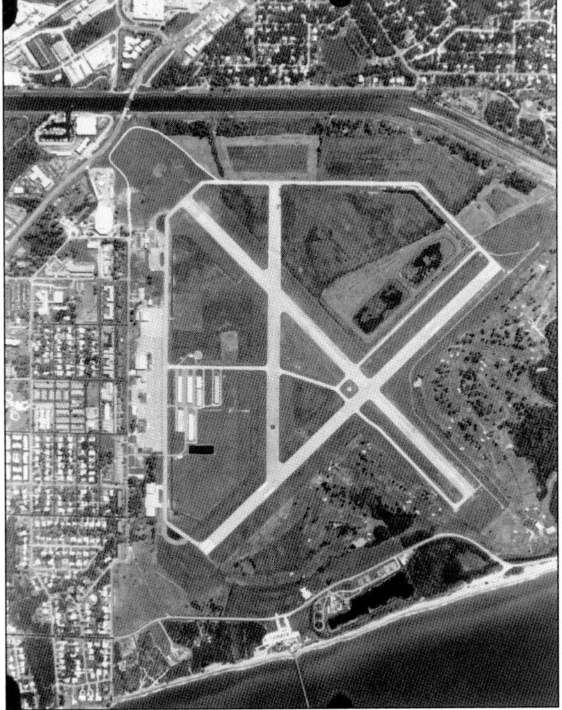

In 1946, the US Army issued a permit for the City of Venice to operate the Venice Municipal Airport, with two runways, hangars, maintenance buildings, and a sewage treatment plant. The remaining property was sold for housing developments. In this 1967 aerial, note Caspersen Beach, new housing, the circus arena, and a single South Bridge crossing the two-year-old Intracoastal Waterway. (PH26.0466, image 2 of 13.)

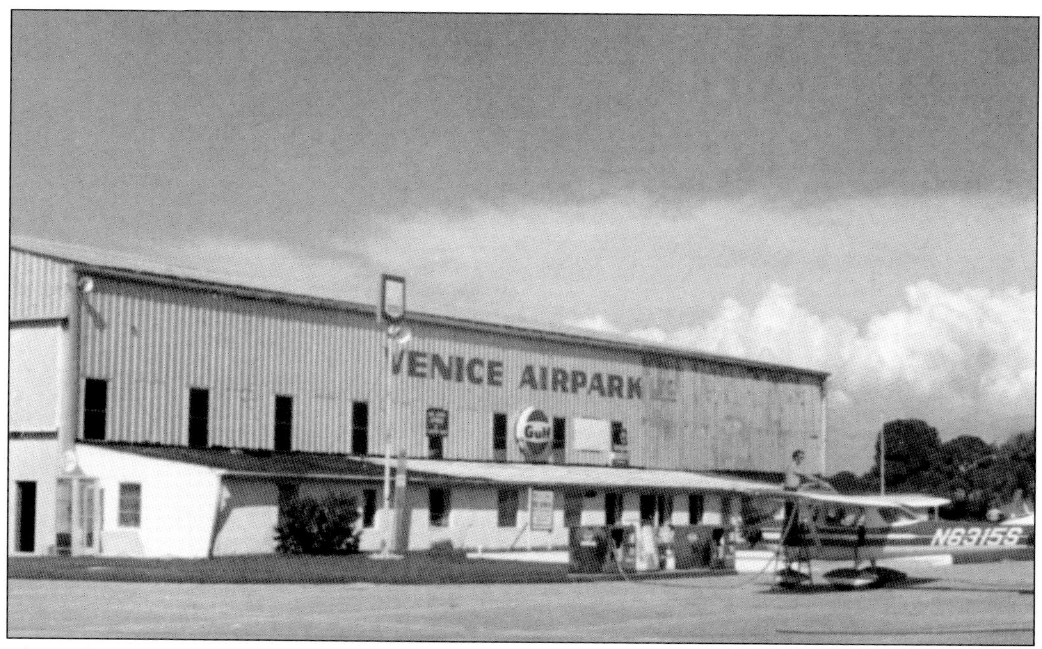

Throughout the years, new hangars, upgraded facilities, a restaurant, expanded operations, and pilot training schools have characterized the municipal airport. The number of flight operations has increased and now includes a significant number of corporate and private jet aircraft. In spite of this increase in traffic, in 2025, the airport continues to be without a control tower. (PH26.0447, image 1 of 4.)

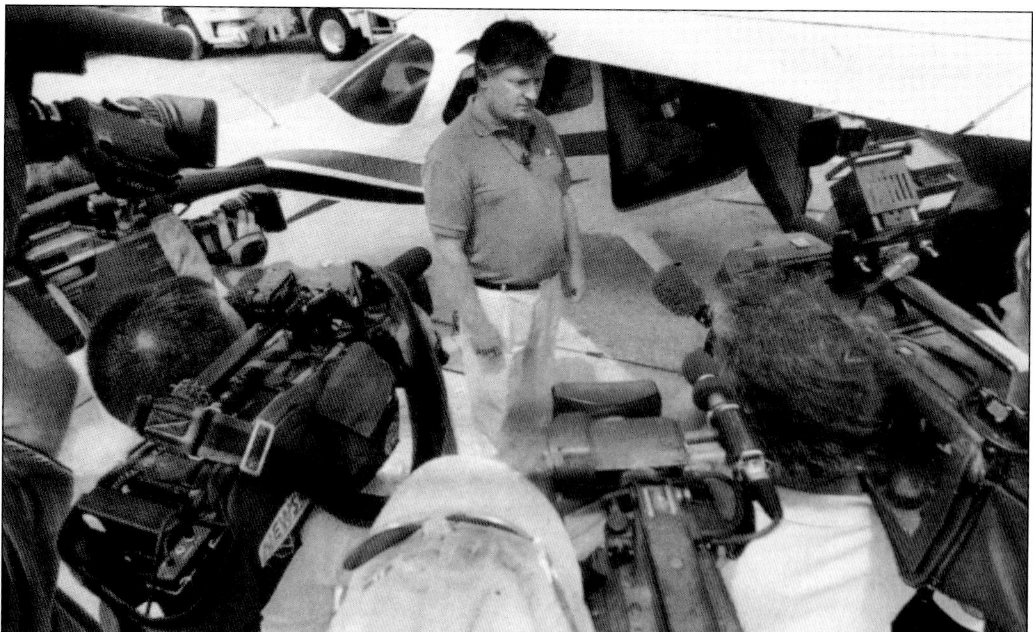

A tragedy occurred on September 11, 2001. Terrorists trained at a flight school based at the Venice Municipal Airport flew planes into the World Trade Center and the Pentagon and crashed in Pennsylvania. The event known as "9/11" shocked and appalled residents and visitors. (*Venice Gondolier* newspaper.)

Seven

Streets, Railroad, and Legacy Trail

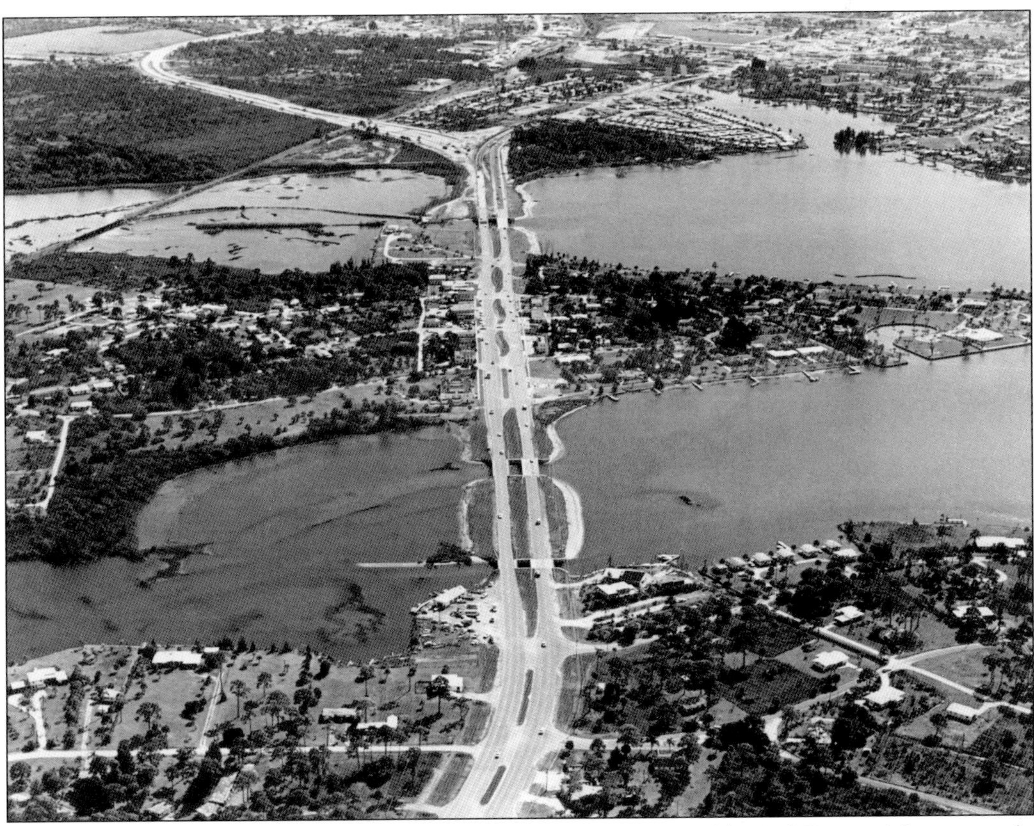

Venice roads have essentially remained as shown in this 1965 aerial by Ted Turner. Moving south, US 41 crosses Dona Bay and then Roberts Bay. The left branch becomes US 41 Bypass. Business 41 turns right toward downtown Venice via the KMI Bridge. Business 41 exits the island on Circus Bridge to meet up with US 41 again. Note the Seaboard Air Line Rail tracks on the top left. (NP1081.)

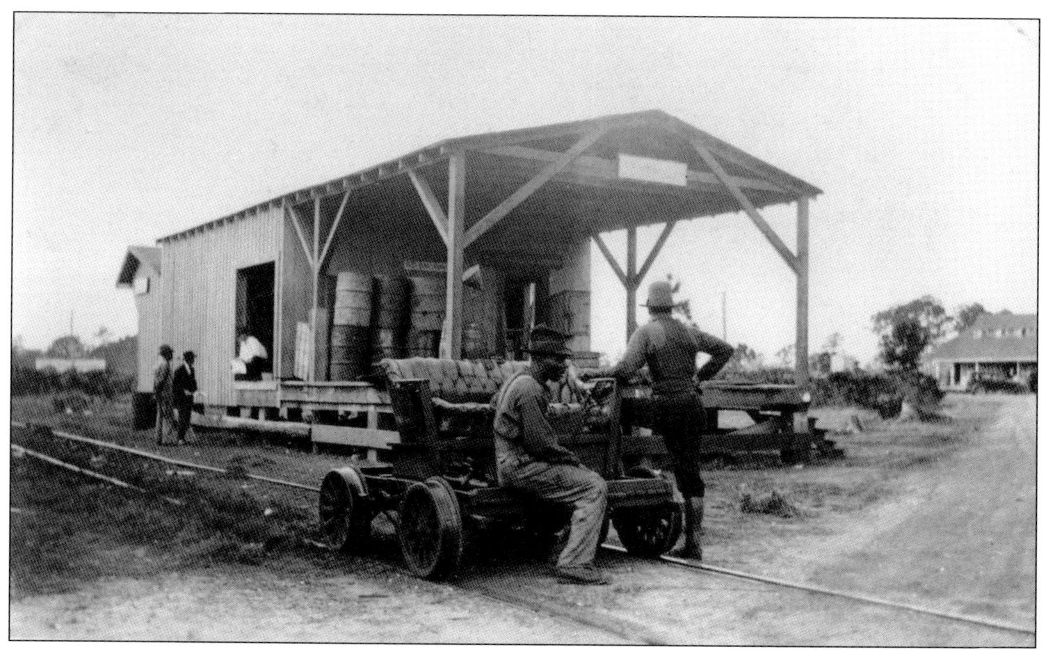

By 1915, the Seaboard Air Line Railroad was extended to a newly named Venice railroad station, conceived by the Palmer family firm, the Sarasota-Venice Company. It was located south of Roberts Bay and would support their planned resorts at Eagle Point and along the Venice coastline. It would also provide southern farmers and cattlemen an easier way to ship products north. (NP0350.)

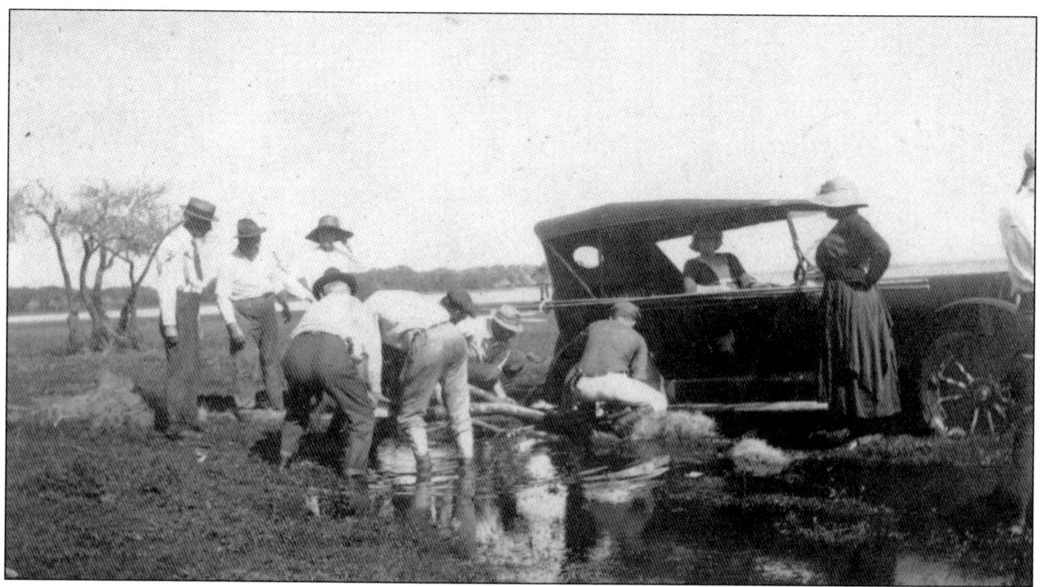

Initially, Native Americans and the first settlers had traveled in shallow boats on the water. Inland trails began as sandy animal trails, expanded into horse trails, and then became wider wagon trails. The late 1880s brought railroads. Finally, paved roads eliminated situations as seen here. (SCHC.)

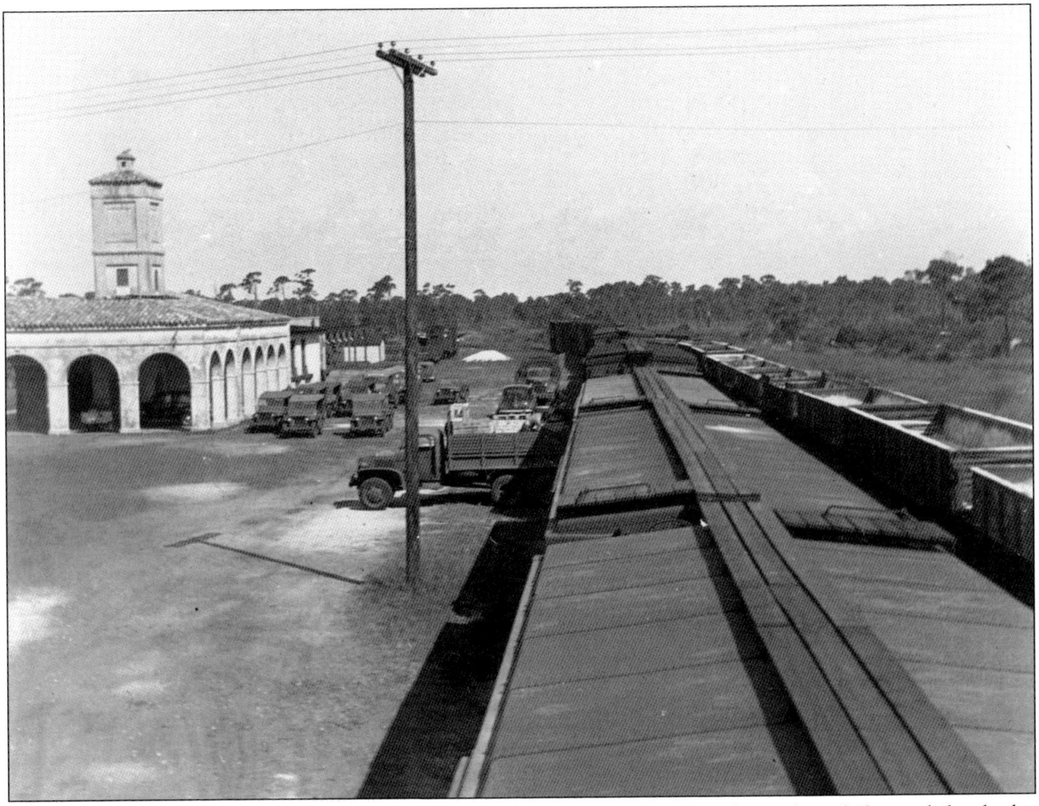

After about 1911, local cattlemen and farmers shipped products on the railroad through both the Nokomis and Venice railroad depots. As shown in this 1942 photograph by George Hauser, the Army Air Corps shipped supplies and men via the Venice Depot. The circus used the railroad from 1960 to 1992. (NP0877.)

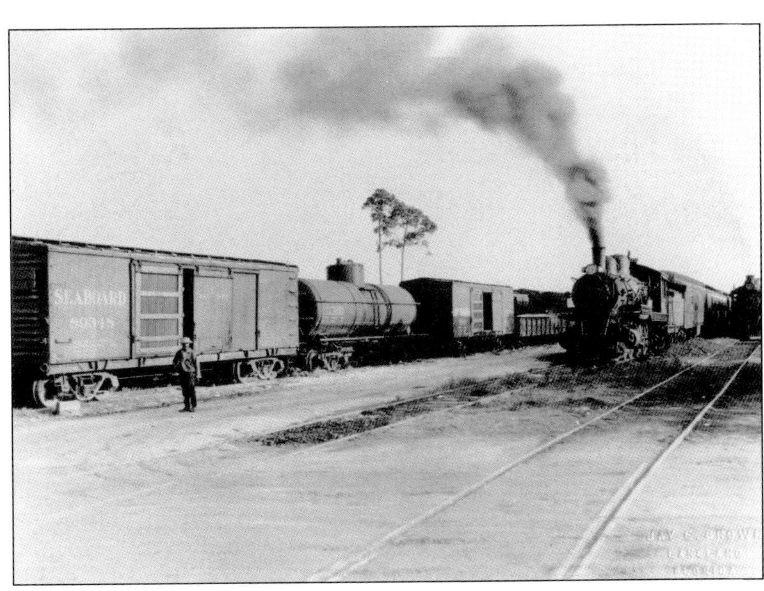

The railroad depot was a busy place, as this 1940s image shows. Produce and livestock moved north every day on dedicated railcars. KMI cadets used the Venice train from 1932 to 1972. Residents and visitors often travelled by rail coach. (2008.21.098, image 30 of 54.)

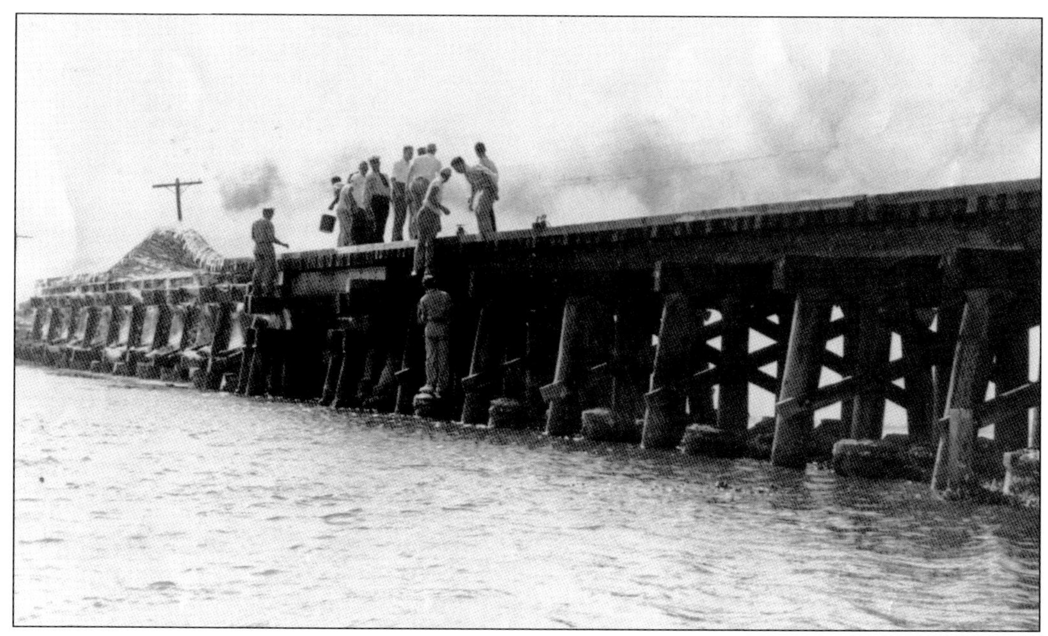

The original railroad line crossed Dona Bay, Roberts Bay, and Hatchett Creek on trestle bridges. In January 1950, part of the trestle over Roberts Bay caught fire, with 120 feet of the 300-foot span destroyed. The fire was near the original Venice-Nokomis High School in Nokomis. (PH06.11.05.01, image 2 of 2.)

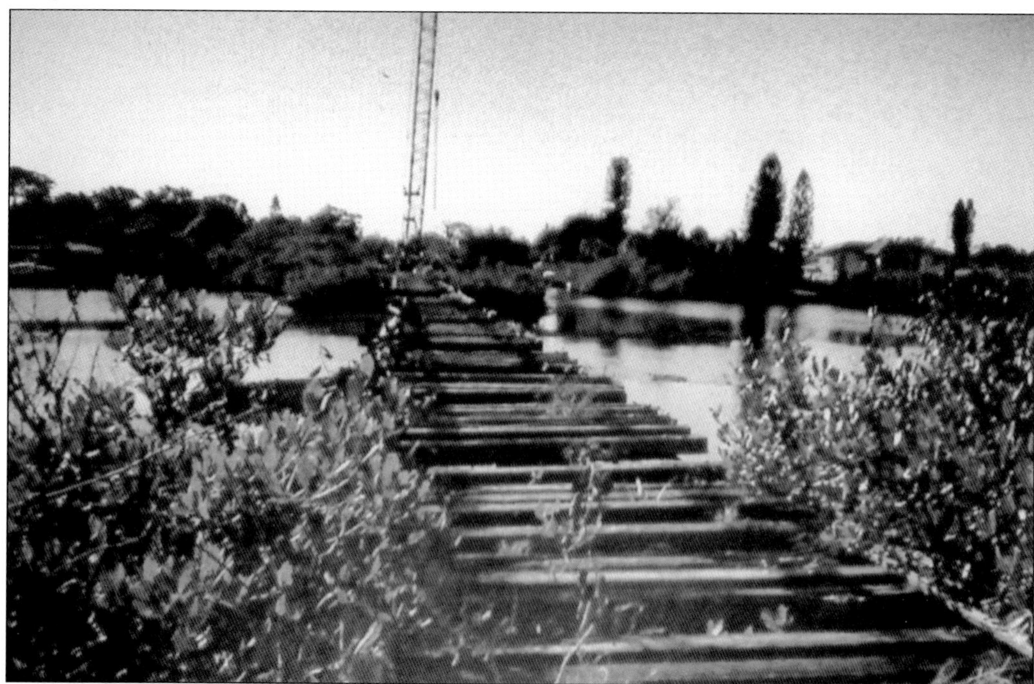

This is the same train trestle over Dona Bay, photographed by Bob Higgens some time after 1998. Farmers and cattlemen were now shipping via trucks, and railroad passenger service had ended in 1971. The depot was closed in 1975, but Ringling Bros. and Barnum & Bailey Circus operated its own trains until 1992. Afterward, only a few freight trains operated until 1997. (PH26.0613.)

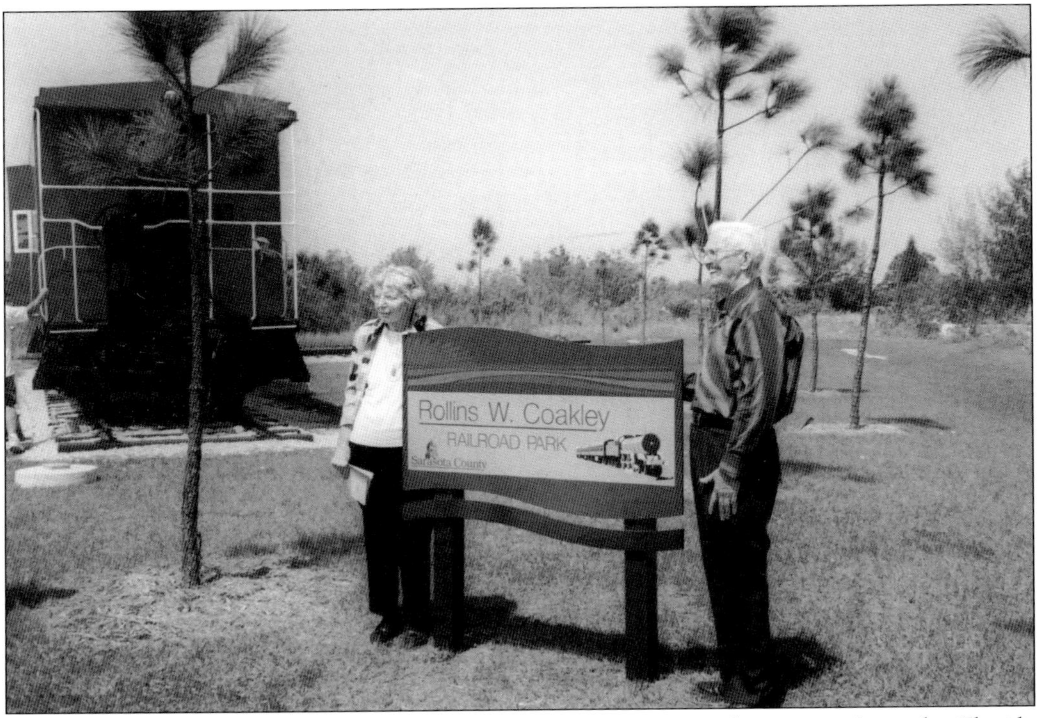

In 1999, Sarasota County purchased the 1927 Venice Depot with support from the Florida Department of Transportation. The renovated station opened in 2003 and was placed on the Venice Register of Historic Places. The Venice Historical Society now maintains an old circus car and a historical caboose. The Rollins W. Coakley Railroad Park was dedicated in March 2005. (PH26.0518, image 2 of 2.)

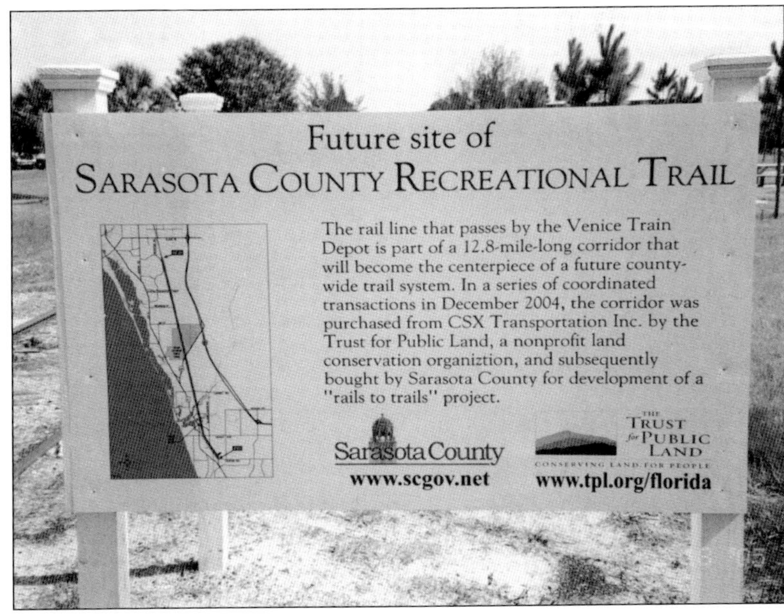

In a "rails to trails" initiative, the Legacy Trail opened in 2008. It was built on the old Seaboard Air Line Railroad tracks, which are now paved for biking and walking. It runs from Sarasota to Venice, with bridges installed over major roads. There are also plans to expand its length. (PH26.0534.)

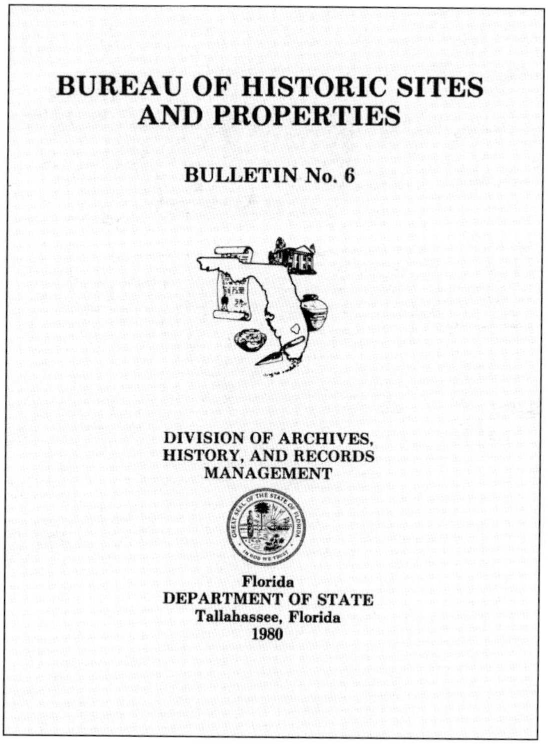

BUREAU OF HISTORIC SITES AND PROPERTIES

BULLETIN No. 6

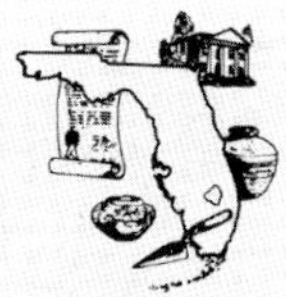

DIVISION OF ARCHIVES, HISTORY, AND RECORDS MANAGEMENT

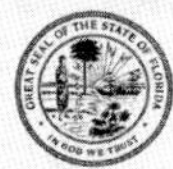

Florida
DEPARTMENT OF STATE
Tallahassee, Florida
1980

Shells deposited by Native Americans on the Gulf Coast of Florida were used for road-making material because initially, concrete, gravel, and stone were not readily available. This bulletin describes where Native Americans or First Peoples built shell mounds beginning perhaps 12,000 years ago. (LIB 930.1 BRO.)

Most of the tall shell mounds are gone. The largest, at Historic Spanish Point in Osprey, was preserved by the John G. Webb family and then by the Bertha Honoré Palmer family. It is hard to determine if this 1926 image by Koons Studios of a BLE shovel is from a shell mound, but it is labeled "Power Shovel Loading Shell that Makes Concrete for Road Bases." (NP0713.)

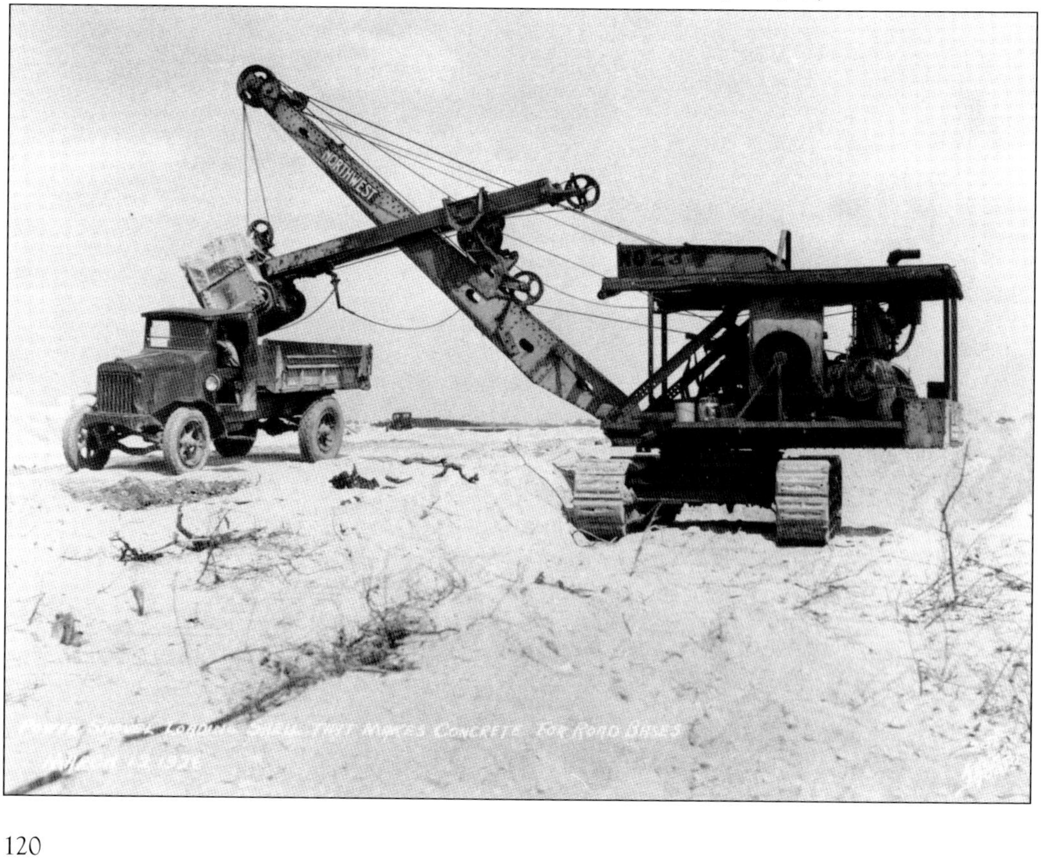

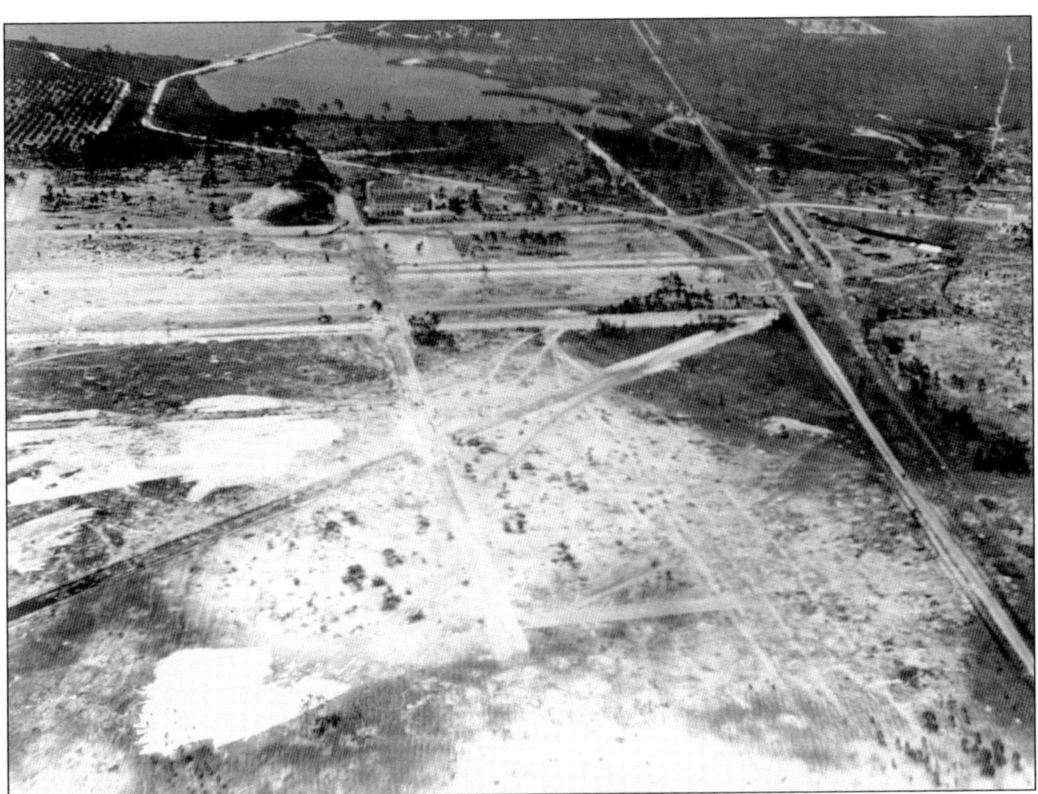

US 41 has an interesting history. First, it was a graded sandy nine-foot-wide road that came south across Roberts Bay, through Eagle Point Resort, and over a causeway to J.H. Lord's citrus grove. It then proceeded down West Bay Drive to St. Augustine Drive at top center above. The route was abandoned by 1927 as US 41 moved farther east. Land deeds still document and complicate purchases. (NP0737.)

Rules and Regulations

Grand Marshal, Hugh Mauck

Marshal from each city represented.

1. Cooperation with marshals requested of all

2. All cars must keep in line and drive to motorists.

3. Cars falling out of line must fall in at right side of Trail.

4. Cars in trouble pull well to right hand side of roadway for aid by repair cars. rear of motorcade.

5. Cars must keep 100 feet distance apart except in cities then close up to ten feet distance apart.

6. Bugle will sound assembly ten minutes before each start.

7. Be sure to service your car each evening.

8. Service truck and mechanics will be in rear of motorcade.

The Fort Myers Press Job Dept.

PROGRAM

Tamiami Trail Opening Celebration

TO HERALD FLORIDA'S NEW CROSS-STATE HIGHWAY THROUGH THE MYSTERIOUS EVERGLADES

April 24, 25, 26, 1928 : Fort Myers, Florida

BARRON G. COLLIER, Chairman
HENRY FORD, Director
THOMAS A. EDISON, Director

CLINTON BOLICK, Executive Secretary

GENERAL COMMITTEE

BARRON G. COLLIER, New York and Everglades, Chairman
MAYOR D. B. McKAY, Tampa, Fla.
W. U. LATHRUP, Bradenton, Fla.
E. P. GREEN, Member S. R. D., Bradenton, Fla.
JOHN RINGLING, Sarasota, Fla.
GEORGE WEBB, Venice, Fla.
WILLIAM H. JOHNSON, Punta Gorda, Fla.
CLINTON BOLICK, Fort Myers, Fla.
GEORGE H. MERRICK, Coral Gables, Fla.
MAYOR E. G. SEWELL, Miami, Fla.
I. E. SCHILLING, Member S. R. D., Miami, Fla.
GRA E. CHAPIN, Fort Myers, Fla., Assistant Secretary.
CAPT. GEO. F. COOK, Coral Gables
SENATOR W. H. MALONE, Key West

PUBLICITY COMMITTEE

HORACE A. DUNN, Fort Myers, Chairman
ED D. LAMBRIGHT, Tampa
WILLIAM ABBOTT, Tampa
JOHN L. HACKNEY, Tampa
RALPH DILLON, Tampa
MISS BEATRICE MAYER, Tampa
BRACK CHESHIRE, Bradenton
WILLIAM T. SIMPSON, Sarasota
C. M. McLENNAN, Venice
VARSITY JOHNSON, Punta Gorda
CHARLES KLINE, Fort Myers
RONALD HALGRIM, Fort Myers
WILLIAM SPEAR, Fort Myers
MISS MARION LUND, Everglades
MORTON MILFORD, Miami
FRANK B. SHUTTS, Miami

ASSISTING AGENCIES

BOARD OF TRADE, Tampa
JUNIOR BOARD OF TRADE, Tampa
TAMPA MOTOR CLUB
CHAMBER OF COMMERCE, Palmetto
CHAMBER OF COMMERCE, Bradenton
CHAMBER OF COMMERCE, Manatee
CHAMBER OF COMMERCE, Sarasota
CHAMBER OF COMMERCE, Venice
CHAMBER OF COMMERCE, Englewood
CHAMBER OF COMMERCE, Punta Gorda
CHAMBER OF COMMERCE, Fort Myers
MUNICIPAL RECREATION BOARD, Fort Myers
BOARD OF TRADE, Bonita Springs
CHAMBER OF COMMERCE, Everglades
CHAMBER OF COMMERCE, Miami Beach
CHAMBER OF COMMERCE Coral Gables
CHAMBER OF COMMERCE, Miami
MIAMI MOTOR CLUB
FLORIDA AUTOMOBILE ASS'N.
AMERICAN AUTOMOBILE ASS'N.
TAMIAMI TRAIL ASS'N.
TAMIAMI TRAIL BLAZERS
TAMIAMI TRAIL IMPROVEMENT ASS'N.
COMMISSIONERS OF HILLSBOROUGH COUNTY
COMMISSIONERS OF MANATEE COUNTY
COMMISSIONERS OF SARASOTA COUNTY
COMMISSIONERS OF CHARLOTTE COUNTY
COMMISSIONERS OF LEE COUNTY
COMMISSIONERS OF COLLIER COUNTY
COMMISSIONERS OF DADE COUNTY
COMMISSIONERS OF MONROE COUNTY

CITY OF TAMPA	CITY OF PUNTA GORDA
CITY OF PALMETTO	CITY OF FORT MYERS
CITY OF BRADENTON	CITY OF NAPLES
CITY OF MANATEE	CITY OF EVERGLADES
CITY OF SARASOTA	CITY OF CORAL GABLES
CITY OF VENICE	CITY OF MIAMI
CITY OF ENGLEWOOD	CITY OF MIAMI BEACH

US 41 has had many names over the years: Sarasota-Venice Road, Hard Road, and the Velvet Highway (after it was paved). Coming through the Venice area in 1927, the Tamiami Trail, which runs from Tampa to Miami, was officially opened on April 25, 1928. It featured a caravan of 300 "first-timers," as this schedule shows. (LAT 5N.)

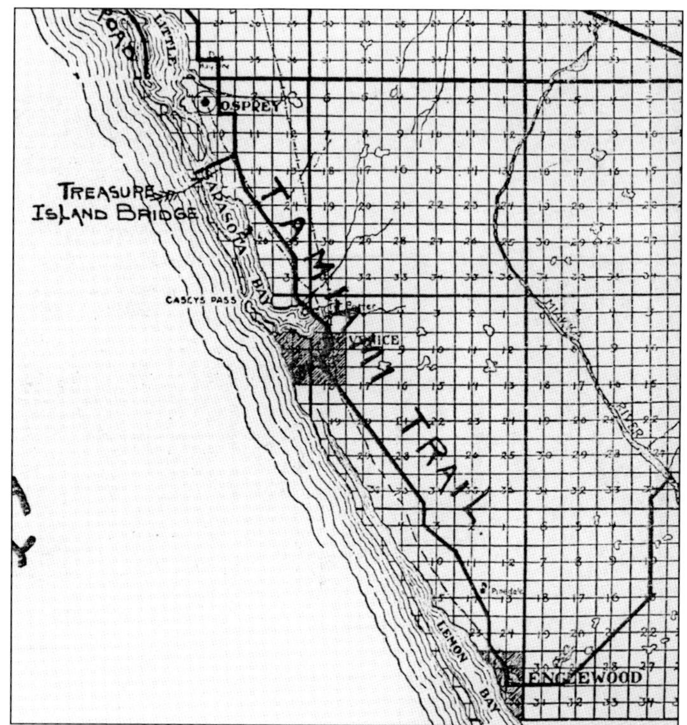

In 1928, the Tamiami Trail (actually a public relations term combining the words "Tampa" and "Miami") was finished with great fanfare. Originally, as shown on this map, it was to go through Englewood. It was dedicated as a scenic highway in 2004. (LAT 5N.)

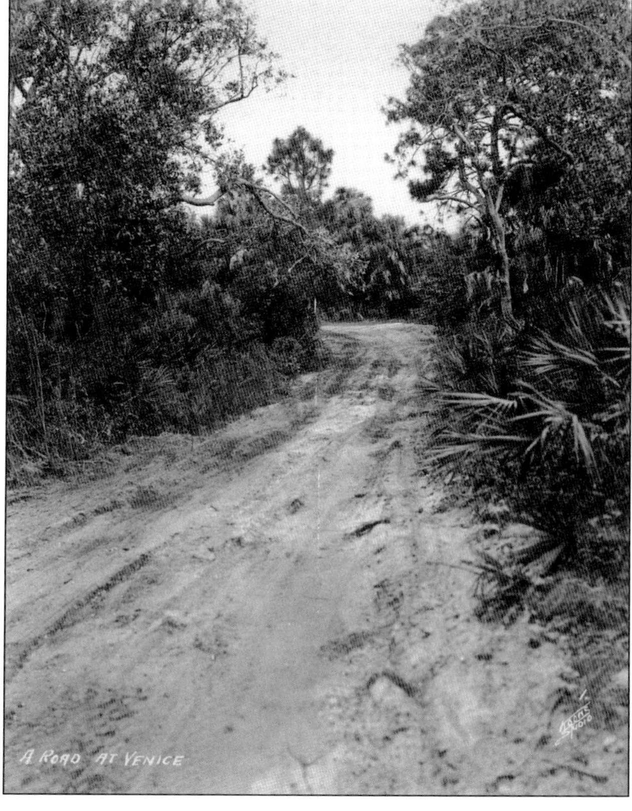

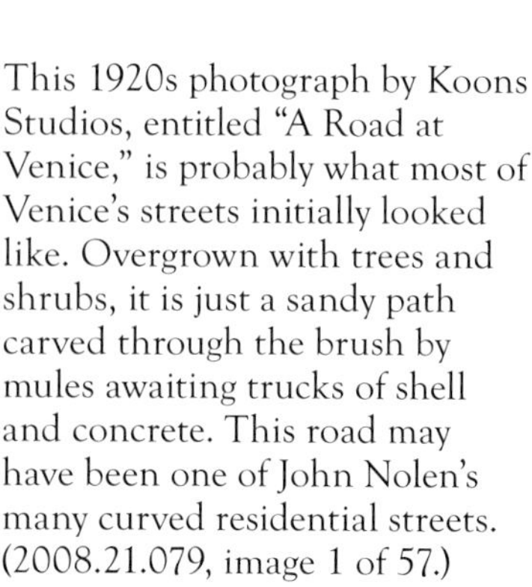

This 1920s photograph by Koons Studios, entitled "A Road at Venice," is probably what most of Venice's streets initially looked like. Overgrown with trees and shrubs, it is just a sandy path carved through the brush by mules awaiting trucks of shell and concrete. This road may have been one of John Nolen's many curved residential streets. (2008.21.079, image 1 of 57.)

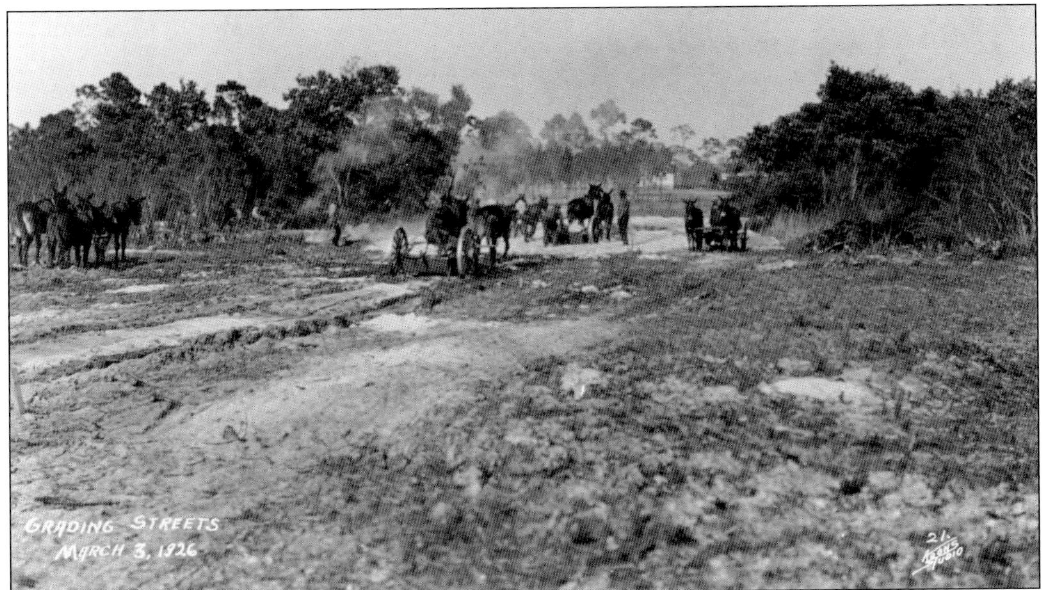

In the 1920s, the BLE built Venice streets in a multistep process. This image by Koons Studios, entitled "Grading Streets," shows the first step in this activity. Mule-drawn equipment leveled and graded the sandy trail. Then, local shell deposits were mixed with sand and cement for the roadway. (NP0711.)

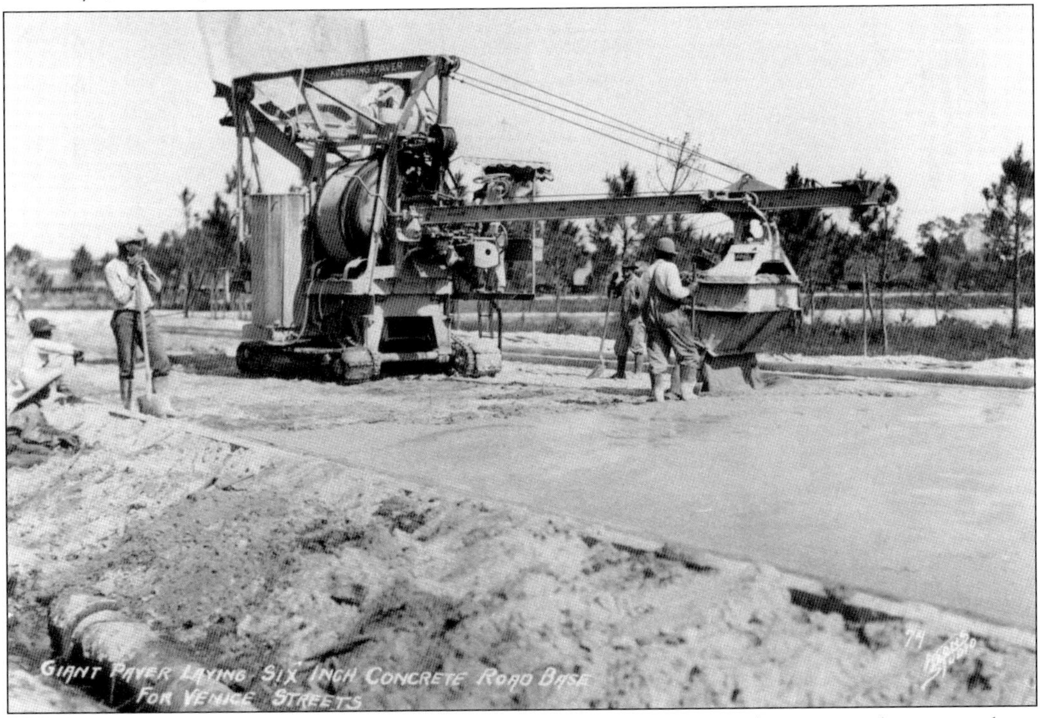

After the shell, sand, and cement mix was made, local laborers operated a concrete laying machine to put down the six-inch-thick roadway, pictured by Koons Studios. This location appears to be Venice Avenue West, because the boulevard in the background is already planted with small trees. (NP0661.)

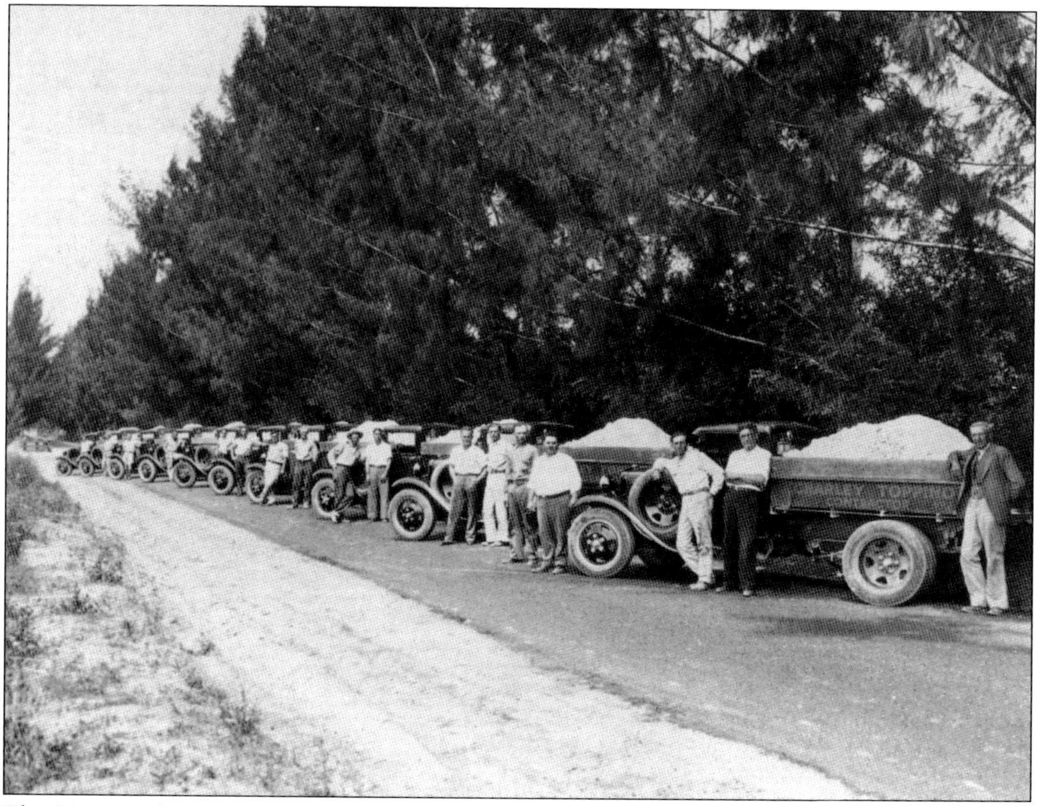

The BLE conducted massive road-building projects from 1925 to 1928. This image by Koons Studios is labeled "Hard Road Building in Venice." The site is uncertain, but it is assumed to be along what is now US 41. Here, it looks like the Hard Road was already built, so perhaps the large number of hoppers full of shells are headed into Venice or elsewhere. (NP0304.)

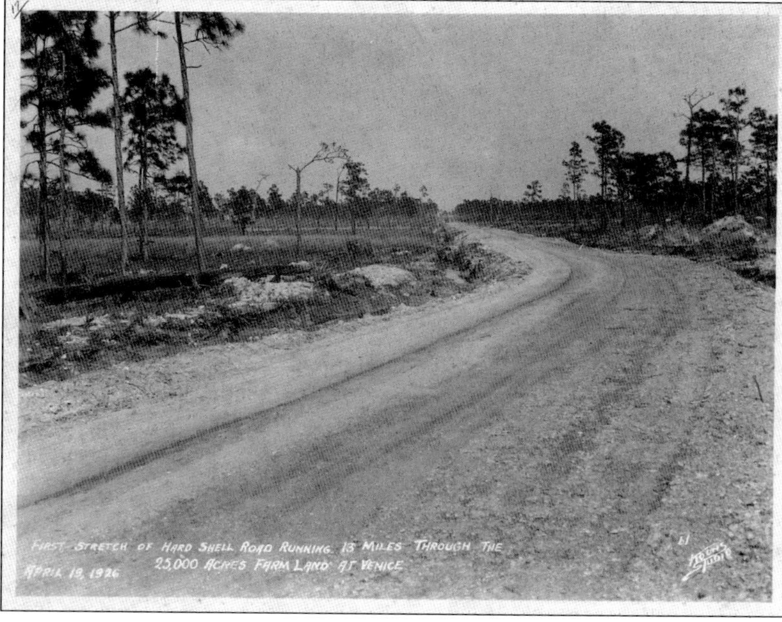

This image from 1926 by Koons Studios, entitled "First Stretch of Hard Shell Road Running 13 Miles through the 25,000 Acres Farm Land at Venice," could be anywhere east of what is now Venice Avenue Bridge. It is about 13 miles from Venice to Sarasota. So perhaps, given the curve, it is what became US 41. (NP0017.)

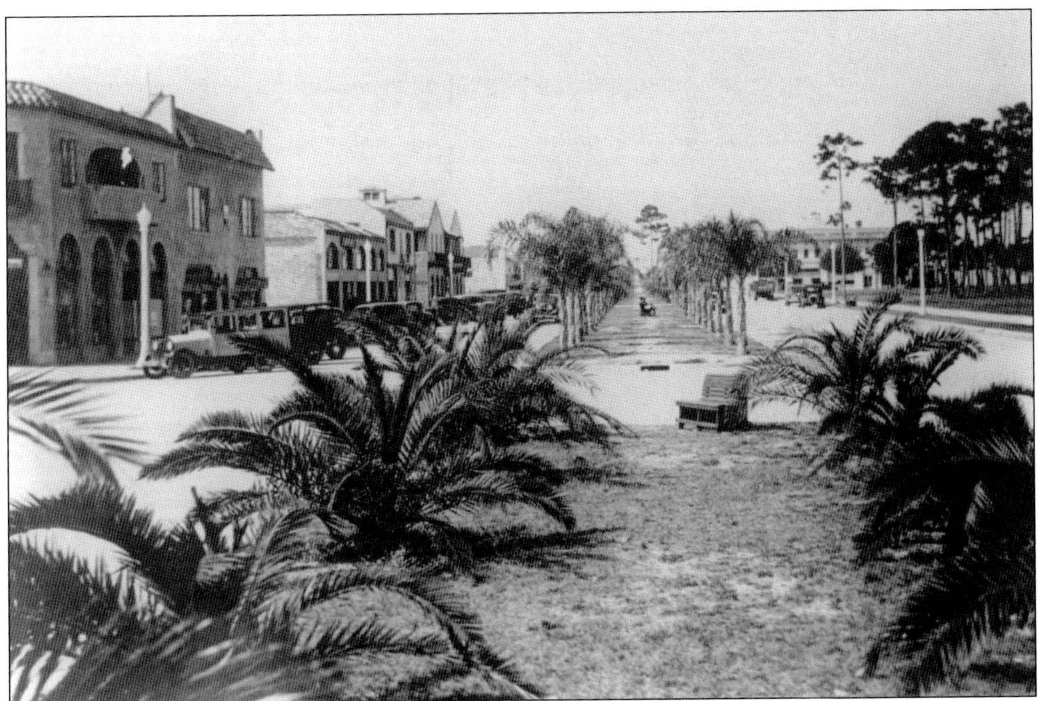

In the John Nolen Plan, West Venice Avenue is the main street. It begins in the historic downtown district and extends west along the Heritage Park boulevard to Venice Beach. Plantings, median designs, and parking plans have changed a number of times. Its history can be traced back to the 1920s through the many images that exist at the Venice Museum & Archives. (NP0975.)

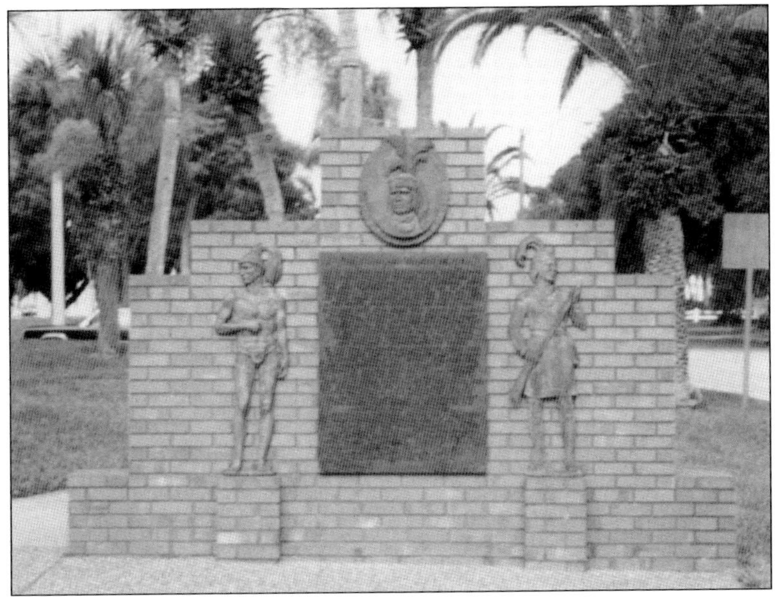

Many historical monuments are located in Heritage Park. The park stretches for several blocks along West Venice Avenue and ends at the beach. One can stop and rest on the accompanying benches or read the plaques along the shaded walkway. It is also a popular spot for dog walking. (PH26.0369.)

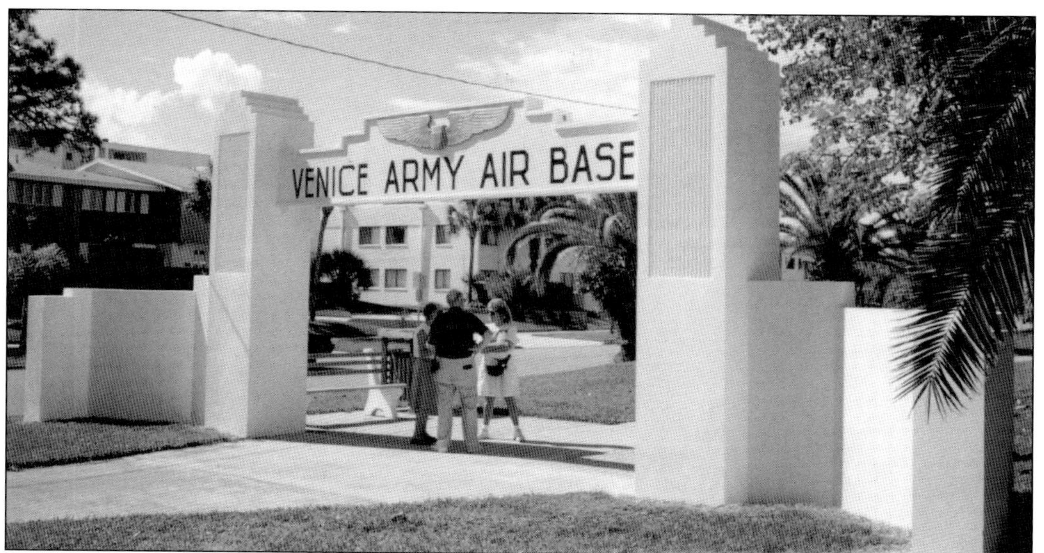

Just east of the veterans and the September 11 memorials is the one-third-sized replica of the Venice Army Air Corps Base front gate. Though the actual base entrance was at The Rialto and San Marco Avenue, it is important to be included in Heritage Park as a reminder of the key role the VAAC played in the development of Venice. (RG102 Box 1.)

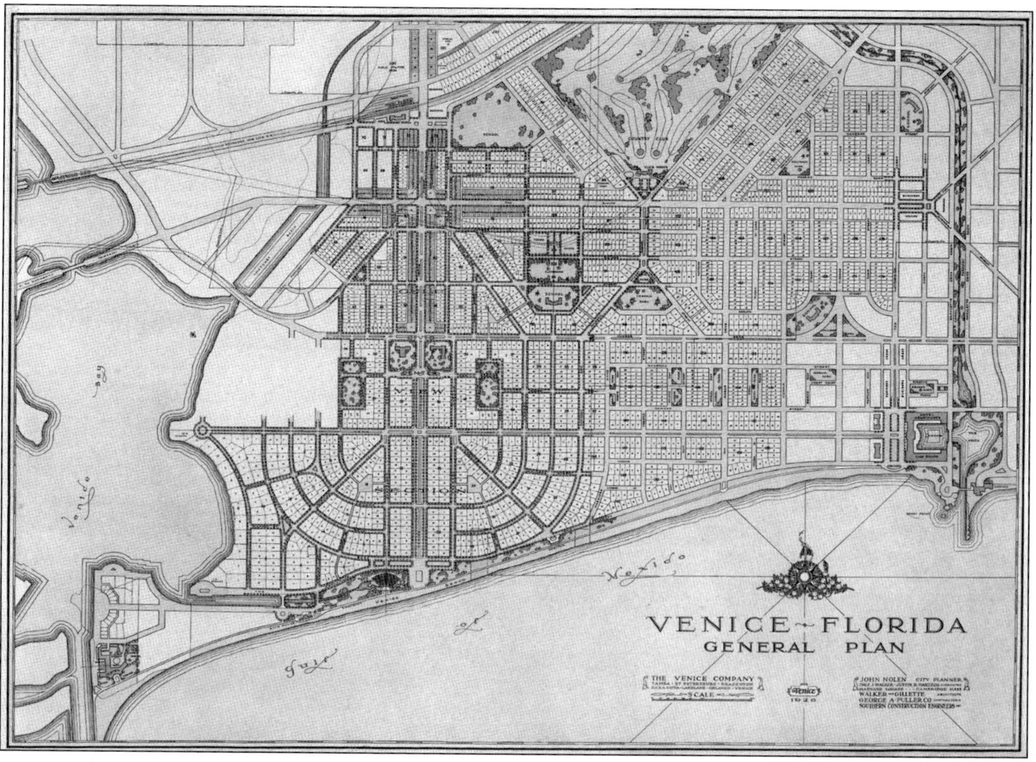

In an informal survey, when asked "Why did you move to Venice?", respondents said they turned onto West Venice Avenue. As they drove past the historic district on the boulevard lined with old trees all the way to the beach, they decided to stay. They did not realize until later that the spell of John Nolen's plan had drawn them to Venice. (LIB 975.96 KOR.)

Bibliography

Antonini, Gustavo A., David A. Fann, and Paul Roat. *A Historical Geography of Southwest Florida Waterways*. Vol. 1, *Anna Maria Sound to Lemon Bay*. Venice, FL: West Coast Inland Navigation District, 1999.

Clayton, Tonya. *How to Read a Florida Gulf Coast Beach*. Chapel Hill: University of North Carolina Press, 2012.

Division of Archives, History, and Records Management. *Bureau of Historic Sites and Properties Bulletin No. 6: Research on Venice Beach Site (8So26)*. Tallahassee: Florida Department of State, 1980.

Higel, George. *Venice before 1925: Nemo Commentaries*. 3 vol. Dorothy Korwek, ed. Venice, FL: City of Venice Archives and Area Historical Collection, 2016.

Humes, Larry. *Venice: A Century on the Gulf*. Charleston, SC: History Press, 2025.

KMI Alumni Association. *Character Makes the Man: The Story of the Kentucky Military Institute, 1848–1971*. DVD. Lexinton: Kentucky Network, 2013.

Korwek, Dorothy. *Building the Intracoastal Waterway*. Venice, FL: Venice Heritage Inc., 2024.

Korwek, Dorothy, and Carl Shiver. *John Nolen Plan of Venice, Florida*. Venice, FL: Triangle Inn Association, 2011.

Manatee River Journal (Bradenton), 1989–2023.

Matthews, Janet Snyder. *Venice: Journey from Horse and Chase: A History of Venice, Florida*. Sarasota, FL: Pine Level Press Inc., 1989.

Sarasota Herald, 1910–2025.

Sarasota Times, 1910–2025.

Stephenson, R. Bruce. *John Nolen: Landscape Architect and City Planner*. Amherst: University of Massachusetts Press, 2015.

Turner, Gregg M. *Venice in the 1920s*. Charleston, SC: Arcadia Publishing, 2000.

Venice Gondolier, 1946–2025.

Young, Tommy R. *Character Makes the Man: The Story of the Kentucky Military Institute, 1848–1971*. Bloomington, IN: Trafford, 2013.

Consistent with our mission to preserve history on a local level, this book was printed in South Carolina on American-made paper and manufactured entirely in the United States. Products carrying the accredited Forest Stewardship Council (FSC) label are printed on 100 percent FSC-certified paper.

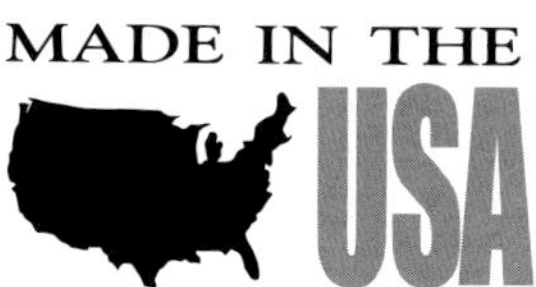